→ Some people pretend to tell that
story - Just like you

MW01056377

p.15 - To stop alienating behavior - court

The Parental Alienation Syndrome

A Guide for Mental Health and Legal Professionals

The Parental Alienation Syndrome

A Guide for Mental Health and Legal Professionals

RICHARD A. GARDNER, M.D.

Clinical Professor of Child Psychiatry
Columbia University
College of Physicians and Surgeons

Creative Therapeutics,
155 County Road, Cresskill, New Jersey 07626-0317

Library of Congress Cataloging-in-Publication Data

Gardner, Richard A.
    The parental alienation syndrome : a guide for mental health and
legal professionals / Richard A. Gardner.
        p.   cm.
    Includes bibliographical references and indexes.
    ISBN 0-933812-24-8
    1. Children of divorced parents—Mental health—Evaluation.
    2. Custody of children—Psychological aspects.   I. Title.
    [DNLM: 1. Child Custody—legislation.   2. Child Psychology.
    3. Mental Disorders—in infancy & childhood.   4. Parent-Child
    Relations.   5. Persuasive Communication.   WS 350 G228pb]
    RJ507.D59G36   1992
    616.85′2—dc20
    DNLM/DLC
    for Library of Congress   91–47859
                                                                CIP

PRINTED IN THE UNITED STATES OF AMERICA

10 9 8 7 6 5 4 3

I dedicate this book to
  my teachers at
  The Bronx High School of Science and
  Columbia College.

My debt to you is enormous,
  not only for what you taught me
  but for serving as models for
  intellectual pursuit, independent thinking, and creativity.

This book, which I consider my
  most creative contribution, is just one
  derivative of your influence and a true
  testament to the success of your efforts.

Other Books by Richard A. Gardner

The Boys and Girls Book About Divorce
Therapeutic Communication with Children: The Mutual
    Storytelling Technique
Dr. Gardner's Stories About the Real World, Volume I
Dr. Gardner's Stories About the Real World, Volume II
Dr. Gardner's Fairy Tales for Today's Children
Understanding Children: A Parents Guide to Child Rearing
MBD: The Family Book About Minimal Brain Dysfunction
Psychotherapeutic Approaches to the Resistant Child
Psychotherapy with Children of Divorce
Dr. Gardner's Modern Fairy Tales
The Parents Book About Divorce
The Boys and Girls Book About One-Parent Families
The Objective Diagnosis of Minimal Brain Dysfunction
Dorothy and the Lizard of Oz
Dr. Gardner's Fables for Our Times
The Boys and Girls Book About Stepfamilies
Family Evaluation in Child Custody Litigation
Separation Anxiety Disorder: Psychodynamics and Psychotherapy
Child Custody Litigation: A Guide for Parents and
    Mental Health Professionals
The Psychotherapeutic Techniques of Richard A. Gardner
Hyperactivity, The So-Called Attention-Deficit Disorder,
    and The Group of MBD Syndromes
The Parental Alienation Syndrome
Psychotherapy with Adolescents
Family Evaluation in Child Custody Mediation, Arbitration,
    and Litigation
The Girls and Boys Book About Good and Bad Behavior
See Abuse Hysteria: Salem Witch Trials Revisited
The Parents Book About Divorce, Second Edition
Self-Esteem Problems of Children: Psychodynamics and Psychotherapy
True and False Accusations of Child Sex Abuse
Psychotherapy of Psychogenic Learning Disabilities
Conduct Disorders of Childhood
Protocols for the Sex-Abuse Evaluation
Testifying In Court: A Guide for Mental Health Professionals

CONTENTS

ACKNOWLEDGMENTS

INTRODUCTION

1 A BRIEF REVIEW OF THE HISTORICAL
   DEVELOPMENT OF THE ADVERSARY SYSTEM   1

   INTRODUCTION   1
   PRIMITIVE SOCIETIES   3
   GREEK SOCIETY   6
   ROMAN SOCIETY   8
   TRIAL BY ORDEAL   9
   TRIAL BY COMBAT (TRIAL BY BATTLE)   11
   TRIAL BY WAGER   14
   FOURTH LATERAN COUNCIL – 1215   16
   THE INQUISITORIAL SYSTEM   17
   THE DEVELOPMENT OF THE ADVERSARY
      SYSTEM FROM THE 13TH TO THE
      17TH CENTURIES   21
      Juries   21
      Witnesses   23
      Judges   24

Lawyers   26
THE DEVELOPMENT OF THE PRESENT-DAY
   ADVERSARY SYSTEM IN ENGLAND   28
THE ADVERSARY SYSTEM IN THE
   UNITED STATES   30

2 **BRIEF REVIEW OF WESTERN SOCIETY'S
   CHANGING ATTITUDES REGARDING
   PARENTAL PREFERENCE IN
   CUSTODY DISPUTES**   37

ANCIENT TIMES TO WORLD WAR II   37
WORLD WAR II TO THE 1960s   41
1960s TO THE MID-1970s   51
MID-1970s TO THE PRESENT   52

3 **THE PARENTAL ALIENATION SYNDROME**   59

INTRODUCTION   59
THE MANIFESTATIONS OF THE PARENTAL
   ALIENATION SYNDROME IN THE CHILD   63
   The Campaign of Denigration   64
   Weak, Frivolous, or Absurd Rationalizations
      for the Deprecation   68
   Lack of Ambivalence   73
   The "Independent Thinker" Phenomenon   74
   Reflexive Support of the Loved Parent in
      the Parental Conflict   75
   Absence of Guilt   76
   The Presence of Borrowed Scenarios   77
   Spread of the Animosity to the Extended
      Family of the Hated Parent   80
   Concluding Comments   82
THE PROGRAMMING MOTHER   82
   Introduction   82
   Programming ("Brainwashing")   83
   Subtle and Often Unconscious
      Parental Programming   99
   Concluding Comments   105
THE PROGRAMMING FATHER   106
THE CHILD'S UNDERLYING PSYCHODYNAMICS   115

Maintenance of the Primary Psychological Bond   115
Fear of Disruption of the Primary
   Psychological Bond   116
Reaction Formation   117
Identification with the Aggressor   117
Identification with an Idealized Person   118
Release of Hostility   119
Infectiousness of Emotions   120
Sexual Rivalry   120
THE MOTHER'S UNDERLYING
PSYCHODYNAMICS   121
Maintenance of the Primary Psychological Bond   121
The Fury of the Scorned Woman   122
Economic Disparity   122
Reaction Formation   123
Projection   125
Elaboration of Preseparation Exclusionary Tactics   127
Overprotectiveness   129
Additional Psychodynamic Factors   132
THE FATHER'S UNDERLYING
PSYCHODYNAMICS   132
Maintenance of the Primary Psychological Bond   133
The Fury of the Scorned Man   134
Economic Disparity   134
Reaction Formation   135
Projection   136
Exclusionary Tactics   137
Overprotectiveness   137
Power   137
The Father's New Woman Involvement   138
Additional Psychodynamic Factors   139
SITUATIONAL FACTORS   140
THE PARENTAL ALIENATION SYNDROME,
   AN EXAMPLE OF FOLIE-À-DEUX   146
THE THREE TYPES OF PARENTAL
ALIENATION SYNDROME   149
Severe Cases of the Parental Alienation
   Syndrome   150
Moderate Cases of the Parental
   Alienation Syndrome   152

Mild Cases of the Parental Alienation
    Syndrome   153
CONCLUDING COMMENTS   154

4 DIAGNOSTIC CONSIDERATIONS FOR
   THE MENTAL HEALTH PROFESSIONAL   157

INTRODUCTORY COMMENTS   157
STRUCTURE OF THE EVALUATION   158
THE STRONGER HEALTHY PSYCHOLOGICAL
    BOND AND "GRANDMA'S" CRITERIA   164
THE INITIAL INTERVIEW   165
THE INDIVIDUAL INTERVIEWS
    WITH THE PARENTS   168
INDIVIDUAL INTERVIEWS WITH
    THE CHILDREN   171
JOINT INTERVIEWS   178
    Mother and Child Together   179
    Father and Child Together   179
    The Family Interview   181
INTERVIEWING HOUSEKEEPERS   182

5 EVIDENCE-GATHERING PROCEDURES
   FOR LEGAL PROFESSIONALS   185

INTRODUCTION   185
LAWYERS   186
JUDGES   190
    Introduction   190
    Intrinsic Weaknesses of In-Camera Interviews
        with Children   190
    Technical Considerations   197
    Interviewing Children with Parental Alienation
        Syndrome   212
GUARDIANS AD LITEM   217

6 PSYCHOTHERAPY OF PARENTAL-ALIENATION-
   SYNDROME FAMILIES   219

INTRODUCTORY COMMENTS   219

THE INITIAL EVALUATION   223
SEVERE CASES OF THE PARENTAL ALIENATION
  SYNDROME   225
  The Mother   225
  The Children   226
  The Father   228
MODERATE CASES OF THE PARENTAL
  ALIENATION SYNDROME   230
  Introductory Comments   230
  The Mother   232
  The Children   236
  The Fathers   242
  Concluding Comments   244
MILD CASES OF THE PARENTAL ALIENATION
  SYNDROME   245
CLINICAL EXAMPLE   245
CONCLUDING COMMENTS   258

7 THE ROLE OF LAWYERS AND JUDGES
  IN DEALING WITH PARENTAL-
  ALIENATION-SYNDROME FAMILIES   261

INTRODUCTION   261
LAWYERS   262
JUDGES   263
  Guidelines for Judges for Making
    Custody Decisions   263
  The Role of the Judiciary in Dealing Optimally
    with Parental-Alienation-Syndrome Children
    and Their Parents   267
  Concluding Comments   274
GUARDIANS AD LITEM   276

8 RECOMMENDATIONS FOR THE FUTURE   279

INTRODUCTION   279
THE EDUCATION OF LAWYERS   280
  Law School Admissions Procedures   280
  Teaching Law Students About the Deficiencies
    of the Adversary System   285

Other Changes in Law School Education That
    Would Benefit Attorneys and Their Clients   300
Concluding Comments   301
THE EDUCATION AND TRAINING OF
    NONLEGAL PROFESSIONALS   302
DO "SEX-BLIND" CUSTODY DECISIONS
    NECESSARILY SERVE THE BEST
    INTERESTS OF CHILDREN?   305
THE STRONGER-HEALTHY-PSYCHOLOGICAL-
    BOND PRESUMPTION   309
AN ALTERNATIVE SYSTEM FOR RESOLVING
    CHILD CUSTODY DISPUTES   312
    Introduction   312
    Mediation   313
    Arbitration Panel   314
    Appeals Panel   316
    Due Process and Constitutional Rights   319
    Final Comments on the Three-Phase Proposal
        for Resolving Child Custody Disputes   321
CONCLUDING COMMENTS   323

CONCLUDING COMMENTS   **325**

ADDENDUM I   **327**

ADDENDUM II   **334a**

REFERENCES   **335**

AUTHOR INDEX   **339**

SUBJECT INDEX   **341**

ACKNOWLEDGMENTS

I am indebted to my secretaries Carol Gibbon, Donna La Tourette, Linda Gould, and Joyce Conforti, who dedicated themselves to the typing of the manuscript of this book.

I deeply appreciate the careful and instructive copyediting of Muriel Jorgensen. Once again, she has respected my ideas and style while providing me with useful criticisms. I appreciate, also, the efforts of Robert Tebbenhoff of Lind Graphics for his contributions to the production of this book from the original manuscript to final volume. I appreciate Barbara Bernstein's careful proofreading of the final page proofs and am grateful to Chris Stawasz for her dedication to the preparation of the index. I am indebted as well to my daughter, Nancy Gardner Rubin, Esq., for her valuable comments on the chapter on the history of the adversary system. I am grateful to Rev. Michael Slusser of Duquesne University for his review of the material relating to the Catholic Church. I appreciate the efforts of my wife, Patricia Lefevere, who took the cover photograph of me (serving as model for a forlorn father) in an empty playground.

My greatest debt, however, is to the children of divorce who have taught me much over many years about the kinds of grief they can suffer. From their parents, as well, I have learned many things that are contained herein. Attorneys have also taught me a great deal about the adversary system, both its weaknesses and strengths (unfortunately, more of the former than the latter). My hope is that what I have learned from these sources will be put to good use in this book and will contribute to the prevention and alleviation of the sorrows of divorce ordeals in others.

INTRODUCTION

During the last 10 to 15 years, we have witnessed a burgeoning of child custody disputes unparalleled in history. This increase has primarily been the result of two recent developments in the realm of child custody litigation, namely, the replacement of the tender-years presumption with the best-interests-of-the-child presumption and the increasing popularity of the joint custodial concept. In association with this burgeoning of litigation, we have witnessed a dramatic increase in the frequency of a disorder rarely seen previously, a disorder that I refer to as the *parental alienation syndrome*. In this disorder we see not only programming ("brainwashing") of the child by one parent to denigrate the other parent, but self-created contributions by the child in support of the preferred parent's campaign of denigration against the non-preferred parent. Because of the child's contribution I did not consider the terms *brainwashing, programming,* or other equivalent words to be applicable. Accordingly, I introduced the term *parental alienation syndrome* to cover the *combination* of these two contributing factors. In the context of this disorder we have more recently been seeing a rash of fabricated sex-abuse allegations, which may serve as an extremely effective weapon in these disputes. Also during the last few years we have become increasingly appreciative of the ubiquity of bona fide sexual abuse of children. Although the sex-abuse factor in the parental alienation syndrome is an important one, I have only made minimal reference to it in this book. Rather, I focus primarily on the etiology, development, manifestations, and treatment of the disorder, having elaborated on the sex-abuse factor in a previous book (Gardner, 1987) and in a forthcoming volume (Gardner, 1992a). So formidable and complex is this component that a separate book was warranted.

In this volume I first trace the historical development of the adversary system, the method most commonly used today to investigate and deal with child custody disputes. I then trace the historical development in western society of parental preference for child custody (mother versus father) following marital dissolution. Appreciation of these historical sequences helps put the reader in a better position to understand and place in proper perspective the problems with which we are dealing today.

I then describe in great detail the clinical manifestations of the parental alienation syndrome. Next, I provide guidelines for mental health professionals who may be involved in evaluating these children. Particular emphasis is given to the importance of the evaluator's serving as impartial examiner, rather than as advocate of one parent, when conducting such evaluations and the value of the joint interview as a source of information about the disorder. In the next chapter I provide guidelines for evidence gathering for lawyers, judges, and other members of the legal profession who may be involved in dealing with such families. Without a thorough knowledge of the etiology, pathogenesis, and manifestations of this disorder, legal professionals are ill-equipped to assess such families judiciously. Over the years I have read numerous *in camera* transcripts of judges interviewing children with parental alienation syndrome and have recognized that many judges have been "taken in" by these children and have accepted as valid their professions of hatred of the denigrated parent. Unfortunately, such receptivity has resulted in what I consider to have been many injudicious rulings regarding child custody placement. Accordingly, I have devoted a section of this book to providing judges with guidelines and specific questions that should enable them to interview more astutely children suffering with a parental alienation syndrome. Obviously, the more knowledgeable and skilled the judge is when interviewing these children, the more judicious will be his (her) conclusions, and the greater the likelihood that a proper decision will be made regarding custodial placement. Next, I provide guidelines for mental health professionals for treating these families and focus especially on the importance of ascertaining in which of the three categories of the parental alienation syndrome a particular family belongs. The next chapter is devoted to legal considerations when dealing with such families, again emphasizing the importance of determining in which of the three categories the disorder should justifiably be placed.

In the final chapter I present guidelines for changes that, if implemented, could contribute significantly to the prevention of the parental alienation syndrome. I discuss the education of lawyers, with particular emphasis on what I consider to be basic weaknesses in the adversary system, especially when it is utilized to resolve child custody disputes. Next, I provide recommendations for mental health professionals and emphasize the importance of their serving as impartial examiners, rather than as advocates, in child custody disputes. I also emphasize the use of mediation as a first step toward resolving such disputes. Specific guidelines are given for both mental health and legal professionals who are involved in dealing with parental-alienation-syndrome children and their parents. The implementation of these guidelines could reduce significantly the incidence of the parental alienation syndrome. I also describe a three-phase proposal for resolving child custody disputes without the necessity of resorting to adversarial litigation. Accordingly, the final chapter (and, in a sense, this book) is basically a proposed contribution to the field of preventive psychiatry.

It has come as a surprise to me from reports in both the legal and mental health literature that the concept of the parental alienation syndrome is often misinterpreted. Specifically, there are many who use the term as synonymous with parental "brainwashing" or "programming." Those who do this have missed an extremely important point regarding the etiology, manifestations, and even the treatment of the parental alienation syndrome. The disorder refers to a situation in which the parental programming is *combined with* the child's own scenarios of denigration of the allegedly hated parent. Were we to be dealing here simply with parental indoctrination, I would have probably stuck with brainwashing and/or programming. Because the campaign of denigration involves the aforementioned *combination*, I decided a new term was warranted, a term that would encompass *both* contributory factors. Furthermore, it was the child's contribution that led me to my theory about the etiology and pathogenesis of this disorder. Moreover, the understanding of the child's contribution is of importance in implementing the therapeutic guidelines described in this book.

Unfortunately, the term *parental alienation syndrome* is often used to refer to the animosity that a child may harbor against a parent who has *actually* abused the child, especially over an extended period. The term has been used to apply to the major categories of parental abuse, namely, physical, sexual, and emotional. Such application indicates a misunderstanding of the concept of the parental alienation syndrome. The term is applicable *only* when the parent has *not* exhibited anything close to the degree of alienating behavior that might warrant the campaign of denigration exhibited by the child. Rather, in typical cases the parent would be considered by most examiners to have provided normal loving parenting or, at worst, exhibited minimal impairments in parental capacity. It is the *exaggeration* of minor weaknesses and deficiencies that are the hallmarks of the parental alienation syndrome. When bona fide abuse does exist, then the child's responding hostility is warranted and the concept of the parental alienation syndrome is *not* applicable.

It is important for examiners to appreciate that a parent who inculcates a parental alienation syndrome in a child is indeed perpetrating a form of *emotional abuse* in that such programming may not only produce lifelong alienation from a loving parent, but lifelong psychiatric disturbance in the child. A parent who

systematically programs the child into a state of ongoing denigration and rejection from the other parent is exhibiting complete
disregard of the alienated parent's role in the child's upbringing.
Such a parent is bringing about a disruption of a psychological
bond that could, in the vast majority of cases, prove of great value
to the child, the separated and divorced status of the parents
notwithstanding. Such a parent exhibits a serious parenting
deficit, a deficit that should be given serious consideration by
courts when deciding primary custodial preference. Certainly
physical and/or sexual abuse of a child would quickly be viewed
by the court as a reason for assigning custody to the nonabusing
parent. Emotional abuse is much more difficult to assess objec-
tively, especially because many forms of emotional abuse are
subtle and difficult to verify in a court of law. The parental
alienation syndrome, however, is most often readily identified,
and courts would do well to consider its presence a manifestation
of emotional abuse by the programming parent. Accordingly,
courts do well to consider the programming parent to be exhibiting a serious parental deficit when weighing the pros and cons
of custodial transfer. I am not suggesting that such a parent
automatically be deprived of primary custody, only that the
pattern be considered a serious deficit in parenting capacity—a
form of emotional abuse—and that it be given serious consideration when weighing the custody decision. In this book, I provide
specific guidelines regarding the situations when such transfer is
not only desirable, but even crucial, if the children are to be
protected from lifelong alienation from the allegedly hated parent.

Since my first publication on the parental alienation syndrome (Gardner, 1985a), I have received many letters and telephone calls in which comments such as the following have been
made, "It's uncanny. What you're describing is exactly what
happened in my family." "I saw my situation on practically every
page. It's almost as if you've been living in my house and taking
notes." Considering the fact that I have received more than a
hundred such communications, I am convinced that my descriptions of this disorder are accurate and that my bringing this

syndrome to the attention of legal and mental health professionals has been warranted. I am certain that there were others who observed the same parent-child phenomena as I did when I first defined the disorder in the early 1980s. I do not believe that I have discovered anything here; rather, I believe that I have provided a name for the disorder and provided understanding of its etiology, pathogenesis, a detailed description of its manifestations, and guidelines for its treatment. I have also provided guidelines for legal professionals for dealing with such families and have formulated proposals for preventing the disorder's development. I would not be surprised if others, as well, have described what I have; however, their work has not yet come to my attention.

The parental alienation syndrome is a relatively new disorder, having evolved primarily from recent changes in the criteria by which primary custodial placement is decided. As is true with all newly described disorders, we are in the early stages of our understanding. I plan to continue to revise and update my publications on the disorder in order to keep readers of my work apprised of new developments.

Comment on Addendum II for the Second Printing—1995

After three years, there is basically nothing in this book that I would modify. What I have said then still holds now. However, there is one important addition related to dealing with mothers and children in the severe category of parental alienation syndrome. My experience has been that the severe category represents about 10 percent of PAS families. Whereas the children of mothers in the mild and moderate categories usually do better remaining with their mothers, many—but not all—the children in the severe category would probably do better living primarily with their fathers. The problem of transfer has been a formidable one. This problem, I believe, has been solved by the proposal included in the back of this book as Addendum II. It describes a series of transitional sites of varying degrees of restriction and supervision that can be very useful, both for deciding where the children shall ultimately live and facilitating their easement into the father's home, if that proves to be the final optimum disposition.

 **ONE**

A BRIEF REVIEW OF THE HISTORICAL DEVELOPMENT OF THE ADVERSARY SYSTEM

INTRODUCTION

Throughout this chapter, when I use the term *adversary system*, I am referring to a legal procedure that prevails in the United States, England, and its former colonies. It is a system based on the principle that the best way of learning the "truth," when two parties have diametrically opposed positions, is for each to present his or her case before an impartial decision maker(s) (a judge and/or a jury). Each side is permitted to withhold (within certain guidelines and procedures) facts that might compromise its position and to present those that support it. The theory is that these opposing presentations provide the impartial evaluators with the best opportunity for ascertaining the truth. In the adversary system, this method of data (evidence) collection is used primarily as a method of dispute resolution. The fact finder (whether it be a judge or jury) serves primarily in a neutral position. Although it originated in criminal proceedings, where the dispute is between a prosecutor and an accused person, it is used in civil proceedings as well, where the dispute is between a plaintiff and a defendant.

When I use the term *European* legal system I am not including

1

the English legal procedure (from which the American is more directly derived) but the European *continental* procedure, which is generally referred to as the *inquisitorial* system. In this system the judge is less neutral and more active in the cross-examination process than the judge in the adversary system. It has been used more extensively for criminal than for civil proceedings. Later in this chapter I will discuss these two systems in greater detail. The adversary system is also the predominant one in countries that were formerly English colonies. Furthermore, countries on the European continent have utilized varying degrees of adversarial procedures within the inquisitorial structure. For example, Spain, Italy, and France utilize systems that are direct derivatives of the inquisitorial procedures from the 15th century, whereas in Germany, the inquisitorial system is fused with a number of traditional adversarial procedures. And the Soviet system, although modeled after the inquisitorial system, has been modified by Marxist principles and restrictions on certain freedoms taken for granted in the West.

It is not my purpose to present here a detailed history of the adversary system. Not only do I not consider myself knowledgeable enough to do this, but it goes beyond the purposes of this book. Rather, I will outline the system's development, with particular emphasis on issues that are relevant to modern-day practices in divorce law and especially custody litigation. My main purpose here will be to demonstrate that we are still using techniques that have their origins in the ritualistic practices of primitive tribes, ancient societies, and the "Dark Ages" (literally) and that these techniques are used in only a small fraction of present societies, namely England (and its former colonies) and the United States. As I trace the historical development of the adversary system, I will point out how some of these early practices have served as the basis for many of our present-day procedures in divorce and custody litigation.

In the preparation of this material, I first sought references from attorneys, friends, and colleagues—many of whom I hold in high regard. I was surprised how little they knew about the historical development of the system, and I was even more surprised to learn that it is rarely taught as a formal course (or even part of a course) in the majority of law schools in the United States. Law students are presented with the adversary system as *the* system for resolving various kinds of disputes. Most are not even told about alternative methods of dispute resolution tradi- tionally used in many other societies. Many, at the time of graduation, automatically assume that the adversary system is the best and the most efficient. And many maintain this unques- tioned allegiance to the system until the end of their professional careers.

The material on the history of the adversary system pre- sented in this chapter was obtained primarily from the compre- hensive articles by Neef and Nagel (1974), Landsman (1983), and Alexander (1984). In addition, some material was obtained from the sections on the legal profession and the law of evidence in the *Encyclopedia Britannica* (1982). These thorough and extensive arti- cles provide numerous references to the primary source material from which this chapter has been derived. I would strongly recommend these articles to those readers who wish more de- tailed information on this subject. In addition to these sources, I present information that has become part of my general knowl- edge and experience, the sources of which are no longer known to me. The reader will soon note that my comments on the adversary system are quite critical. This is the result, I believe, of the fact that my experiences with it have primarily been in its utilization in divorce/custody proceedings. I recognize that its utilization in other kinds of cases may be less psychologically damaging to the clients. Accordingly, the reader does well to keep this in mind when reading this book and to recognize that the reforms I will recommend at the end relate primarily to its utilization in custody/visitation disputes. I suspect, however, that its utilization in other areas may also be psychologically traumatic and that the criticisms I present here may very well be applicable to these areas of utilization as well.

PRIMITIVE SOCIETIES

Our knowledge of the kinds of dispute-settling mechanisms utilized by primitive societies is largely speculative. There are, however, some general principles subscribed to by those who have investigated this area. One cannot put a particular date on this phase. What is described here is a *developmental theory* that ascribes a sequence of procedures utilized for dispute resolution. The sequence began at different times in different places, and there are some societies today still operating in accordance with these primitive principles.

In the earliest primitive societies, wherein the whole society lived in a small cluster in which everyone knew one another, the general method for dispute resolution was through compromise. The purpose was to reach a solution that would enable the individuals to live as harmoniously as possible with one another after the settlement of the dispute. Such groups avoided any system that might result in residual animosity between the disputants. This was especially important because the extended families of the disputants might harbor residual animosity toward one another, which could be even more detrimental to the survival of the small group. Accordingly, compromise techniques were utilized rather than the winner-take-all principle that the modern adversary system employs. Although many judges attempt to get the disputants to compromise, if they are unsuccessful and the dispute goes to trial there is often a winner-take-all victory for the party that prevails. Present-day compromise analogies are labor management disputes and disputes between businessmen and customers, wherein both parties recognize that, following the dispute, they may still have to have a relationship with one another. It is only when communities become larger and individuals are able to remove themselves entirely from one another that a more adversarial and permanently divisive arrangement comes to prevail.

Another method of primitive dispute resolution that could insure cohesiveness was one in which leaders imposed punishments in accordance with speculations regarding what ghosts, dead ancestors, and other spirits considered to be justifiable punishments. In this way, the punishers were not viewed as being personally responsible for implementing the punishment, but were merely considered to be the vehicles through which these higher powers operated. As a result, the system still allowed for a certain amount of cooperation between the accusers and the accused, between the punishers and the punished. The system was also a reflection of the ignorance of tribal leaders. By ascribing wisdom to spirits and other unseen powers, tribal leaders compensated for their own lack of understanding of the complex and even unknown issues that were involved.

As societies became larger and more complex, the likelihood increased that the disputants would not subsequently have to live with one another. Under these circumstances, other methods of dispute resolution evolved. However, the aforementioned method by which supernatural powers were brought into play served in later phases as well. Invoking these unseen powers served to protect the accusers and the punishers from the acrimony of the guilty party and thereby allowed for ongoing cooperation between the parties.

I believe it was unfortunate that more complex and recent societies developed systems that did not take into proper consideration the factor of ongoing cooperation between the disputants. Had they done so, we might not have gone so far afield regarding our methods of dispute resolution; we might have maintained the systems of compromise first utilized by the earliest societies. In a sense, these most primitive methods were the most advanced in that they were the methods most likely to insure resolutions that promised ongoing conciliation.

In many Asian societies the mediation/conciliation notion is very much present to this day. In Japan, for example, people who are unable to resolve their disputes themselves generally take them to mutually respected elders who attempt to resolve the dispute privately. People who are unable to resolve their disputes by themselves or with the help of elders are generally viewed as socially atypical and may be stigmatized. The fear of such social stigma deters them from carrying the dispute further. When, however, a situation does warrant intervention by third parties, they may resort to neighborhood dispute-resolution centers. It is rare that individuals must go further and use attorneys to resolve their disputes. This is one of the reasons why there is now only one attorney for every 10,000 people in Japan; in the United States there is one attorney for every 320 people.

In recent years we have witnessed evidence of increasing appreciation of conciliatory procedures in the United States. Alternative methods of dispute resolution are now being taught in some law schools, and divorce mediation has also gained some limited popularity recently (Coogler, 1978; Folberg and Taylor, 1984).

GREEK SOCIETY

The ancient Greeks, as the first step toward the resolution of a dispute, submitted the conflict to an arbitrator. This was the earliest form of dispute resolution used by the ancient Greeks. The arbitrator was often paid a small fee and his goal was to try to reconcile the parties. One could not go to court before one had gone through the arbitration process. As is the case with the inquisitorial system, all the information from both the disputants and the witnesses was submitted to the court in written form before the trial began. This information was sealed in a special box and opened when the court was ready to hear the case. These documents were read by a panel who decided the case on the basis of this written material. It is of note here that at that point in Greek history the disputants did not confront one another. Residua of this absence of confrontation is to be found in the inquisitorial system used in the Middle Ages. And it may be that some residua of this is present in our present-day adversary system, where there is still some restriction on the disputants confronting one another, although they are certainly in the courtroom together.

As the Greek society became more complex, the disputants were permitted to be represented by orators or rhetors (people who used rhetoric). It was in this setting that there developed the practice of dramatic presentations, a practice that probably has its counterpart in modern-day courtroom lawyers, especially those who pride themselves on their oratorical skills. When used in moderation, this residuum of the Greek system is probably of benefit to the client; however, when the dramatizations reach the point of bombast, then the courtroom becomes the stage for melodrama, hyperbole, and even a circus-like atmosphere.

It is important for the reader to note that I am referring here only to free men of ancient Greece, not to slaves. Slaves could not hope to get redress in court or bring suit against another person unless they could find a citizen to represent them. On occasion, however, a slave could be a witness. The assumption was generally made that slaves lied. Accordingly, their testimony was often accompanied by torture in order to extract the "truth." This practice discouraged masters from allowing their slaves to testify because they might be worthless as workers following their testimony. (It would seem to me that if it were indeed true that all slaves automatically lied, then a more judicious and humane way of dealing with their testimony would be to assume that the *opposite* of what they said was true. This would save both the tortured and the torturer much time and trouble.) Sometimes an ordeal (see below) was utilized when the judges were unable to arrive at a decision.

Juries were used in the Greek courts, but they voted secretly (as they do today in the United States). Following the jury's decision, the accused and the accuser together were permitted to suggest to the court a reasonable punishment, suggestions which were given serious consideration. This practice is often seen in courtrooms today when both sides are given the opportunity for input to the judge before sentencing.

Among the ancient Greeks, trial by ordeal was commonly used as a method of ascertaining whether or not a party was guilty or innocent of a crime. It generally involved subjecting the accused to a wide variety of pains and tortures. Guilt or innocence was established on the basis of the accused's reactions to the ordeal. Ordeal by water was especially popular among the ancient Greeks. This system operated in a world that was viewed as anthropomorphized, i.e., inanimate objects were considered to contain spirits, and to have wills, thoughts, and feelings. The Greeks assumed that if the accused were to float in the river, then it indicated that the river found the accused objectionable and did not wish to embrace him or her. If the accused sank, this indicated that the individual was innocent and good and that the river thereby wanted to embrace him or her. Attempts were usually made to pull the sinking innocent to safety. In contrast, the person who floated would be punished for the crime, often by being put to death.

Ordeal by fire was also common among the ancient Greeks. The accused might prove innocence by walking on fire, swallowing fire, or passing through flames unharmed. Boiling liquids and hot irons were also used to determine guilt or innocence, based on the extent of the injuries sustained after exposure. Other ordeals involved the use of snakes, swords, and poisons. Girls whose virginity was questioned were compelled to descend into a cavern in which a poisonous snake had been placed. If they were bitten by the snake, it indicated that they were no longer virgins. Among the ancient Greeks, male nonvirgins were not considered to have committed a crime. This attitude toward male nonvirginity persists in many societies to this day, and there are many societies today that basically do not deal with *female* nonvirgins any differently than the ancient Greeks did.

ROMAN SOCIETY

In *early* Rome a priest was generally considered crucial when dealing with legal matters. Priests were considered to be the ones most knowledgeable about how to deal with the problems of finding out which of the disputants was telling the truth. The priests kept their laws and techniques in personal secret books. Gradually, however, lawyers did evolve, replacing the priests. They advised their clients and pleaded for them in court. The parties rarely engaged in direct confrontation with each other in the courtroom. As was true in Greek society, slaves, as a matter of course, were tortured on the witness stand. Juries were used, but only in cases involving senators and equites (horse-mounted warriors with status halfway between senators and common men). Either the defendant or the plaintiff could object to the selection of certain jurors at his trial (a practice still in operation today).

Like the Greeks, the Roman lawyers enjoyed their orations. Sometimes a client would have many lawyers representing him, each of whom would provide elaborate speeches to the magistrate and jury. Histrionics were accepted and even considered desirable. It was not uncommon to display the wounds of a client and bring injured children before the court. Lawyers were in oversupply and they often competed with one another to obtain clients. They were allowed to hawk their wares in the streets and often hired "clappers" to applaud their orations in the courtroom. They hoped thereby to enhance their reputations and obtain more clients. Although the judge and jury might decide that a defendant was guilty, it was the accuser's responsibility to impose the punishment, and sometimes he did not have the means to do so.

In the early fourth century A.D. a new development took place in Roman law. Whereas previously trials were open and public, they now became secret. This was rationalized by the argument that members of the judicial hierarchy were beyond criticism, were dedicated to work honestly and efficiently, and could be trusted to make judicious decisions. They also rationalized secret judicial decisions as necessary for the stability of the empire. Accordingly, prior to the downfall of the empire, the Romans abandoned a very complex and sophisticated courtroom system for a somewhat totalitarian one. It regressed thereby from a more democratic and egalitarian legal system to one that infringed much more on the freedom of individuals. However, certain aspects of the Roman system persisted and can be found in the legal profession today, e.g., lawyers representing their clients, juries and jury selection, and lawyers advertising.

TRIAL BY ORDEAL

Trial by ordeal was one of the three commonly used methods of trial used in the Middle Ages. Reference was made to it in my discussion of ancient Greek society. However, in the Middle Ages it became much more commonly used. Trial by ordeal is based on the belief that God will intervene and by a miraculous sign indicate whether the litigant undergoing the ordeal was in the right. It has appeared in many countries and at different times. Ordeal by fire is an ancient tradition. The accused might establish innocence by walking on fire, swallowing fire, or passing through the flames unharmed. In many societies the ordeal was only used after the judge or jury found itself unable to arrive at a decision. Trial by ordeal was especially popular during the Middle Ages in Europe and England. A priest usually administered an oath before the ordeal, and quite frequently the ordeal was conducted on Church grounds. Of the three forms of trial used in the Middle Ages (trial by battle and trial by wager being the others), trial by ordeal was the most likely to be under church auspices. In England common forms of ordeal required the litigant to carry a red-hot iron bar a certain distance or place an arm in boiling water for a prescribed period. If the litigant's burns did not fester after a prescribed period (usually three days), he or she was considered to be in the right. A typical example of trial by ordeal was to place the litigant's arm in a seething cauldron. Afterward, it was carefully enveloped in cloth, sealed with the signet of the judge, and three days later was unwrapped. The guilt or innocence of the party was ascertained by the condition of the hand or arm. The theory was that the guilty individual's arm would be infected or seriously scarred and the innocent person would remain unhurt.

Immersion in deep water was another common form of ordeal. The person was considered to be in the right if he or she sank rather than floated. Ordeal was used for women who were charged with witchcraft. In the Middle Ages (and subsequently) women charged with witchcraft were often assumed to have had sexual intercourse with Satan. In the course of such sexual relations, part of his spirit was considered to have entered into and invested them. Their human attributes were considered to be altered by his spirit, which, because it is lighter than air, lightens the body. The woman charged with witchcraft was dropped into a river with her hands and feet tied. If she sank she was considered innocent, because the presumption was made that the devil had not invested her. If she floated she was considered guilty and punished, sometimes by being burned to death. The Salem Witchcraft water-dunking ordeal is an example of the utilization of trial by ordeal in America.

Trial by ordeal is basically a statement of mankind's feelings of impotency and appreciation of ignorance regarding dispute resolution and the determination of whether or not an alleged perpetrator did indeed commit a crime. In trial by ordeal the assistance of supernatural powers is brought into play. There is a certain grandiosity in trial by ordeal in that it is based on the assumption that the deity, the Great Judge, is paying attention to the particular ordeal and manipulating the events in the service of helping the good or the innocent survive the ordeal.

Trial by ordeal was generally an earlier phenomenon than trial by battle (to be discussed below). In trial by ordeal the individual is helpless in playing a role in his or her fate, and it is left entirely in the hands of higher powers. In trial by combat, which generally came later, some power was placed in the hands of the combatants in the decision regarding guilt and/or innocence.

Trial by ordeal in English society was traditionally for the lower classes, whereas trial by combat was for the upper classes. This was especially the case because trial by combat required the ownership or utilization of horses and often involved disputes concerning land ownership (which poor people, obviously, did not have). Trial by ordeal was declared unacceptable in England and on the Continent in 1215 by the Fourth Lateran Council (to be discussed below). Once the Church removed priest participation, the practice quickly fell into disuse. However, residua of the method, I believe, exists today in adversary proceedings. Many attorneys, by design, will subject witnesses to ordeals of exhausting and painstaking interrogation. The individual is brought to the point where he or she may not even realize what is being said. Such tactics could also be viewed as a method of extracting a confession by subjecting the individual to such an ordeal. Here, verbal whips are used as the method of torture.

TRIAL BY COMBAT (TRIAL BY BATTLE)

Trial by combat (or trial by battle) was a common form of trial utilized in the Middle Ages, especially on the Continent. In trial by battle the disputants or their representatives (sometimes referred to as *champions*) engaged in physical combat until one side yielded or was subdued. The party who prevailed was considered to be telling the truth. The defeated party could admit defeat by speaking the word "Craven" (*Middle English, cravant:* overthrown, coward) or by stopping the battle when it was obvious that that party was defeated. Or the battle continued until one party no longer had the capacity to go on or was slain. In certain serious criminal matters, it was understood from the outset that the fight would continue until one party was indeed killed. The fight was overseen by judicial officers, and the combat began only after each of the combatants had taken a solemn oath that his cause was just. Each party would invoke the judgment of God and declare that he did not use sorcery or enchantment. A fundamental assumption of trial by combat is the notion that being right is expected to be productive of the just result. This is related to the belief that justice will prevail and that God will see to it that good will win out over evil.

In this form of trial, as in trial by wager (to be discussed below) and trial by ordeal, divine intervention was considered to be the important determinant as to who would prevail. There was no presentation of evidence. The individual was often permitted to be represented by a substitute, called a champion. Accordingly, trial by combat has also been called trial by champion. Because women and children were considered unable to fend for themselves, they were almost routinely provided with champions. Professional champions were available to fight for anyone who paid them. The battle would begin when the challenger threw down a glove and the person who accepted the challenge picked it up. Sometimes the weapons used were not designed to be lethal; rather they were made of wood, bone, or a horn. In criminal cases, however, the loser was hanged or mutilated. In civil cases the loser would cry "Craven," which meant that he had perjured himself, was a liar, and was guilty. He then paid a fine and came to be known as a liar. On occasion the two combatants would continue to fight until nightfall ("before the stars appeared"), at which point the battle would be discontinued and the person who appeared to be prevailing was considered the innocent party. This practice protected people from being killed. Sometimes champions were individuals who had proven themselves successful in previous trials by battle. Trial by battle clearly favored the rich, who either had better martial skills or could afford to hire those with such skills. Trial by battle was common throughout most of northern Europe in the early Middle Ages and was introduced into England from France after the Norman Conquest in 1066. It was never a very popular or influential form of adjudication in England.

In one form of trial by combat the accuser might have been a public prosecutor. He would then battle the accused, the defendant. Accordingly, the accuser was not only a prosecutor, but in many cases also served as the executioner. This was especially the case when champions were not used. Although champions were probably used earliest for women or children because women and children were less capable of "fighting their own battles" and thereby less capable of proving their innocence, champions later came to be used by men as well. The use of champions came after the realization that it didn't seem reasonable that the taller, stronger, and more powerful defendants would almost invariably be innocent.

An interesting tradition evolved in trial by battle. In criminal proceedings between an accuser and an accused, the men themselves would fight. However, if the dispute was about ownership of land, then the battle was fought by champions who represented the disputants. This was done because, if the participants themselves fought and both died in battle, there would be no owner for the land in dispute.

It was not until 1819 that trial by combat was abolished in England, but it had fallen into disrepute long before that time. The last recorded trial by champion took place in England in 1571. Many critics of the adversary system (including the author) claim that it is a direct extension of trial by battle. Those who defend the system claim that this is not the case, for the following reasons: (1) trial by battle was basically outlawed in England by the 13th century, (2) there is no evidence for its use beyond the 16th century, and (3) adversarial proceedings in their present form did not emerge until about the 18th century. However, the tradition in trial by battle of the litigants being represented by another party has its equivalent in the adversary system. I believe that we have not moved as far from trial by combat as many proponents of the adversary system profess. In many cases it is still very much a "bloody battle." Peoples' lives have literally been destroyed by the system. Many have been drained completely of all financial resources. Many have suffered irreparable psychological damage over the course of protracted litigation. The practice of ending the battle at sunset, and making a decision then, is in a sense more humane than the system today where litigation can go on for years.

TRIAL BY WAGER

Trial by wager and ordeal were more common in England than trial by battle. Trial by wager required each of the litigants to take an oath that his or her claims were true and to produce other persons, usually referred to as *compurgators*, to support the litigant's oath by making their own oaths. It was also called *trial by compurgation*. It was basically a "character test" in which the oath taker established his or her case by demonstrating good standing in the community. The compurgators were not asked to provide testimony about the facts of the case, but only served to guarantee that the oath taker was an honest person. The more compurgators who would swear on behalf of a litigant, the greater the chances of acquittal.

In trial by wager the person took an oath. Such an oath involved invoking supernatural powers, who were allegedly listening to the oath, operating at the time of the trial, and who would intervene on behalf of the person who was innocent or right. There was an appeal here to a supernatural power, with the implication that if one was not telling the truth, God would somehow punish the individual. The participants did not expect that God would rule immediately; instead the perjurer would be punished at some future date. Such oaths were taken seriously by primitive peoples. They were also taken seriously by people in the Middle Ages, who genuinely believed that if they lied, there might be some punishment in the hereafter.

Residua of trial by wager exist today. The oath that we take in court with our hand on the Bible is a derivative of this system, as is the use of character witnesses. There is little reason to believe that the vast majority of people who take such oaths today under the European/American system take them seriously and can be relied upon not to perjure themselves from the fear that they will be punished by God. They might fear punishment by the court for perjury, but not punishment by a supernatural power. Perjuring oneself before a court of law is routine nowadays and most often promulgated by the attorneys (the champions). Recent examples of this are the Watergate hearings and the more recent Iran-contra congressional hearings. On the basis of my own experiences with divorce/custody litigation, I would say that 80 to 90 percent of all the clients I have seen will lie in court without any hesitation or guilt. Although attorneys profess publicly that it is unethical for them to encourage their clients to perjure themselves, this is routinely done. One method is to foster lies of omission. Because there may be some readers who are not familiar with the difference between lies of omission and lies of commission, I will define this important distinction here. A lie of omission is simply a kind of deceit in which an individual knowingly omits data in the service of misleading the listener. In a lie of commission the individual adds fabrications toward the same goal, namely, that of misleading the listener. Lies of commission are not permitted by the adversary system, but lies of omission are not only permitted but actively encouraged. As I see it, a lie of omission is no less a lie than a lie of commission; it is a form of deceit. A man who does not tell a woman with whom he is amorously involved that he has a sexually transmitted disease is lying by omission. A woman who does not tell her husband that he is not the biological father of the child she is bearing is also lying by omission. Obviously, the consequences of such silences may be grave. Although the system will not uniformly condone all such egregious examples of lies of omission, its principle of sanctioning such withholding of vital data often produces similar grievous results. But clients and their attorneys often go further and actively support lies of commission as well. Even character witnesses are generally not uncomfortable perjuring themselves. Accordingly, the residua of trial by wager are primarily ritualistic. They exist in the oath taken on the Bible and in the character witnesses. And, like most rituals, their original purposes have long since passed into oblivion.

In recent years, some states have changed their courtroom procedure and no longer require a witness to take an oath on the Bible and/or may omit the word "God" from the oath taken before testifying. In some European countries witnesses are allowed to object to taking an oath and are permitted to substitute a solemn affirmation. In Denmark, oaths in legal procedures have been abolished. In the Soviet Union, consistent with the antireligious position of the government, oaths or solemn affirmations are prohibited in the courtroom.

FOURTH LATERAN COUNCIL — 1215

The three methods of trial used in the Middle Ages were not mutually exclusive and often coexisted in the same area. Often the accused could choose the method of trial. All three methods were based on the premise of Divine intervention. Direct heavenly intercession was postulated for ordeal and battle, and eternal damnation was supposed to enforce trial by wager. The emphasis was on the judgment of God rather than on the judgment of man. Very little use of evidence was considered necessary, nor were fact-finding procedures considered important. Because of the heavy reliance on Divine intervention, there was little concern with the appellate process. Active participation by both the accused and the accuser was central to the three medieval methods, as it is to the adversary system. Such participation is not central to the inquisitorial system (to be discussed below).

In the year 1215, the Fourth Lateran Council prohibited Church participation in trial by ordeal. The Lateran Councils were ecumenical councils held in the Pope's palace in Rome (the

Lateran Palace) between 1123 and 1517. Pope Innocent III's 1215 edict against trial by ordeal ended the practice, because priestly participation had been one of its fundamental components. At the same time, both ecclesiastical and secular critics began a series of sustained attacks on trial by wager and trial by battle, but these were not prohibited. These systems of determining guilt or innocence did, however, become far less frequently utilized. As a result, a partial vacuum was created that permitted the development of alternative systems for ascertaining whether or not an accused did indeed commit a crime. On the Continent the inquisitorial system emerged as the predominant system, as is the situation today. In England, however, other systems evolved, culminating in the adversary system, which took its present form in the 18th and 19th centuries. I will first discuss briefly the inquisitorial system and then discuss in greater detail the evolution of the adversary system, first in England and then in the United States.

THE INQUISITORIAL SYSTEM

As mentioned, in 1215 the Fourth Lateran Council banned Church participation in ordeals. In addition, trial by wager and trial by battle were also on the wane. On the Continent the inquisitorial system evolved. This procedure was the product of combining certain aspects of the laws of ancient Rome (Roman law) with judicial principles developed in European ecclesiastical circles (canonical law). By the 16th century this amalgam of Roman and canonical approaches was dominant throughout continental Europe. A central element in this approach was active inquiry by the judge in order to uncover the truth. He wielded great power, so much so that it became prudent to limit his authority by means of strict evidentiary requirements. Generally, the judge could only convict a criminal defendant under two circumstances: (1) when two eyewitnesses were produced who observed the crime or (2) when the defendant confessed. Circumstantial evidence was generally not considered sufficient to warrant conviction. However, under these same laws, judges were authorized to use torture to extract the necessary confessions. Torture came to be viewed as an excellent and reliable method of finding out "the truth." Thus, torture became a tool of judicial inquiry and was used to generate the evidence upon which the defendant would be condemned.

At this point I will discuss some of the reasons why the inquisitorial system developed on the Continent and why the adversary system evolved in England. In 1215, the same year that the Fourth Lateran Council convened, the English barons forced King John to sign the Magna Carta, which guaranteed certain rights and liberties to Englishmen (men, not women; nobility, not lower classes). Certain rights of individuals (upper class) were thereby established, and a precedent was set for the democracy that ultimately evolved in England. In contrast, on the Continent, derivatives of Roman law still prevailed—especially the notion of the centralized authority of the state. Another factor that contributed to the expansion of the inquisitorial method on the Continent was the Catholic Church's fear of the spread of anti-Catholic movements.

One of the earliest and most powerful of the anti-Church groups was the Albigenses (a name derived from the city of Albi in southern France), who spread anti-Church doctrines throughout Europe (especially southern Europe) in the 11th and 12th centuries. They posed such a threat to the Church that a special crusade, the Albigensian Crusade (1208-1213) was organized in the attempt to exterminate them. In addition, the earliest papal inquisition, the medieval Inquisition, was set up to bring to trial and execute these and related groups of heretics. These proved successful in obliterating almost completely the Albigensians and related movements.

However, in the late 15th century the Spanish Inquisition was established in Spain to extinguish Jews and Muslims, who were then considered to be a threat to the Church. And in the 16th century the Roman Inquisition was set up, this time to stem the rising tide of Protestantism. The methods utilized by the medieval and Spanish Inquisitions were much more brutal and sadistic than those used by the later Roman Inquisition. The methods described below were more typical of the two earlier inquisitions than the third. All three, however, served in part, as models for the secular inquisitorial systems that developed on the Continent.

The Church did not consider the relatively primitive judicial systems operative at that time to be sufficient to handle the widening threat of the anti-Catholic movements. The key word here is *heresy*, and the inquisitions were constantly searching for heretics who were then brought before them. Heretics were rounded up, persecuted, and tried for their heresy. There was little concern for evidence and veracity of witnesses. Accused individuals did not know the names of the witnesses against them, for fear of retaliation. Witnesses in support of the accused were not permitted to appear. There was no confrontation (cross-examination) of witnesses. Death by fire was made the official punishment for heretics, and they were usually burned at the stake. If they warranted special clemency, they were sentenced to life imprisonment. However, because life imprisonment was a much more expensive proposition, it was rarely utilized. Torture was used to elicit confessions. The Church and the State worked together, with the Church authorizing the torture and the State being the arm of enforcement. The inquisitors could excommunicate and label as heretic any civil magistrate who refused to inflict the punishment the inquisitors prescribed. The methods of torture commonly used to elicit confessions included the rack, thumbscrew, and flogging. There was an extremely high rate of conviction; acquittal was rare. Archbishops traveled throughout the Continent and would force people to denounce one another. Those who refused risked being considered heretics themselves. Often the cases were judged without the names of the accused or witnesses. The inquisitions were not universally embraced. It was not utilized in Scandinavian countries, nor did it take root in England. This is partly related to the fact that these countries were geographically isolated from the Continent. Also, the Albigenses and related sects did not spread as far north as Scandinavia or across into England. Thus, there was little need for the utilization of the medieval Inquisition in these areas. In addition, as mentioned, a parallel system of adjudication was developing in England, one based more on individual rights.

Whereas the adversary system is based on the premise that truth will emerge as an outgrowth of a clash between adversaries, the inquisitorial system is based on the assumption that truth is most likely to emerge as a result of an inquiry by neutral persons, such as judges. The judge in the inquisitorial system is a fact finder, but a very active fact finder. It is he who controls the mechanisms of inquiry. In the American and English adversarial system, the lawyers collect and present the facts and the judge is a more neutral hearer of the facts, although he does have some power of inquiry.

In the European system, both sides generally provide all pertinent information to the court and to one another prior to the onset of the proceedings. In the adversary system, each side tries to keep "aces up its sleeve" in order to catch the other side off guard and limit opportunity for response. In the adversary system, the attorneys call in the witnesses. In the European system, the judge calls in the witnesses and interviews them in the presence of the attorneys and the clients. Whereas in the adversary system the witnesses are generally selected because they are likely to support a particular side's position, in the European system the witnesses are more neutral and are generally called in by the judge.

In the inquisitorial system the judge is an active fact finder. The European trial is more an investigation rather than a battle of two opposing sides. The judge collects all the information before the trial and is given information by both attorneys. Witnesses are not interviewed by the attorneys for either side before the trial begins. Rather, they are interviewed by the judge. They do not belong to either side; rather, they belong to the judge. The witnesses testify in an uninterrupted narrative. The judge is the one who questions the witness. After the judge interrogates the witness, the lawyers can do so but not in the restrictive cross-examination type of inquiry used in the United States and England.

As a person who has appeared as a court-appointed expert

on many occasions, I am sympathetic to the inquisitorial system's practice of giving witnesses (expert and nonexpert) free rein to present their testimony. The argument given by proponents of the adversary system that such restriction ultimately balances out and that all the facts are ultimately presented to the judge is a myth. I have never been involved in a case where this has proven to be true. What usually happens is that only a fraction of opposing arguments are presented to the court. But even those that are brought forth are usually presented at some other date, long after the judge (no matter how brilliant and no matter his or her memory) has forgotten the initial points.

THE DEVELOPMENT OF THE ADVERSARY SYSTEM FROM THE 13TH TO THE 17TH CENTURIES

The foundations of our present-day adversary system in England and the United States were laid down primarily between the 13th and the 17th centuries. As mentioned, the Fourth Lateran Council created a partial vacuum with regard to methods of dispute resolution and determination of guilt or innocence. On the Continent conditions prevailed that led to the development of the inquisitorial system. In England, for reasons already stated, the climate was one in which the adversary system gradually evolved. Four institutions developed that served as foundations for the system: juries, witnesses, judges, and lawyers. I will discuss each of these separately and then describe how they coalesced into the adversary system, first in England and then in the United States. Of course, discussing them separately is somewhat artificial in that each influenced the others.

Juries

The Normans probably brought the jury system to England at the time of the Norman Conquest in 1066. The jury has served many different functions over the years. In the 11th century juries served to inform the court of cases it should try because jurors, as friends and neighbors of the parties involved in the litigation, were more likely to know what was going on in the community. The early jurors, however, were not really peers of the litigants because they were generally freeholders (landowners and titled individuals). They were free men, and they were often higher on the social ladder than those on trial.

Originally jurors were not the neutral fact finders they are today, listening to others present the facts; rather, they were actively involved in collecting evidence. Traditionally, they were individuals who lived in the same community as the litigants and were thereby more likely to have information about the events to be dealt with at the trial. In fact, not to have such knowledge was considered reason for disqualification. In addition, there was often a time gap between the assignment of the jury members and the beginning of the trial, during which time the jurors were expected to collect facts relevant to the dispute. They were empowered to make investigations, to ask questions, and to acquaint themselves with the details of the case. Accordingly, Divine guidance was replaced by collection of pertinent data. Jurors could be punished if the judge decided that their decision was the "wrong" one. This check on the jury system enhanced dedication and honesty and was probably a factor in its survival. The growth of the jury system as a method of fact finding reduced and obviated the utilization of torture, another method of fact finding. The jury, then, was the adversary system's means of fact finding, in contrast to torture, which was the inquisitorial system's method of obtaining information.

From the 13th to 15th centuries, the practice evolved that the litigants could challenge the jurors; if the jurors were found to be biased, they could be removed. From the 15th century onward, jurors generally became less involved in out-of-court investigations and began to rely upon facts presented in court as the basis for their decision. The use of a considerable volume of evidence had the effect of shifting the function of the jury from active inquiry to passive review and analysis. Juries also evolved from being the king's representatives to being independent entities, unconnected with the objectives and influences of the government. It was not until 1705 in civil cases and 1826 in criminal cases that jurors could be drawn from places other than the immediate locality in which the dispute arose. This was done to reduce the likelihood that jurors would enter the courtroom with preliminary, and possibly prejudicial, information. Our present-day grand jury is similar in its function to the earlier juries (prior to 1705); it is primarily an inquisitorial body that seeks evidence in order to determine whether a trial should be held.

In the late 1300s and early 1400s contact between the litigants and the jurors after the submission of a case were significantly curtailed to reduce the possibility of prejudice and influence. Separation of the litigants from the jury is a central element in the adversary process and is one of the ways in which the jury system laid the foundation for the development of the adversary system.

By the 18th century the jury was not only viewed as a neutral and passive fact-finding group but as a check on judicial despotism. The Constitution of the United States, fashioned in the 1780s, specifically incorporated the right to jury trial as a check on other institutions of government, not only the judiciary, but those who chose the judges and wrote the laws. The juries served as monitors of the laws by having the power to control the judges empowered to implement them.

Witnesses

Up through the 15th century the testimony of witnesses was held in low esteem. In fact, witnesses were not generally used in English trials until about 1500. Voluntary testimony was viewed with suspicion, and witnesses could not be compelled to testify against their will. However, in the 16th century the presentation of testimonial evidence grew dramatically. The information provided by witnesses came to replace private juror inquiry as the basis for decisions in criminal cases. Prior to 1555 witnesses were not compelled to testify, but after 1565 witnesses were compelled to do so. This change more deeply entrenched the role of the jury as a passive fact-finding group, and the witnesses became primary sources of information for the court. Attention shifted away from the juror's private knowledge toward witnesses' testimony as a primary source of evidence.

In the mid-1500s, we see the beginnings of the development of rules governing the presentation of evidence, especially by witnesses. During that period rules were developed that prohibited the use of data from untrustworthy informants, such as proven perjurers. In addition, wives were not permitted to testify against their husbands. Other rules that came into being were the *best evidence rule* (the court must only consider evidence that has high credibility and must deem as inadmissible evidence of low credibility), the *opinion rule* (the court has the power to give priority to the opinions of experts over those who have no expertise in a particular area), and the *hearsay rule* (the court has the power to give priority to testimony based on direct observations of the witness as opposed to information transmitted indirectly and/or via second and third parties). The opinion rule defined the kinds of testimony lay people could provide and the kinds experts could provide—with strict definitions for each. It was not until the 18th and 19th centuries, however, that the rules of evidence became more formalized and stringent.

Judges

During the 12th and 13th centuries the offender was generally forced to pay the family or his victim compensation for causing the victim's death or injury. However, it gradually evolved that the state became viewed as the wronged party, because offenses were viewed as breaches of the "king's peace." Judges then became viewed as representatives of the king. By the 13th century English law and procedure had become sufficiently technical to warrant the designation of fulltime judges. Before 1300, judges were civil servants, often appointed by the king. After 1300, judges were appointed *only* from among the ranks of the serjeants (sic), a small group that constituted the elite of the bar.

The aforementioned changes notwithstanding, judicial procedures between 1300 and 1700 were not truly adversarial. In the typical trial of the 1500s and 1600s, the judge served as an active inquisitor, whereas the jury was passive. The judge would directly question the defendant and the witnesses. Following these inquiries there was a kind of freewheeling discussion among the witnesses, defendant, and judge. When the judge was satisfied that he had heard enough, he would summarize the case to the jury, charge them to decide it, and they were generally not allowed to eat or drink until a decision had been rendered. Lawyers were not involved in the judicial process to an active degree. The defendant was not usually represented by counsel and was often prohibited from having legal representation. The defendant was not allowed to call witnesses, conduct any real cross-examination, or develop an affirmative case. The judge wielded great power over the jury and was free to urge a verdict upon the jury. Up until 1670, jurors who refused to follow the judge's directions could be jailed or fined. There was no appellate procedure by which the litigants could secure review of the decision. These procedures did, however, have certain precursors of the adversarial system: they were orally contentious, were decided upon by the evidence of witnesses, and were judged by a neutral and passive jury. However, the emphasis was not upon adversarial presentation of evidence. The judge was a very active participant, the protection against misleading prejudicial evidence was minimal, and appellate review was not available. The focus was not so much on accurate data collection and evidence, but on the development of legal principles of procedure.

In the latter part of the 17th century, judges became less active fact finders and took a more passive role in the courtroom. They devoted themselves more to serving as an umpire. Judges today in the English and American adversarial system are neutral. Their duties are to interpret the laws by which the contestants are operating and to enforce the rules of procedure during the trial. They do, however, have great power in that they can manipulate the court procedures in a manner prejudicial to the party he or she believes to have the better case.

In the United States, since the beginning of the 19th century, further developments insured that judges would remain neutral and passive fact finders. They were required to adopt a neutral political stance, could not run for office, and were discouraged from supporting political candidates. They were also required to adhere strictly to rules of evidence and were limited as to the kinds of remarks that they could make in the course of a trial.

In the 19th century the appellate courts developed. They were designed to be the guardians of the adversary system, insuring that judges complied with the rules of evidence and procedure. If not, the appellate courts could reverse a decision in order to insure compliance with the new principles. In addition, appellate courts could reverse what they considered to be the trial court's misinterpretation or misapplication of the law.

Lawyers

About the beginning of the 14th century, requirements were established regulating the education and conduct of those who would be allowed to argue cases in the king's courts. In time, the advocates formed special organizations, called Inns of Court, for training members of the bar. In the 15th and 16th centuries, as the jury's investigative role diminished and juries became more passive, the responsibilities of the advocates increased. Lawyers undertook the job of supplying the jury with the evidence upon which the decisions would be based. By 1600, lawyers had established for themselves their special status as masters of the evidence-gathering process.

It was around 1577 that an important change occurred that became central to the development of our present-day adversary system. It was at this time that the concept of attorney-client privilege came into being. It granted lawyers special exemption from the obligation to provide evidence that had been provided by clients, if divulgence of such evidence might compromise the client's position. Lawyers then developed a special status of immunity from certain courtroom obligations. I consider this to be a mixed blessing. On the one hand, it increased the likelihood that the client would be honest with the attorney in a manner similar to the confidential relationship that patients have with their doctors. On the other hand, it gave sanction to lies of omission, a practice that reflects a basic weakness in the system that has produced grief for many over the centuries.

During the 15th through 17th centuries lawyers were generally less concerned with gathering accurate evidence than they were with narrowly defining various legal principles. The lawyers involved themselves in endless nitpicking about formal legal rules and procedure. They wasted incredible amounts of time arguing fine points of law rather than the substance of their cases.

Codes governing lawyers' behavior are basically products of the 18th and 19th centuries. One of the central ethical conflicts was this: On the one hand, attorneys were expected to be officers of the court and speak the truth. On the other hand, they were expected to be loyal advocates on behalf of their clients. This problem has been resolved, primarily, by allowing attorneys to withhold from the court any information that might compromise their client's position. This is basically a lie of omission. It is justified on the grounds that the adversary is also permitted to engage in lying by omission. At the same time, both sides are encouraged to present before the court those arguments that support their clients' positions. Presumably, such evidence will also include what each side has attempted to withhold. The assumption, then, is that all the data and evidence will ultimately be brought before the court. In practice, this assumption is rarely realized because of the complexity of the process and the fact that very few can afford the indulgence of a trial in which all pertinent evidence is brought before the court. Furthermore, lies of commission are frequent. If one sanctions lies of omission, one cannot be surprised if lies of commission soon follow. The result of all of this, I believe, is that attorneys are trained in law school to be liars. In Chapters Seven and Eight I will discuss in detail further views of mine on the lawyer's role in adversary proceedings, especially with regard to their participation in bringing about stress and psychopathology in their clients.

THE DEVELOPMENT OF THE
PRESENT-DAY ADVERSARY SYSTEM
IN ENGLAND

The development of the adversary system, which prides itself on giving the accused and the accuser the opportunity to confront one another directly in an open courtroom, was retarded significantly in 1487 by Parliament, when it established the judicial proceedings that came to be known as the Star Chamber proceedings. The Star Chamber proceedings were established at the instigation of King Henry VII in order to curb the power of feudal nobles. The council met in the royal palace of Westminster in a room decorated with stars on the ceiling, thus the name *Star Chamber.* Initially, Parliament defined the Star Chamber's jurisdiction over riots, unlawful assembly, and other events beyond the power of ordinary courts to control. Subsequently it widened its jurisdiction to include any other issues with which its judges or the king wished to deal. Juries were not used, the meetings were often secret, rumor was accepted as evidence, and torture was often utilized to obtain testimony. Rising resentment resulted in Parliament abolishing the Star Chamber in 1641. On the one hand, the Star Chamber's dictatorial and repressive habits played a role in suppressing the development of the adversary system. On the other hand, when the Star Chamber was finally discontinued, memory of its repressive tactics encouraged reforms that resulted in the guarantees of openness central to adversary proceedings.

The present-day adversary system dates its origins to the mid-17th century, the time of the abolishment of the Star Chamber. By the end of the 18th century the adversary system, as we know it today, was established both in the United States and England. It was during this 150-year period that both judge and jury came to conform closely to the ideals of neutrality and passivity. By 1700 decisions could be reversed and a new trial ordered if the judge believed that evidence was insufficient to warrant a verdict. By 1756 the retrial mechanism was effectively extended to all cases. After 1705, in civil cases, there was an abolishment of the requirement that juries be drawn from the exact neighborhood in which the case arose. This reduced the likelihood that jurors would have any private information to rely on when making their decisions.

In the 19th century we see the development of cross-examination. The lawyer's obligation to provide zealous representation and loyalty to his or her client's cause was the product of the 18th and 19th centuries. However, lawyers were restricted from harassing or intimidating an opponent. As proceedings became more adversarial, however, conflicting ethical demands were exerted upon lawyers. On the one hand, attorneys were expected to be officers of the court and to seek the truth; on the other hand, they were expected to be keen advocates on behalf of their clients. In the mid-19th century the emphasis shifted to zeal and loyalty (denials notwithstanding), and this is the present state of affairs. In the 19th century we see the development of courts set up for the sole purpose of deciding appeals. They reviewed trial records and determined whether errors warranting reversal had occurred. They did not conduct open hearings with clients or witnesses.

Over the last 300 years, three sets of rules have evolved that are generally considered crucial for the successful utilization of the adversary system. First, there are the *rules of procedure,* which are designed to produce in an orderly fashion a climactic confrontation between the parties in the trial. The *rules of evidence* protect the integrity of the evidence. They prohibit the use of evidence that is likely to be unreliable and might bring about misleading information to the judge and jury. These rules also prohibit the use of evidence that poses a threat of unfair prejudice against one of the parties. Last, there are certain *ethical rules* designed to serve as guidelines and controls for the attorneys. They require, for the clients' protection, that counsels zealously protect the clients' interests at all times. They require the attorney to be loyal to the client. Because of the danger that attorneys will become excessively swept up in the battle, they are not permitted to harass or intimidate an opponent. Courts of appeal insure that litigants and judges will comply with these mandated procedures.

THE ADVERSARY SYSTEM
IN THE UNITED STATES

In the early days of colonization the legal systems were very much like those of primitive societies, because there were few individuals in any particular setting and the need for compromise was very great. Because of the separation of the various colonies and their colonization by different countries, there was little uniformity in their legal procedures. However, arbitration was commonly used. Many of the emerging middle class who came to America had been abused by the aristocratic government in England. Because many colonists came to America with a feeling of antagonism toward the status quo and the entrenched establishment, there was resistance against the incorporation of English law into the colonies. The colonists were intent on preventing the formation of another aristocracy. This reluctance predictably became even more pronounced at the time of the American Revolution. The American system of government is based heavily on the concepts of self-reliance and individualism. Accordingly, there was great distrust of a central authority, and the judiciary was the target of such distrust. Any move toward centralization was resisted, and individuals were viewed as capable of defending themselves in courts. However, in time the English adversary system came to be viewed favorably because the judge, as umpire, exerted far less authority than the magistrates under Continental law. The adversary system came to be viewed as the best protection of the middle class against the aristocracy. It was viewed as excellent protection against judges becoming arms of the state. The framers of the Constitution, then, included such revisions as due process, the right to a trial by jury, habeas corpus, the right to counsel, the right to bail, and the privilege against self-incrimination. It would be an error to conclude that the founding fathers were particularly interested in the protection of the lower classes of society; they were interested in protecting the middle class's commercial and entrepreneurial interests.

During the pre-revolutionary period judges and juries became increasingly independent of political and governmental influence. This was one of the cornerstones of the American Constitution. The founding fathers were adamant in their belief that trial by jury was a central protection for the freedom of individuals. But juries had to be established that were independent of government control (while still complying with the law). Prior to the 1800s, judges were likely to have been political partisans who openly advertised their opinions in court. After Thomas Jefferson was elected, his supporters removed a number of incompetent or partisan Federalist judges from office. Supreme Court Chief Justice John Marshall became the standard by which the propriety of judicial behavior came to be measured. He was the first of the truly impartial chief justices. Since the early 1800s, judicial conduct was controlled by applying strict rules of evidence and by placing exacting limits on the types of remarks that could be made at the close of a case.

The adversary system has flourished in the United States, so much so that it is reasonable to say that there is no other country in the world in which it has enjoyed such widespread utilization. It is also reasonable to say that the United States, at this time, is the most litigious country on earth. Lieberman (1981) devotes significant sections of his book to a description of the reasons why litigation has burgeoned in the United States. He states that the further one goes back in history, the more individuals have considered themselves to be at the mercy of nature and the less likely they were to view calamities that befell them to be related to indignities they suffered at the hands of other human beings. As man gained more control over the environment, other individuals came to be blamed more frequently for the traumas and catastrophes that inevitably befell humans. If one views botulism, for example, to be God-sent, then one cannot blame fellow human beings for one's suffering. However, if one considers the disease to be caused by food contamination, which was the result of negligence on the part of those who packaged the food, then the blame is easily traced back to some human agent. In such situations the sufferer is likely to want retribution, or at least to prevent the recurrence of the event. Because the United States has been one of the countries at the forefront of modern scientific advances and its associated environmental control, this shift of blame from God to mankind has been particularly evident here, especially in the last century.

Another factor that has contributed to the litigiousness of the American people relates to the fact that we are a "melting pot." In the countries from which our immigrants came, there was generally a greater degree of homogeneity among the population than exists in the United States. Accordingly, there was general unanimity with regard to what customs and traditions should be adhered to. In the United States, however, we have a potpourri of traditions that are often in conflict with one another. Thus there has been a greater need to utilize higher powers to enforce uniformity of behavior. In a democratic country, the imposition of rules by a dictator, monarch, aristocrat, or group of oligarchs is not considered to be a viable source of such regulation. Rather, the rule of law, equally applied to all, has been the guiding principle for bringing about compliance with social standards.

With an ever-enlarging body of laws, there has been an ever-growing number of methods for challenging and altering the legal structure. This is an intrinsic concomitant to the growth of a democratic system governed by laws. Accordingly, since the earliest days of our government, litigation has been ubiquitous. Although the democratic countries of Europe have also witnessed a significant growth in the body of their laws, there has been an important difference with regard to the growth of litigation. Specifically, in the past, only those highest in the social hierarchy enjoyed the protection of the laws, and it was only they who were significantly involved in litigation. In America, however, every person, no matter how low on the social scale, has the right to the protection of the law and can litigate. Although poorer people were (and still are) less likely to enjoy the services of the most skilled attorneys, the route to litigation was (and is) very much available to them—a situation that did not prevail in Europe where the litigation potential was enjoyed primarily by the aristocracy.

Another factor that has contributed to the litigiousness of

Americans is our individualism, which lessens the likelihood that people will submit to more community types of dispute settlement. Our spirit of individualism has gone so far that people are increasingly representing themselves in court and refusing the assistance and guidance of attorneys. Part of this practice relates to the expense of engaging professional counselors, but part relates to a system that allows individuals to represent themselves pro se. Although there is some general recognition that one is likely to do better in litigation when one is represented by an attorney, the court systems provide ready vehicles for pro se representation.

Since World War II, litigation has expanded in other ways in the United States. Whereas in the past it was generally considered unethical for attorneys to solicit litigants (this is generally referred to as *ambulance chasing*), this is no longer the case. At the time of this writing there is approximately one practicing lawyer for every 320 people in the United States. In the U.S. in February 1991, there were 777,119 practicing lawyers (American Bar Association, 1991) in a population of 249,632,692 (U.S. Census Bureau). Obviously, competition is keen, and under these circumstances it is not surprising that soliciting litigants has become an acceptable practice. For example, a well-known American litigator recently instituted a suit against the Union Carbide Company for the death of thousands of Indians in Bhopal as the result of a leakage of lethal chemical gases from one of its plants there. He is asking for 15 billion dollars. If successful, he can conceivably retain as his fee one-third of this amount. Although it is not clear from newspaper accounts whether this lawyer solicited clients in India, with incentives such as this, it is no surprise that other attorneys quickly found their way to India to sign up clients in the streets, hospitals, and their homes. Of course, personal monetary gain is denied as the primary motivating factor for these gentlemen; rather, they self-righteously proclaim that innocents must be protected from the negligence of giant corporations and that they are thereby serving in justice's cause.

At one time in the United States there was an adage, "You can't fight City Hall." This is no longer the case. One cannot only sue City Hall; one can sue local governments, states, civic officials, and even the federal government. People who are only tangentially and remotely involved in a case may be sued. People can be liable for acts undertaken by others. For example, the National Broadcasting Company (NBC) was sued by a girl's family because her rape followed a film depicting a similar assault from which they claim the assailant obtained his ideas. Law suits may be initiated on mere suspicion, the extent of the injury may remain unknown, and the plaintiff's lawyer may hope that a discovery procedure may force the defendant to prove the case against himself (herself). Recently, I saw a magazine cartoon depicting a man watching a salesman giving his pitch on television. The caption: "Having trouble with your next-door neighbor? Sue; it's less trouble than you may think." A court may impose a liability on an entire industry because the wrongdoer could not be identified. In such a setting it is no surprise that litigation is ubiquitous and that most of the best law schools are flooded with applicants.

The adversary courtroom battle is often viewed as a sport similar to that of a traditional sporting event. Each side has its attorney(s), client(s), and witness(es). The court's rules of procedure, evidence, and lawyer ethics have their analogies in the rules of the various sports. People cheer for their side, especially if brought to public attention. Attorneys get swept up in their clients' battles, and the name of the game is to win. The game or sport theory becomes even more apparent when a trial is brought to public attention and gets significant coverage in the public media. The litigants, however, may not view the adversary trial as a game; rather, they might justifiably view themselves as the pawns in the game.

One could argue that the adversary system is indeed a blessing and that it is a manifestation of the most powerful and effective way that individuals in a democratic society can protect themselves from indignities, whether they be inflicted by other individuals or by the government. If a government is oppressive, then should we not have a means of fighting back? If someone breaks a contract, should we not have the means of enforcing commitment?

One cannot deny that individuals should have a means of fighting back, and it may very well be the case that the adversary system provides us with the best method for protecting ourselves. However, it is not well designed to deal with situations in which there was no intrinsic opposition at the outset. When the doctor's intent is to help and he errs, should one make him or her an adversary? Should two parents who have differences regarding who is the better parent utilize the adversary system to make this decision? In our conflictual society we create conflicts when there may initially not have been any. Courts working within this system are not permitted to decide disputes that are not brought to them by genuinely adverse parties. A controversy *must* be created—even if there was none before—if the courts are to consider hearing the case. For example, courts decide whether or not to remove life-sustaining machinery from terminally ill comatose patients. Adversaries are created in order to function within the structure of the adversary system. The courts thereby manufacture an adversarial situation out of one that is not intrinsically adversarial for the purposes of fitting individuals into the Procrustean bed of the adversary courtroom proceeding.

As mentioned, the adversary system is based on the assumption that the truth can best be discovered if each side strives as hard as it can to bring to the court's attention the evidence favorable to its own side. It is based on the assumption that the fairest decision can be obtained when the two parties argue in open court according to carefully prescribed rules and procedures. They face each other as adversaries in a kind of constrained battle procedure. Criticism of this method of dispute resolution dates back to ancient times:

> Both Plato and Aristotle condemned the method. They considered the advocate as one who was paid to make the better cause appear the worse, or endeavor by sophisticated tricks of argument to establish as true what any man of common sense could see was

false. The feeling against advocacy in the criminal law was so strong that, at least in the case of the more serious kinds of crime, a right to representation by a trained advocate was nowhere generally recognized until the 18th century A.D. (Encyclopedia Britannica, 1982).

In this chapter I have provided a brief survey of the adversary system's development, with particular focus on what I consider to be its weaknesses. In the next chapter I will focus more specifically on the utilization of the system as a method of dealing with divorce and custody disputes.

 # TWO
BRIEF REVIEW OF WESTERN SOCIETY'S CHANGING ATTITUDES REGARDING PARENTAL PREFERENCE IN CUSTODY DISPUTES

ANCIENT TIMES TO WORLD WAR II

A brief review of the criteria used in Western society to determine custody will enable the reader to place in better perspective our present situation regarding custody determination. Again, I will not simply present historical data, but will present my opinions regarding the significance of the various developments.

In the days of the Roman Empire, fathers were automatically given custody of their children at the time of divorce. (Divorce was quite common, incidentally, when the empire was at its peak.) Mothers had no education or reasonably marketable skills, and so were not considered as fit as fathers to care for their children alone. Fathers had such power that they could, at their whim, sell their children into slavery and, after proper release from councils convened for the purpose, literally kill their children. The power of fathers to kill their children extended up to the 14th century, but the power to sell children into servitude was retained for another 100-200 years (Derdeyn, 1976). Serfs on feudal manors were often children who were sold into slavery. However, divorce was extremely uncommon because there was no easily available route to it, either via secular or ecclesiastical channels. People like King Henry VIII could defy papal authority and provide themselves with a divorce, but lesser souls had to "hang in there" and remain married until the end of their days.

In the 17th and 18th centuries we see the introduction of the notion that custody involved not only *rights* but *responsibilities* as well. If the father (still the automatic custodial parent) showed evidence that he was not capable of or interested in assuming parental responsibilities, then the state considered its right to assume the role of the parent in order to protect the children. This concept became known as the *doctrine of parens patriae* (*Latin:* parenting by the state). In England this concept was incorporated in 1839 in *Talfourd's Act,* in which the court was given power to determine custody of children under the age of seven. The state, operating through the courts, would then assign the child to the parent who could provide better protection. In some cases this would be the mother. However, such designation was rare because divorce was rare.

In 1817, in a well-publicized case, Percy Shelley, the poet, lost custody of his children because of his "atheism" and "immorality" (specifically, marital infidelity). It is reasonable to assume that it was not the adultery alone that caused him to lose his children: If that were the case, there would have been few fathers retaining custody. It is reasonable to assume also that it was not the atheism alone that caused him to lose his children, in that there were many atheists in England at that time who were not losing custody. It was probably the *combination* of adultery *and* atheism (if one can imagine such a terrible combination coexisting in a *single* human being) that "did him in." In addition, it is reasonable to assume that there were many other adulterous atheists in England who were still retaining custody, but that Shelley, as a well-known figure, probably served well as an example to other would-be adulterous atheists to mind their manners and mend their ways.

But Shelley's was an isolated case. It was not until the middle of the 19th century that we see the first indications of what came subsequently to be called (in the 20th century) the *tender-years presumption.* The courts began to work under the presumption that there were certain psychological benefits that the child could gain from its mother that were not to be so readily obtained from its father. The notion of wresting a suckling infant from its mother's breast came to be viewed as somehow injudicious and "wrong." Accordingly, mothers began to be given custody of their infant children. But when the children reached the age of three or four (the age at which breast-feeding was usually discontinued in the 19th century), they were considered to have gained all that they needed from their mother, and they were transferred to their father, their "rightful and just" parent.

We also see in the mid-19th century the increasing utilization by the courts of the concept of *parent culpability* when considering custody disputes. Specifically, before granting custody the court not only considered which parent would provide the child with better treatment but also made the assumption that the parent who obeyed marriage vows was more likely to provide the child with a proper upbringing. Although this might initially appear to have been an advance, the main vow that was under consideration by the courts was the vow not to commit adultery. Furthermore, it was most often the adulterous mother who was deprived of custody, rather than the adulterous father. Punitive attitudes toward adulterous mothers were certainly prevalent until the 1950s and 1960s. It has only been since the 1960s that adultery (adultery by mothers or fathers) has not been given serious weight in determining parental capacity. The courts generally appreciate that private sexual activities, which do not directly affect the children, are not likely to have any significant and/or immediate effect on parenting capacity. However, parents who expose their children to sexual activity are generally considered to be demonstrating a parental deficiency.

In the late 19th century we see the birth of the Women's Liberation movement. Women began to wrest entrance into educational institutions and gained training in various skills (to a very limited degree, however, in the 19th century). By the end of the 19th century, little headway was made regarding custody of children. This was primarily related to the notion (supported by the courts) that to give a mother custody of the children while requiring the father to contribute significantly, if not entirely, to their financial support was unjust to the father. And the courts ultimately reflect prevailing notions of what is just and unjust. What we accept today as perfectly reasonable was beyond the comprehension of the 19th-century father. Until this change in attitude came about, mothers could not reasonably hope to gain custody. The only women who could hope for custody were those who had the wherewithal to support their children independently.

The change in attitude came about by what was possibly an unanticipated route – the Child Labor laws, passed in the early part of this century. Prior to the 20th century, children were an important economic asset. Before the appearance of the Child Labor laws, children as young as five or six years of age worked in such places as factories and mines and contributed to the family's support. In agricultural communities they were used as farm hands as well. Fathers, therefore, had the power to keep – and were very desirous of keeping – these important economic assets. With the passage of the Child Labor laws, children became less of a financial asset and more of a liability. These laws made fathers more receptive to giving up their children to their ex-wives and were an important factor in the 20th-century shift in attitude. Fathers no longer rallied around the flag of "injustice" when asked to support children in the homes of their ex-wives (Ramos, 1979).

In the 1920s the states gradually changed their laws, and custody was no longer automatically given to fathers. Rather, in many states the sex of the parent was not to be considered a factor in determining parental preference. Only criteria related to parental capacity – regardless of sex – were to be utilized. This change was incorporated in England in 1925 in the *Guardianship of Infants Act*, in which mothers and fathers were considered to be equal regarding the right to have custody of their children. During the next 50 years these statutes were generally interpreted in favor of mothers. A father had to prove a mother grossly unfit (e.g., an alcoholic, drug addict, or sexual "pervert") before he could even hope to gain custody. The notion that mothers were

PARENTAL PREFERENCE IN CUSTODY DISPUTES   **41**

intrinsically preferable to fathers as child rearers came to be known as the *tender-years presumption*. To the best of my knowledge this term was introduced by Justice Benjamin Cardozo (Finlay v. Finlay, 1925). For the reader who is not appreciative of the significance of the word *presumption* as used in the law, the term generally refers to the principle that the judge, when making a decision regarding custody, must *presume* that the mother is the preferable parent. Under this presumption, the only way a father can get custody is if he is able to provide compelling evidence that the mother is unfit to bring up the children. It is the father, then, who had an uphill fight in custody disputes, not the mother. From the mid-1920s to the mid-1940s, i.e., until the end of World War II, the divorce rate was relatively low. Accordingly, custody litigation was not too common. Since World War II, however, there has been a progressive increase in the divorce rate as well as a burgeoning of divorce litigation, especially custody litigation. Accordingly, after World War II we entered into what (at least from many lawyers' points of view) could be called the "Golden Age" of divorce and custody litigation. At no point in the history of the legal profession has there been a greater opportunity to earn "gold" from divorcing litigants than the mid-to-late 20th century.

WORLD WAR II TO THE 1960S

From the post-war period until the mid-1960s, the adversary system was the main one utilized in divorce cases. This was consistent with the concept that the kinds of indignities complained of in divorce conflicts were minor crimes called *torts* (*Latin:* wrongs). Because they were viewed as crimes, divorce conflicts were justifiably considered in the context of adversary proceedings. Divorce laws in most states were predicated on concepts of guilt and innocence, i.e., within the context of punishment and restitution. The divorce was granted only when the complainant or petitioner proved that he or she had been wronged or injured by the defendant or respondent. In most states the acceptable grounds for divorce were very narrowly defined and, depending upon the state, included such behavior as mental cruelty, adultery, abandonment, habitual drunkenness, nonsupport, and drug addiction. The law would punish the offending party by granting the divorce to the successful complainant. During this period, as was true at other times in history, adultery was one of the more common grounds for suing for divorce. But one had to have proof if one was to use this complaint successfully in the divorce litigation. Accordingly, it was common for people to bring in as evidence photographs taken in motel rooms. Sometimes these were bona fide, in that the spouse was actually involved in such an extra-marital escapade. On occasion, however, a prostitute was used to provide the "photographic evidence" when there had been no actual infidelity.

If the court found that both the husband and the wife were guilty of marital wrongs, a divorce could not be granted. If *both* parties, for instance, had involved themselves in adulterous behavior, they could not get a divorce. Therefore, in such situations, the parties often agreed to alter the truth in a way that would result in their obtaining a divorce. Frequently one party would agree to be the adulteress or the adulterer, or agree to be considered the one who had inflicted mental cruelty on the other. "Witnesses" were brought in (usually friends who were willing to lie in court) to testify in support of the various allegations, and everyone agreed to go through the theatrical performance. Even the judge knew that the play was necessary to perform if he or she was to have grounds to grant the divorce. All appreciated the cooperation of the witnesses, and there was practically no danger of their being prosecuted for their perjury. Although such proceedings rarely made headlines in the newspapers, the records were available for public scrutiny and distribution. The knowledge of this possibility became an additional burden to the person who, because of the greater desire for the divorce, was willing to be considered guilty while allowing the spouse to be considered innocent. In addition, there were possible untoward psychological sequelae resulting from the acceptance of the blame, and this could contribute to residual psychological problems following the divorce.

People involved in custody litigation are fighting. They are fighting for their most treasured possessions – their children. The stakes are extremely high. Litigation over money, property, and other matters associated with the divorce produce strong feelings of resentment and anger. However, they are less likely to result in reactions of rage and fury than are conflicts over the children. Children are the extensions of ourselves, our hopes for the future, and thereby closely tied up with our own identities. Fighting for them is almost like fighting for ourselves. The two may become indistinguishable, and the fight becomes a "fight for life."

The adversary system, which professes to help parents resolve their differences, is likely to intensify the hostilities that it claims it is designed to reduce. It provides the litigants with ammunition that they may not have realized they possessed. It contributes to an ever-increasing vicious cycle of vengeance – so much so that the litigation may bring about greater psychological damage than the pains and grief of the marriage that originally brought about the divorce. Although some attorneys appreciate well the terrible psychological trauma that may result from protracted adversary proceedings, other attorneys do not. For the latter, the name of the game is to win. They believe their reputations rest on their capacity to win, and they fear that if they appear to be moderate and conciliatory, they will lose clients. Lawyers recognize that the more protracted the litigation, the more money they are going to earn. In addition, they may lose perspective once they are swept up in the battle, so intent are they on winning. Nizer, in his book *My Life in Court* (1968), states: "All litigations evoke intense feelings of animosity, revenge and retribution. Some of them may be fought ruthlessly. But none of them, even in their most aggravated form, can equal the sheer, unadultered venom of a matrimonial contest." I would add to this the following: Of all the forms of marital litigation, the most vicious and venomous by far is custody litigation! The stakes are higher than in any other form of courtroom conflict in that the parents' most treasured possessions – the children – are at stake. Conflicts over money and property pale in comparison to the ruthlessness with which parents will fight over the children.

Weiss (1975) states the problem well:

> It is possible for lawyers to negotiate too hard. In pursuit of the best possible agreement for their clients, some lawyers seem to worsen the post-marital relationship of their clients and the clients' spouses. They may, for example, actively discourage a client from talking with his or her spouse for fear that the client will inadvertently weaken his or her negotiating position, or will in thoughtless generosity make concessions without obtaining anything in return. Or they may take positions more extreme than their client desires in order eventually to achieve an advantageous compromise, but by so doing anger the client's spouse and further alienate the spouse from the client. Some separated individuals reported that until negotiations were at an end, their relationship with their spouse became progressively worse.

Gettelman and Markowitz (1974) provide a good example of the problem:

> For many divorcing couples, their biggest headaches begin after they retain their respective attorneys. Recently we talked with the ex-wife of a famous and wealthy stage actor. It had taken her three years to obtain a divorce in California, which is one of the more progressive states! In her words, "Once the lawyers smelled money, they acted in cahoots to bleed us and draw out the proceedings." Although their separation had started out amicably, they grew to loathe each other; she believed that both his lawyers and her own successfully manipulated her and her husband into feeling victimized by each other.

Sopkin (1974) describes in dramatic terms how sordid and sadistic such litigation can be. He focuses particularly on the role of attorneys in intensifying and prolonging such conflicts. In his article "The Roughest Divorce Lawyers in Town" (although the "town" referred to by Sopkin is New York, the legal techniques described are ubiquitous and by no means confined to that city), he describes a brand of attorney often referred to in the field as a "bomber." Sopkin quotes one such bomber (Raoul Lionel Felder, a New York City divorce attorney) as saying: "If it comes to a fight, it is the lawyer's function using all ethical, legal and moral means to bring his adversary to his knees as fast as possible. Naturally, within this framework the lawyer must go for the soft spots." The kinds of antics that such lawyers utilize and promulgate are indeed hair-raising. One husband is advised to hire a gigolo to seduce his wife into a setting while a band of private detectives are engaged to serve as witnesses. Another husband is advised to get his English-born wife deported because she is not yet a citizen.

Elsewhere Sopkin states:

> Getting a lawyer out of his office is expensive, but to crank up a bomber, pump him full of righteous indignation and ship him down to the matrimonial courts can be terribly expensive—running from 15-, 20-, or 25-thousand dollars. . . .Bombers are in business to accommodate hate. . . .But the incontrovertible fact remains that if there is big-time money at stake, or serious custody questions at stake, or you want to leave your husband/wife with nothing but a little scorched earth, get a bomber.

Although Sopkin's examples are not typical, they are not rare either. In litigation, winning is the name of the game. The lawyer with a reputation for being a "softie" is not going to have many clients. Although more humane and less pugilistic attorneys certainly exist, even their "fighting instincts" often come to the fore when they are caught up in adversary proceedings. Although the more sensitive may even then not be willing to stoop to the level of the bombers, they still are likely to utilize a variety of deceptive maneuvers to win for their clients.

One attorney, Glieberman, in his book *Confessions of a Divorce Lawyer* (1975) states:

> I made sure that each client I handled—whatever else he or she thought about me—came away feeling two things. One, I was thorough as hell. Two, I was out to win. Frankly the second was easy. I love to argue and win. . . .

If a divorce was what someone wanted then my client and I became a team, did everything in our power, not just to win but to win big. . . .

There's only one rule on divorce settlements: If you represent the wife, get as much as possible. If you represent the husband, give away as little as possible. . . .

Now, as I walk through the outer door of my office heading for the courtroom, I know that I'm walking to a case where there will be no compromises, no conciliations, no good feelings to balance the bad. This will be an all-out confrontation, a real tooth and nail fight. I'll love it. . . .

Now finally we're here. And it's a real circus. The other side has two accountants, a tax lawyer, three expert witnesses and a defendant; our side has one accountant, a comptroller, no tax lawyer because I've become an expert at that, and seven expert witnesses.

The criticisms of the adversary system as applied to divorce and custody proceedings come not only from mental health professionals, but from some lawyers and judges as well. A judge, Forer (1975), criticizes the legal profession's own Code of Professional Responsibility—a criticism that is most relevant to divorce and custody litigation:

A lawyer is licensed by the government and is under a sworn duty to uphold and defend the law and the Constitution of the United States. Despite the license and the oath, the role of the lawyer is by definition and by law amoral. . . .He must press the position of his client even though it is contrary to the public good, popular opinion and widely accepted standards of behavior. Canon 7 of the Code of Professional Responsibility promulgated by the American Bar Association declares in part, "The duty of the lawyer, both to his client and to the legal system, is to represent his client zealously within the bounds of the law." In other words, the skilled judgment of the lawyer that his client's case is spurious or without merit is irrelevant. The lawyer must, therefore, be a Hessian, a mercenary, available for hire to do the bidding of whoever pays him. . . .If the client wishes to sue or contest a claim, the lawyer must either zealously pursue his client's interest or withdraw from the case. If Lawyer A withdraws, Lawyer B will accept the case and the fee.

Another judge, Lindsley (1980), is critical of the utilization of the adversary system in custody disputes. He states:

> The adversary process, historically effective in resolving disputes between litigants over contracts, torts, business matters, and criminal charges, where objective evidentiary facts have probative significance, is not suited to the resolution of most relations problems. In family disputes, the evidence that we would find most meaningful is more likely to consist of subtle, subjective human relations factors best identified and discerned by psychologists and behaviorists who do not approach the inquiry as antagonists. When you add the concept of "fault" as the necessary basis for deciding questions relating to the family, I think it is fair to say that no other process is more likely to rip husband, wife, father, mother, and child apart so thoroughly and bitterly.

A highly respected judge who has concerned himself deeply with mental health issues, Bazelon (1974) holds that the adversary system is not necessarily detrimental to clients. Its ultimate aim, he states, is to gain knowledge and resolve differences. It attempts to resolve differences through the opposition of opposing positions. Its ultimate aim is resolution, and the cross-examination process is one of the important ways in which information is gained. I am in agreement with Bazelon regarding the methods and aims of the adversary system. I am not, however, in agreement with his statement regarding the risk of detriment to clients. His statement that the adversary system is "not necessarily" detrimental implies little risk for the development of psychopathology. My experience has been that in divorce, and especially custody cases, the risk for the development of psychopathology is extremely high. Elsewhere (Gardner, 1986a) I have described in detail a wide variety of psychopathological reactions to protracted divorce and/or custody litigation. Bazelon's position is idealistic in that he does not make reference to the sly tricks, duplicity, courtroom antics, and devious maneuvers that lawyers will often utilize in order to win. He makes no mention of attorney's attempts to unreasonably discredit the experts, cast aspersions on their characters, and try to make them look silly or stupid.

Although Judge Bazelon's view is that of the majority of jurists today, there are dissenters among the judiciary. One of the most outspoken critics of the use of the adversary system in solving custody disputes is Judge Lindsley, who states (1976):

> The adversary process, historically effective in resolving disputes between litigants where evidentiary facts have probative significance, is not properly suited to the resolution of most family relations problems. . . .Where there are children and the parties cannot or will not recognize the impact of the disintegration of the marriage upon the children, where they fail to perceive their primary responsibilities as parents—i.e., custody and visitation— we make it possible for parents to carry out that struggle by the old, adversary, fault-finding, condemnation approach. . . .This kind of battle is destructive to the welfare, best interests, and emotional health of their children.

Berger, a Cleveland attorney, has made what may be the most compelling statement about adversarial proceedings in divorce/custody litigation (1985):

> In all that is decent. . .in all that is just, the framers of our Constitution could never have intended that the "enjoyment of life" meant that if divorce came, it was to be attended by throwing the two unfortunates and their children into a judicial arena, with lawyers as their seconds, and have them tear and verbally slash at each other in a trial by emotional conflict that may go on in perpetuity. We have been humane enough to outlaw cockfights, dogfights, and bullfights; and yet, we do nothing about the barbarism of divorce fighting, and trying to find ways to end it. We concern ourselves with cruelty to animals, and rightfully so, but we are unconcerned about the forced and intentionally perpetrated cruelty inflicted upon the emotionally distressed involved in divorce. We abhor police beating confessions out of alleged criminals, and yet we cheer and encourage lawyers to emotionally beat up and abuse two innocent people and their children, because their marriage has floundered. Somewhere along the line, our sense of values, decency, humanism and justice went off the track.

I fully appreciate that many attorneys begin their involvement with divorcing litigants by attempting to calm them down and bring about some compromises in their demands. However, when such efforts fail, many get swept up in the conflict and join their clients in trying to win the battle and punish the spouse. (Taking the children away is one predictable way of implementing such punishment.) The training of lawyers primes them for such encounters. Therapists, because of their orientation toward understanding and reducing hostility, are less likely to rise so quickly to a patient's cry for battle and lust for vengeance. Accordingly, lawyers are often criticized for inflaming their clients, adding to their hostility, and thereby worsening divorcing spouses' difficulties. A common retort to this criticism is: "We're only doing what our clients ask us to do." Such lawyers claim that they are just the innocent tools of their clients and that their obligation is to respond to their clients' wishes, even though such advocacy may be detrimental to the client, the spouse, and the children.

I believe that this response is a rationalization. I believe that lawyers have greater freedom to disengage themselves from a client's destructive behavior than they profess. I believe that financial considerations often contribute to their going along with the client. (I fully recognize that there are physicians, as well, who recommend unnecessary medical treatment. For both professions the practice is unconscionable.) There are attorneys who discourage their clients from litigating in court with the professed reason that it may be psychologically damaging. This may only be a coverup. In actuality they appreciate that they may reduce their income per hour if they go to court—because only the wealthiest clients can afford the formidable expense of protracted courtroom litigation. To the wealthy client, the latter consideration does not often serve as a deterrent for the lawyer, and the psychological considerations are then often ignored.

There are many couples who, at the time of the separation, make a serious attempt to avoid psychologically debilitating litigation. Having observed the deterioration of friends and relatives who have undergone prolonged litigation, they genuinely want to make every attempt to avoid such unnecessary and traumatic sequelae to their own divorce. Unfortunately, many such well-meaning couples, in spite of every attempt to avoid such a catastrophe, gradually descend into the same kind of psychologically devastating experience. An important contributing element to such unfortunate disintegration relates to the anger and rage engendered by their having involved themselves in protracted adversary proceedings. The system fosters sadism. The aim of simply *winning* often degenerates with each side bent on depleting the other of funds, producing psychological deterioration, or even destroying the other party. The result, however, is most often a Pyrrhic victory in which both sides lose, even though one may ostensibly be the winner.

Venting anger tends to feed on itself. The notion that anger merely needs to be dissipated, and then the individual is free from it, is probably an oversimplification. The fact that some expression of anger is necessary and that its release can produce some feeling of catharsis is certainly the case. However, it appears that another phenomenon may also be operative, especially when anger is great. Here the expression of anger does not result in its dissipation but rather in its intensification. When a person starts to "roll" with anger, more anger may be generated. It appears to have an existence of its own. An extreme example of this is the murderer who stabs the victim to death with a knife thrust into the heart. Although the victim is now dead, the murderer continues to stab the dead body repeatedly. Obviously, there is no further useful purpose for such anger release. In less dramatic ways individuals, once angry, tend to perpetuate the process. And protracted divorce litigation is an excellent demonstration of this phenomenon. The fight intensifies and rolls on for months and even years, having a life of its own, almost independent from the original issues that began the litigation in the first place.

A common result of parents being swept up in such litigation is that they blind themselves to the stupidity of what they are doing. A father, for example, may be so blinded by his rage that he fails to appreciate that he is giving far more money to his attorney (and possibly his wife's, in that he may be paying her lawyer as well) than he would have given to his wife had he agreed to her original request at the outset. The depletion of funds to his wife not only compromises her psychological stability but that of his children as well. The more psychologically and/or financially debilitated she is, the more impaired will be the children's upbringing. One mother, who lived in a large house with the children, made every attempt to increase her husband's bills as much as possible. She turned on the heating system to maximum capacity and, simultaneously, turned on every air conditioning unit in the house. Both systems would operate simultaneously, sometimes up to 24 hours a day. Every electrical outlet was used to maximum capacity at the same time, to the point where the house was blazing with light for days and weeks, especially on vacations. All this was done with the knowledge and support of her lawyer! Every form of destructive act known to mankind has been perpetrated by one parent upon the other in the course of custody litigation—and even murder is not unknown (I myself had such a case recently).

1960S TO THE MID-1970S

In the 1960s we began to witness greater appreciation by state legislatures of the fact that the traditional grounds for divorce are not simply wrongs perpetrated by one party against the other, but that both parties have usually contributed to the marital breakdown. In addition, the kinds of behavior complained of by the petitioner came to be viewed less as crimes and more as personality differences, aberrations, and/or psychopathology.

With such realization came the appreciation that adversary proceedings were not well suited to deal with such conflicts. Accordingly, an ever-growing number of states have changed their laws regarding the grounds for divorce and the ways in which people can dissolve their marriages. These recent statutes are generally referred to as *no-fault divorce laws.* They provide much more liberal criteria for the granting of a divorce. For example, if both parties agree to the divorce, their living apart for a prescribed period may be all that is necessary. (And the period may be shorter if no children are involved.) One does not have the problem of designating a guilty and an innocent party. Some states will grant a divorce on the basis of "incompatibility." The term may not be defined any further, and it may be quite easy for the couple to demonstrate that they are incompatible. The latest phase of such liberalization enables some individuals to divorce entirely without legal assistance. In California, a state that has often been at the forefront of such liberalization, a couple can now obtain a divorce via mail and the payment of a small fee, if they have no children and there is no conflict over property.

The passage of no-fault divorce laws has been, without question, a significant step forward. By removing it from adversary proceedings, a divorce is more readily, less traumatically, and usually less expensively obtained. However, many no-fault divorce laws require the agreement of *both* parties to satisfy the recent liberal criteria. Divorce can rarely be obtained unilaterally. If one party does not agree, then adversary proceedings are necessary if the person desiring the divorce is to have any hope of getting it. In addition, the new laws have not altered the necessity of resorting to adversary proceedings when there is conflict over such issues as visitation, support, alimony, and custody. Although no-fault divorce laws have considerably reduced the frequency of courtroom conflicts over divorce, litigation over custody is not only very much with us, but for reasons to be described soon, is on the increase. And the adversary system—a system designed to determine whether an accused individual has committed a criminal act—is being used to determine which of two parents would better serve as custodian for their children.

MID-1970S TO THE PRESENT

In the mid-1970s we began to see a male "backlash" to the tender-years presumption. Maternal preference is "sexist" complained many fathers. The notion that a woman is automatically a preferable parent, they claimed, is as much a sexist concept as the idea that a man should automatically be considered the preferable parent. The courts were asked to look again at the laws with which they were working and to apply more closely what was stated therein. In many states the old statutes, passed in the mid-1920s, were applicable and were interpreted more strictly along "sex-blind" lines. In most states, however, new statutes were passed that clearly stated that the sex of a parent should not be a consideration when courts were asked to settle custody disputes. The tender-years presumption was replaced with the *best-interests-of-the-child presumption.* And the assumption was made that children's interests would be best served if the courts were "sex blind" in their ruling on custody disputes. (In Chapter Eight I will discuss in detail my views on the judiciousness of the concept that sex-blind custody decisions necessarily serve the best interests of the child.)

Suddenly, fathers who had previously thought that they had no chance of gaining custody found out that they had. But love of the children and concern for their welfare was not the only motive for fathers who were now beginning to fight for custody. Less noble motives such as vengeance, guilt assuagement, and competition were now allowed expression and possibly even realization. Since the mid-1970s children have become "open territory" in child custody conflicts. The frequency of such litigation is burgeoning, and there is no evidence for a decline in the near future. New interpretations (or, strictly speaking, reexamination) of the original statutes have increased the complexity of such litigation as well. As A.P. Derdeyn (1978) points out, courts now have to work much harder. Traditional formulas all fell along what would now be considered sexist lines. Using such formulas made the judge's work easier. The child automatically went either to the father or the mother, depending on the particular period in history. Now a detailed inquiry into each parent's parental assets and liabilities is necessary before anything approaching a judicious decision can be made.

During the half-century (the mid-1920s to the mid- 1970s) when the tender-years presumption prevailed, fathers recognized that they had little chance of gaining custody of their children following separation and divorce. During that period a father might say to his lawyer, "Look, she's making inordinate financial demands. They're crazy. Let's do this. Let's go for custody of the children and then, at the final negotiations, we'll give up our

demand for custody if she'll come down on her financial requests." The lawyer might then ask the father whether his wife
was a prostitute, drug addict, chronic alcoholic, was sexually
promiscuous in front of the children, had been committed to an
insane asylum, etc. If the answer to these questions were all
negative, then the lawyer would inform the client that there was
absolutely no chance that he could gain custody.

However, under the best-interests-of-the-child presumption,
such a father need not prove that his wife exhibits profound
impairments in parenting capacity. Presumably, he comes before
the court as an equal to his wife and presumably has as much a
chance as she for gaining custody. Presumably the courts are
operating on the principle that the sex of a parent shall not be a
consideration when ruling in such disputes. I have repeated and
emphasized the word *presumably* here because, in fact, courts
have not rejected the tender-years presumption so quickly. Many
so-called old-fashioned judges still hold that a mother is intrinsically superior to the father when it comes to raising children.
(Later in this book I will comment on this idea.) We see then,
when we look back over the span of history, that there was only
a 50-year period—from the mid-1920s to the mid-1970s—when
mothers were viewed to be the preferable custodial parent
following divorce. Prior to that time fathers were generally
considered to be the preferable parent, and since then mothers
and fathers have been considered to be equally capable, at least in
the eyes of the law.

In the late 1970s and early 1980s we see the development of
another phenomenon that has markedly affected judicial procedures regarding custody determinations. This has been the increasing popularity of the joint custody concept. The idea that
one parent should be designated the sole custodial parent and the
other the visitor came to be viewed as inequitable in that the
visiting parent could not but feel inferior regarding his or her
status as a parent contributing to the child-rearing process. The
basic theory of the joint custody concept is that every attempt
should be made to approximate as closely as possible the kind of
situation that prevailed in the marital home, a situation in which

both parents contributed to the child's upbringing. The concept has become so popular that in some states the judge must order a joint custodial arrangement unless there are compelling reasons to consider another custodial plan. Ideally, in order for the joint custodial concept to work, both parents must be able to communicate and cooperate well with each other and to be equally capable of assuming child-rearing responsibilities. Furthermore, their living situation must be one in which they can both participate in bringing the children to and from school. Central to the concept is that there is no specific schedule. Rather, the determination as to where the children will be at any particular point is decided by criteria relevant to the needs and obligations of the parent and, to a lesser degree, the desires of the children.

The main drawback of granting joint custody so frequently and automatically is that it may do many children more harm than good. For example, it increases the chances that they will be used as weapons or spies in parental conflicts. Because no restraints are placed on noncooperating parents, such use of the children is likely. Children then become used like ropes in a tug of war. They are in a no-man's land in which they are "up for grabs" by either parent. Obviously, in such situations the children may suffer formidable psychological damage. Certainly the sole custodial arrangement cannot protect children entirely from being so used, but it does reduce the opportunities for parents to involve their children in such manipulations. Furthermore, automatic awarding of joint custody seldom takes into consideration the logistics of school attendance. Therefore, it can cause problems in the educational realm as well. Parents now litigate for joint custody. I believe that if one litigates for joint custody one is not a candidate for the arrangement. A meaningful joint custodial arrangement requires the parents to be able to cooperate and communicate well with one another, especially with regard to caring for their children. Parents who resort to litigating for custody have proven themselves incapable of cooperating with one another and, in most cases, are not communicating well either.

Strong proponents of the joint custodial concept hold that it circumvents the loss of self-esteem suffered by the parent who is designated the visitor and makes him or her (usually him) feel like a second-class citizen when compared to the parent who is designated to have primary or sole custody. I believe that the attempt to enhance self-esteem by giving an individual a different label is psychologically naive. Self-esteem is far too complex an issue to be affected significantly by this relatively minor factor. Yet there are individuals who will litigate for joint custody because they believe that such designation will thereby enhance their feelings of self-worth. Although I am basically in sympathy with the joint custodial concept I believe that its injudicious utilization has contributed to the burgeoning of divorce litigation that we have witnessed since the concept came into vogue.

Joint custody decisions enable judges to avoid a complex and difficult fact-finding task by offering a seemingly benevolent resolution. It certainly is easier for a judge to award joint custody than to deliberate about all the mind- boggling issues involved in a custody conflict. And judges who circumvent such challenges often justify their actions by considering themselves advanced and modern thinkers, in tune with the sexual egalitarianism of today's society. It is for these reasons that many family lawyers and psychiatrists are beginning to view joint custody as a judicial "cop-out."

And this is where we stand today in the late 1980s. At no time in the history of Western civilization has there been more litigation over custody and, unfortunately, the adversary system—a system designed to determine whether an accused party has committed a criminal act—is the method most commonly used to determine which is the preferable parent. In most cases, the people primarily involved in making such decisions—judges and attorneys—have little, if any, training in child development and psychology. Yet it is they who have traditionally been left with the decision as to who is the better parent for custodial purposes, working within the context of a system that may be one of the poorest yet devised to help investigate and deal with such disputes. Many forms of psychopathology result from the utilization of this system as a method for resolving divorce and/or custody conflicts. I have described these in greater detail elsewhere (Gardner, 1986a, 1989b). In the next chapter I will focus on the parental alienation syndrome, one of the most common forms of psychiatric disorder that results from the attempt to deal with divorce/custody disputes within the adversary system.

▢ THREE
THE PARENTAL ALIENATION SYNDROME

INTRODUCTION

Prior to the early 1980s, I certainly saw children whom I considered to have been brainwashed by one parent against the other. However, since that period I have seen—with increasing frequency—a disorder that I rarely saw previously. This disorder arose primarily in children who had been involved in protracted custody litigation. It is now so common that I see manifestations of it in about 90 percent of children who have been involved in custody conflicts. Because of its increasing frequency and the fact that a typical pattern is observed—different from simple brainwashing—I believe a special designation is warranted. Accordingly, I have termed this disorder the *parental alienation syndrome*.

I have introduced this term to refer to a disturbance in which children are preoccupied with deprecation and criticism of a parent—denigration that is unjustified and/or exaggerated. The notion that such children are merely "brainwashed" is narrow. The term *brainwashing* implies that one parent is systematically and consciously programming the child to denigrate the other. The concept of the parental alienation syndrome includes the brainwashing component, but is much more comprehensive. It includes not only conscious but subconscious and unconscious factors within the programming parent that contribute to the child's alienation from the other parent. Furthermore (and this is extremely important), it includes factors that arise within the child– independent of the parental contributions–that play a role in the development of the syndrome. In addition, situational factors may contribute, i.e., factors that exist in the family and the environment, that may play a role in bringing about the disorder.

It has come as a surprise to me from reports in both the legal and mental health literature that the concept of the parental alienation syndrome is often misinterpreted. Specifically, there are many who use the term as synonymous with parental brainwashing or programming. Those who do this have missed an extremely important point regarding the etiology, manifestations, and even the treatment of the parental alienation syndrome. The disorder refers to a situation in which the parental programming is *combined with* the child's own scenarios of denigration of the allegedly hated parent. Were we to be dealing here simply with parental indoctrination, I would have probably stuck with the term *brainwashing* or *programming.* Because the disorder involves the aforementioned *combination,* I decided a new term was warranted, a term that would encompass *both* contributory factors. It was the child's contribution that led me to my theory about the etiology and pathogenesis of this disorder. Furthermore, the understanding of the child's contribution is of importance in implementing the therapeutic guidelines described in this book.

Unfortunately, the term *parental alienation syndrome* is often used to refer to the animosity that a child may harbor against a parent who has *actually* abused the child, especially over an extended period. The term has been used to apply to the major categories of parental abuse, namely, physical, sexual, and emotional. Such application indicates a misunderstanding of the concept of the parental alienation syndrome. The term is applicable *only* when the parent has *not* exhibited anything close to the degree of alienating behavior that might warrant the campaign of denigration exhibited by the child. Rather, in typical cases the parent would be considered by most examiners to have provided normal loving parenting or, at worst, exhibited minimal impairments in parenting capacity. It is the *exaggeration* of minor weaknesses and deficiencies that is the hallmark of the parental alienation syndrome. When bona fide abuse does exist, then the child's responding hostility is warranted and the concept of the parental alienation syndrome is not applicable. Perhaps this point was not stated clearly enough in previous publications (Gardner, 1985a, 1986a, 1987, 1989a), although it certainly is strongly implied. In this book this important point will be clearly spelled out.

The parental alienation syndrome is a relatively new disorder, having evolved primarily from recent changes in the criteria by which primary custodial placement is decided. As is true with all newly described disorders, we are in the early stages of our understanding. I plan to continue to revise and update my publications on the disorder in order to keep readers of my work apprised of new developments. I plan to include these in my forthcoming books as well as in inserts that I have typically had placed in my books.

There are two important reasons for the recent dramatic increase in the prevalence of this syndrome. First, since the mid-to-late 1970s, courts have generally taken the position that the tender-years presumption (that mothers are intrinsically superior to fathers as parents) is sexist and that custodial determinations should be made on criteria relating directly to parenting capacity, independent of a parent's sex. This concept became known as the *best-interests-of-the-child presumption*. Second, in the late 1970s and early 1980s, the joint custodial arrangement became increasingly popular. The notion that one parent be designated the *sole* custodian and the other the *visitor* was considered inegalitarian; joint custody promised a more equal division of time with the children and of decision-making powers. Both of these developments have had the effect of making children's custodial arrangements far more unpredictable and precarious. As a result, parents are more frequently brainwashing their children in order to ensure "victory" in custody/visitation litigation. And the children themselves have joined forces with the preferred parent in order to preserve what they consider to be the most desirable arrangement, without the appreciation that in some cases primary custody by the denigrated parent might be in their best interests.

These changes have placed women at a disadvantage in custody disputes. Under the tender-years presumption, mothers were secure in the knowledge that fathers had to prove compellingly significant deficiencies in their wives' parenting capacity before they could even hope to wrest custody of the children. Under the best-interests-of-the-child presumption, especially when the sex-blind doctrine was used in its implementation, mothers' positions became less secure. And, with the subsequent popularization of the joint custodial concept, their positions became even more precarious. Accordingly, mothers have been more likely than fathers to attempt to alienate their children in order to strengthen their positions in custody/ visitation conflicts. Moreover, following a divorce mothers are generally in a far more disadvantageous position financially than fathers. One of the effects of this disadvantage is that they are less capable of affording attorneys who will be as effective in child custody litigation. The resulting sense of helplessness and impotency has also played a role in their resorting to the programming of their children in order to prevail in the custody conflict. Last, for reasons to be elaborated upon, children have been supporting their mothers much more than their fathers, thereby providing their own contributions to the parental alienation syndrome.

Because of this clinically observed difference, namely, that mothers are more likely than fathers to be the alienators ("brainwashers"), I will, for simplicity of presentation, refer more frequently to the mother as the preferred or "loved" parent and the father as the rejected or "hated" parent. I place the words *loved* and *hated* in quotes because there is still much love for the so-called hated parent and much hostility toward and fear of the allegedly loved one. This does not preclude my observation that on occasion (in about 10 percent of cases) it is the father who is the preferred parent and the mother the despised one. It would be an error for the reader to conclude that the designation of the mother as the preferred parent and the father as the hated one represents sexist bias on my part. Rather, it is merely a reflection of my own clinical observations and experiences as well as of others who work in the field. It also would be an error for the reader to conclude that my belief that mothers, more often than fathers, are the active contributors to the brainwashing components necessarily implies condemnation of these women. Actually, as I will discuss later, I am in sympathy with most of these mothers and believe that they have been shortchanged by the aforementioned recent developments. I will, however, describe some situations in which fathers were the primary programmers and mothers were subjected to the children's deprecations.

I will first describe the most common manifestations of the parental alienation syndrome. I will begin with the description of the syndrome's manifestations in the child and then describe the ways in which mothers may contribute to the development of the disorder. I will, however, devote some discussion to fathers as primary programmers. I will then describe the psychodynamic factors I consider to be operative in bringing about the disorder. I divide such contributing factors into three categories: (1) the child's contributions, (2) the mother's contributions (again, with some discussion of the father's contributions), and (3) situational factors. More recently, I have come to appreciate that there are three distinct types of parental alienation syndrome (with some overlap, of course), and that such differentiation is not only important diagnostically but is crucial to appreciate if one is to deal with such families, both from the therapeutic and legal points of view. In subsequent chapters, I will discuss approaches to the prevention and the treatment of the disorder.

THE MANIFESTATIONS OF THE
PARENTAL ALIENATION SYNDROME
IN THE CHILD

It is important for the reader to appreciate that in the parental alienation syndrome, as is true for all psychiatric disorders, there is a continuum from the mildest, through the moderate, to the most severe. Here, I present a rather comprehensive statement of manifestations that I myself have observed, as well as some descriptions from others who have seen such children. Although one could say that I am describing here the classical case, obviously no single child is going to exhibit all of these symptoms. Rather, what is presented here is a composite of many full-blown cases, especially in the moderate to severe categories. As I will discuss subsequently, it is important for the evaluator to make an attempt to divide these children into the mild, moderate, and severe categories—especially because such differentiation is important both with regard to the therapeutic approaches utilized and the legal decisions regarding primary custodial assignment.

The Campaign of Denigration

Typically the child is obsessed with "hatred" of a parent. (As mentioned, the word *hatred* is placed in quotes because, as will be discussed, there are still many tender and loving feelings felt toward the allegedly despised parent that are not permitted expression.) These children speak of the hated parent with every vilification and profanity in their vocabulary—without embarrassment or guilt. The denigration of the parent often has the quality of a litany. After only minimal prompting by a lawyer, judge, probation officer, mental health professional, or other person involved in the litigation, the record will be turned on and a command performance provided.

Typical comments of such children include: "I hate him and I never want to see him again in my whole life," "He's mean and he's stupid and I don't care if I ever see him again," and "If I have to see him I'll see him once a month for an hour. That's all I can stand." A father who was once doting and loving becomes transformed into a noxious individual or a nonperson. A father with whom there were joyous experiences is now referred to as boring. When asked about the activities the child engaged in with the father prior to the separation, the child will often say, "I don't remember." When the examiner asks incredulously about the child's lack of memory for all events that occurred prior to the father's departure, the child claims complete amnesia. It is as if that segment of the child's brain in which were embedded memories of life with father prior to his departure have been totally obliterated.

When the therapist invites everyone for a family interview (separated parental status notwithstanding), the child(ren) and mother will typically be sitting on one side of the waiting room and the father on the other. The mother and child(ren) act as if the father were not even present in the waiting room. Then, when they come into the evaluator's consultation room, the child(ren) almost invariably sits next to the mother, who tries to find a position most remote from the father.

The professions of hatred are most intense when the child(ren) and the loved parent are in the presence of the alienated one. However, when the child is alone with the allegedly hated parent, he (she) may exhibit anything from hatred, to neutrality, to inhibited (but certainly not exuberant) expressions of affection. Not surprisingly, visitation transfer times are periods in which these problems are most likely to exhibit themselves. When the father comes to the home for visitations, the child will often refuse to go with him providing the most frivolous excuses, which are supported by the mother. Later, when these children are alone with the hated parent, they may let their guard down and start to enjoy themselves. Then, almost as if they have realized that they are doing something "wrong," they will suddenly stiffen up and resume their expressions of withdrawal and animosity.

Commonly, these children will be most comfortable when making a sharp division between their clothing, toys, and other possessions in each of the two homes. They are particularly concerned with the transfer of such items from one home to the other, especially from the father's home to the mother's. There is a vague feeling that the object has been somehow contaminated in the father's home and that this contamination will spread into the mother's home if the object is brought therein. Sometimes the children appreciate that anything brought from the father's to the mother's home will serve as a reminder of the father to the mother and thereby engender her hostile reaction, which may spill over onto them. Less common, in my experience, is the child's hesitating to bring objects from the mother's into the father's home lest they be "contaminated" there. The child may not clearly understand the reasons for this separate-but-equal division of property. When children who engage in this practice are asked *why* they insist upon this sharp division, they may respond: "My father makes me do it." Then, when the father is asked about this, he routinely denies that this is the case. In such cases the children are generally providing a rationalization that not only provides them with a seemingly logical reason but also serves the purposes of the father's denigration.

A related phenomenon is the child's changing clothing upon arrival at the father's home. This clothing, which stays in the father's home, is worn during the visit. Then, before return to the mother's house, the child changes back into the original clothing, which was worn at the time of arrival. Here again, there is a vague and often ill-understood feeling that bringing father's clothing into mother's home will somehow contaminate her premises. This sometimes protects the child from the mother's criticisms about how dirty the clothing has become in the father's home. I have seen a few situations in which the mother sends the children in old clothing in the hope that the father will be turned off by the old clothes and return the children in newly bought clothes. In some cases this may be the only way in which she can get him to pay for such clothing. In other cases it is one manifestation of her compulsion to exploit him. In some cases the mother has refused to allow the father to take any of the children's clothing from the home at the time of his departure. The purpose here is to interfere with the smooth flow of visitations and contribute to his having "a hard time" when he is with the children. Although it is a small bit of ammunition, it is ammunition nevertheless. The father, whether justifiably or not, may then change the children's clothing upon their arrival, dress them in more presentable clothing, and then return them in the unkempt manner in which they arrived. The children, in such circumstances, may then fall into the pattern and automatically change clothing upon arrival at the father's house without realizing the original reasons for the pattern. Because of the many reasons for such a practice (which is quite common), the examiner does well to make a detailed inquiry about the origins and the reasons for this practice.

On occasion, one sees a family in which the children have been split, some siding with the mother and some siding with the father. Although this may initially appear to be yet another example of a divided family in which the children have been split up into two warring camps, the introduction of the children's own scenarios warrant the parental alienation syndrome designation. In one such family that I saw, the two brothers sided with the father and the sister sided with the mother. In accordance with this division, the court ordered a split custodial arrangement even though, in my testimony, I strongly urged that all three children reside primarily with the mother because the father was clearly the individual who was programming the boys against the mother. When I interviewed the boys, they both told me: "The good kids go with the good parent and the bad kids go with the bad parent." The boys, however, did reluctantly agree to visit with their mother. However, during visitations they would not speak directly with her, but through their sister. It was almost as if she were serving as a translator, even though all parties were speaking the same language. They would never look their mother in the face nor answer her questions directly. Rather, they would say: "You tell mommy that I don't want to go to the movies with her today" and "You tell mommy that I'm hungry." We see here a typical maneuver of a child with this disorder. By not speaking directly with the mother, they can satisfy their father that they are indeed exhibiting hostility toward her. However, the hostility is not that great that it precludes visitation entirely nor does it preclude enjoying one of her meals.

Another maneuver commonly seen in these children is the child's claiming affection for the parent being spoken to and professing hatred of the other. The parent to whom the affection is being expressed is asked to swear not to reveal the professions

of hatred to the other parent. And the same statements are made
to the other parent with a similar extraction of a promise that the
divulgences not be revealed to the absent parent. In this way
these children "cover their tracks" and thereby avoid the disclosure of their schemes. Such children may find family interviews
with therapists extremely anxiety provoking because of the fear
that their manipulations and maneuvers will be divulged. The
loved parent's proximity plays an important role regarding what
the child will say to the hated one. When the child is with the
hated one, the closer the loved parent the greater the likelihood
the hated parent will be denigrated. When seen alone in consultation, the child is likely to modify the litany in accordance with
which parent is in the waiting room. Judges, lawyers, and mental
health professionals who interview such children should recognize this important phenomenon.

Weak, Frivolous, or Absurd
Rationalizations for the Deprecation

Typically, these children provide irrational and often ludicrous justifications for their alienation from their fathers. Even
years after they have taken place, the child may justify the
alienation with memories of minor altercations experienced in the
relationship with the hated parent. These are usually trivial and
are experiences that most children quickly forget, e.g., "He
always used to speak very loud when he told me to brush my
teeth." "He used to tell me to get his things a lot." "She used to
say to me 'Don't interrupt.' " "He used to make a lot of noise
when he chewed at the table." When these children are asked to
give more compelling reasons for the hatred, they are unable to
provide them. Frequently, the loved parent will agree with the
child that these professed reasons justify the ongoing animosity.

It was the presence of incredible rationalizations that first led
me to the conclusion that what I was seeing here was not simply
the result of parental programming, but the child's own contribution playing an important role. I remember, very specifically,
one of the earliest children (in the early 1980s) who had to miss

an appointment because of the death of his paternal grandfather. At the beginning of our first session the next week, the following interchange took place:

> *Gardner:* I'm very sorry to hear that your grandfather died.
> *Patient:* You know, he just didn't die. My father murdered him.
> *Gardner* (incredulously): Your father murdered your grandfather, his own father?
> *Patient:* Yes. I know he did it.
> *Gardner:* I thought he was in the hospital? I understand that he was about 85 years old and that he was dying of old age diseases.
> *Patient:* Yeah, that's what *my father* says.
> *Gardner:* What do *you* say?
> *Patient:* I say he murdered him in the hospital.
> *Gardner:* How did he do that?
> *Patient:* He sneaked into the hospital, at night, and did it while no one was looking. He did it while the nurses and the doctors were asleep.
> *Gardner:* How do you know that?
> *Patient:* I just know it.
> *Gardner:* Did anyone tell you any such thing?
> *Patient:* No, but I just know it.
> *Gardner* (now turning to the mother who is witness to this conversation): What do you think about what he said?
> *Mother:* Well, I don't *really think* that he did it, but I wouldn't put it past him.

Even this mother, who hated her husband with every cell in her body and who was fostering a parental alienation syndrome, did not go along with this particular allegation, although she was not beyond stretching the truth in her receptivity to believing the child's criticisms of the father. I still recall this interchange as one that played an important role in my recognition that children were creating scenarios of their own, above and beyond what their programming parents were providing. Such contributions warranted my introduction of the concept of the parental alienation syndrome.

Therapists should routinely ask these children to provide the exact reasons why they harbor such acrimony toward their fathers. It is in this way that the inconsequential reasons will be provided. One child, who was alienated from his mother, as a result of programming by his father, complained that he did not want to see his mother because she embarrassed him. The following interchange then took place:

> *Gardner:* I would like to know *exactly* how your mother embarrasses you.
> *Patient:* Well, she once embarrassed me at Little League practice.
> *Gardner:* Tell me exactly what happened there.
> *Patient:* Well, she sprayed us all with bug stuff, stuff that kills bugs.
> *Gardner:* Were there bugs around?
> *Patient:* Yes.
> *Gardner:* Were the bugs bothering everybody?
> *Patient:* Yes.
> *Gardner:* It would seem to me that everybody would have been happy that she sprayed the bug stuff. Were the other boys happy about it? Did the other boys complain?
> *Patient:* No.
> *Gardner:* Were the other boys happy to be sprayed?
> *Patient:* I think so, but she still embarrasses me. She just should have stayed by the side with the other parents and watched.

Although this boy, like many eight-year-olds, are easily embarrassed by a parent who steps out of the crowd and does anything different, no matter how minor, his embarrassment did not justify the degree of animosity he professed.

One 11-year-old boy, who was refusing to go with his father, gave this as one of his reasons for not wanting to visit with him: "He doesn't make the decisions where we should go. He's always asking me where we should go." One could more easily see the child making the opposite complaint, namely, that the father imposes the decisions on him. Interestingly, the same child made this complaint: "Two years ago, he made me go to Europe with him and I hated every minute of it." This boy was continually placing his father in a no-win situation. Here, when he would give the boy the option of deciding where to go, he was criticized for not making the decisions himself. And, when he made the decisions himself, he was criticized for that. Such fathers frequently complain that "they can do no right" and that no matter what decision they make, it's the wrong one.

Another common complaint is that the hated parent is always breaking promises. When asked specifically what promises have been broken, one will get answers such as: "He promised to take me to the zoo and he didn't." On further inquiry one learns that there were heavy downpours that day and that no sane person was bringing children to the zoo that day to get drenched while looking at animals. Visits broken because of compelling time conflicts such as the attendance at funerals, car breakdowns, crucial business meetings, etc., are provided as examples of the broken promises. Sometimes the promises that were allegedly broken were never even made in the first place. This, of course, leaves the father with even a greater sense of impotence.

Insisting that the child do household chores may be used as the reason for refusal to visit: "He made me help make the bed," "He made me watch my little sisters while he was washing the dishes," "He made me help wipe the dishes," etc. Although the same child performs these chores at the mother's home, with little beyond the normal degree of resistance, at the father's home they become onerous tasks, examples of exploitation, and justifications for nonvisitation. Other examples: "The bike at my mother's house is better than the one at my father's house," "At his house I have to sleep in the same room as my brother; at my mother's house we each have our own rooms," and "Now that he lives in an apartment, I can't bring my dog with me." One child (who was alienated against his mother by his father) stated that he only wanted to see his mother "for one hour, once a month." When I asked him why he wanted to see her so infrequently, he said, "We'd both go crazy." When I asked him specifically in what ways they would drive each other crazy, he was not able to give me a specific answer other than to say, "I just know that it'll happen."

One child claimed that his reason for not wanting to see his father was "because he says bad things about my mother. He says she brainwashed me. He says that she tells me lies about him." In this situation the mother was indeed brainwashing the child and telling him lies about the father. The father's attempts to correct these distortions and to exonerate himself were then used as ammunition against him in the service of the child's campaign of denigration. Another girl stated, "My father said he'd get the police if I didn't go visit with him. So I stopped going after that." Again, the father's threat to get the police was made in the hope of enlisting their aid in enforcing the visitation schedule. The child, as is often the case with these children, was completely oblivious to the benevolent intent of the threat to bring the police; rather, she used this in the service of providing a justification for refusing visits entirely. Unfortunately, this child's refusals were supported by a well-meaning but misguided guardian ad litem who proudly stated that her job was to support her client's wishes. Another child stated that one of her reasons for not wanting to visit with her father was, "He showed up at the Christmas play and he wasn't supposed to." Here, again, the father's love that motivated him to break the mother's rule (and it was only hers and not the court's) was completely ignored by the child. Rather, she used this demonstration of his deep affection as an excuse for refusing to visit him.

In the course of child custody litigation one can rely upon the mother's attorney to collect all of these reasons and detail them in their briefs and motions. Because it is their obligation to select those that most support the mother's position, they can be relied upon to select those that they consider the most compelling. In a typical case of parental alienation syndrome the list consists primarily, if not exclusively, of frivolous reasons similar or identical to those presented above. The failure to be able to provide more compelling reasons and the listing of a series of these inconsequential ones is pathognomonic of the disorder. It is

The nite before July 4, 97, Dan "wanted" to return to Mom - Ricky followed his lead, + E. went to Albany + took Dan out of school - He didn't want "to be ⊆ me. ???

almost as if the attorney provides here convincing evidence for the diagnosis.

Lack of Ambivalence

Another symptom of the parental alienation syndrome is complete lack of ambivalence. All human relationships are ambivalent, and parent-child relationships are no exception. The concept of mixed feelings has no place in these children's scheme of things. The hated parent is all bad and the loved parent is all good. Most children (normals as well as those with a wide variety of psychiatric problems), when asked to list both good and bad things about each parent, will generally be able to do so. When children with parental alienation syndrome are asked to provide the same lists, they will typically recite a long list of criticisms of the hated parent, but will not be able to think of one positive or redeeming personality trait. In contrast, they will provide only positive and endearing qualities for the preferred parent and claim to be unable to think of even one trait they dislike. The hated parent may have been deeply dedicated to the child's upbringing, and a strong bond may have been created over many years.

The hated parent may produce photos that demonstrate clearly a joyful and deep relationship in which there was significant affection, tenderness, and mutual pleasure. But the memory of all these experiences appears to have been obliterated. When these children are shown photos of enjoyable events with the hated parent, they usually rationalize the experiences as having been forgotten, nonexistent, or feigned: "I really hated being with him then; I just smiled in the picture because he made me. He said he'd hit me if I didn't smile." "She used to beat me to make me go to the zoo with her." The aforementioned amnesia for all enjoyable experiences with the hated parent, prior to the separation, is another example of this lack of ambivalence. This element of complete lack of ambivalence is a typical manifestation of the parental alienation syndrome and should make one dubious about the validity of the professed animosity.

The "Independent Thinker" Phenomenon

Many of these children proudly state that their decision to reject their fathers is their own. They deny any contribution from their mothers. And the mothers often support this vehemently. In fact, the mothers will often state that they want the child to visit with the father and recognize the importance of such involvement. Yet, such a mother's every act indicates otherwise. Such children appreciate that, by stating that the decision is their own, they assuage mother's guilt and protect her from criticism. Such professions of independent thinking are supported by the mother, who will often praise these children for being the kinds of people who have minds of their own and are forthright and brave enough to express overtly their opinions. Frequently, such mothers will exhort their children to tell them the truth regarding whether or not they really want to see their fathers. The child will usually appreciate that "the truth" is the profession that they hate the father and do not want to see him ever again. They thereby provide that answer—couched as "the truth"—which will protect them from the the their mother's anger if they were to state what they really wanted to do, which is to see their fathers. It is important for the reader to appreciate that after a period of programming the child may not know what the truth is anymore and come to actually believe that the father deserves the vilification being directed against him. The end point of the brainwashing process has then been achieved. I recall once observing the following "conversation" between a mother and her seven-year-old boy regarding the question of his visiting with his father.

> *Mother:* Now, Billy, I want you to tell me *the truth*. Do you *really* want to see your father?
> *Billy:* (child remains silent)
> *Mother* (voice now getting louder): Billy, you can tell me the truth. What is it?
> *Billy:* (still silent)
> *Mother* (voice now getting even higher): You don't have to be afraid of me, Billy. All I want you to do is tell me *the truth*. *Do you* or do you *not* want to see your father? You don't have to be afraid

to say that you don't want to see your father. Do tell me now, what's the truth, what do you really want? You can say it.

Billy: I don't want to see my father.

Mother (turning now to me): You see, doctor, it's like I said. He really doesn't want to see his father and that's his *own* opinion. I haven't talked him into it. (Mother now turning to Billy.) Isn't that right? Isn't that your *own* opinion?

Billy: Yes, that's my *own* opinion.

Unfortunately, after a few interchanges of this kind, a child in this situation will ultimately come to believe that the refusal to see the father is indeed his (her) own opinion and always has been. They do not seem to appreciate, however, that the frequent appearance of borrowed scenario words and phrases (see below) belies completely their professions of independent thinking. In extreme cases such mothers will hire lawyers for the children and go to court in order to support what is ostensibly the child's own decision not to visit. The realities are that, with the exception of situations in which the father is indeed abusive, there is no good reason for a child's not wanting to have at least some contact with a father. Children are not born with genes that program them to reject a father. Such hatred and rejection are environmentally induced, and the most likely person to have brought about the alienation is the mother.

Reflexive Support of the Loved Parent in Parental Conflict

In family conferences, in which the children are seen together with both the loved and hated parent, the children reflexly take the position of the loved parent—sometimes even before the other has had the opportunity to present his (her) side of the argument. Even the loved parent may not present the argument as forcefully as the supporting child. These children may even refuse to accept evidence that is obvious proof of the hated parent's position. For example, one boy's mother claimed that her husband was giving her absolutely no money at all. When the father showed the boy cancelled checks, signed by him and endorsed by the mother, the boy claimed that they were "forged." Commonly these children will accept as 100 percent valid the allegations of the loved parent against the hated one. One boy's mother claimed that her husband had beaten her on numerous occasions. The child presented this as one of the reasons why he hated his father. The father denied that he had ever laid a finger on the mother; in contrast, he claimed that the mother on a number of occasions had struck him. When I asked the child if he had even *seen* his father hit his mother, he claimed that he had not, but that he believed his mother and insisted she would never lie to him. I pointed out to the child that he was not at all considering the possibility that his mother might be lying and that it was his father who was telling the truth. He responded that his father always lied to him and that his mother never did so. When I asked him to give me examples of his father's lies he stated, after giving the request some thought, "I don't remember now, but I know he's a liar." In this situation, as a result of an exhaustive evaluation, I concluded that the father's rendition was far more likely to have been valid.

Absence of Guilt

The child may exhibit a guiltless disregard for the feelings of the hated parent. There will be a complete absence of gratitude for gifts, support payments, and other manifestations of the hated parent's continued involvement and affection. Often these children will want to be certain the alienated parent continues to provide support payments, but at the same time adamantly refuse to visit. Commonly they will say that they *never* want to see the hated parent again, or not until their late teens or early twenties. To such a child I might say, "So you want your father to continue paying for all your food, clothing, rent, and education — even private high school and college — and yet you still don't want to see him at all, ever again. Is that right?" Such a child might respond, "That's right. He doesn't deserve to see me. He's mean and paying all that money is a good punishment for him." Probably one of the best examples of this phenomenon is the child who knowingly and consciously participates with the mother in promulgating a false sex abuse accusation. In such situations fathers' lives have literally been destroyed and many have been sent to jail, even for years. The lack of guilt here is not simply explained by cognitive immaturity (often the case, especially for very young children), but is a statement of the degree to which children can be programmed to such points of cruelty that they are totally oblivious to the effects of their sadism on innocent victims. Elsewhere, in my discussion of the accusing children in the Salem witch trials (Gardner, 1991a), I have elaborated on this point.

The Presence of
Borrowed Scenarios

Not only is there a rehearsed quality to these children's litanies, but one often hears phraseology that is not commonly used by the child. Many expressions are identical to those used by the loved parent. A father tries repeatedly to call home in order to communicate with his children. Each time he calls, the mother screams, "Stop harassing us!" and hangs up. The four-year-old child, then, when asked why he does not want to see his father, responds, "He harasses us." One four-year-old girl told me that she did not want to visit with her father because "He makes me watch R-rated movies." When I asked her exactly what are R-rated movies, she replied, "I don't know." Another child said to me, "I have bad dreams when I go to my daddy's house." When I asked her to please tell me what were in those dreams, she replied, "I don't know. My mommy says I have them there."

Sometimes, and this is especially true of younger children, they will not appreciate that they are providing the exact source of their programmed information when providing good examples of borrowed scenarios: "My mommy says that he touched my peepee," "My mommy says he sexually molested me." One five-year-old told me, "His new girlfriend's a whore." One seven-year-old girl, whose father alienated her from her mother, complained that she was "cooped up" when she visited with her mother and did not feel "cooped up" when she stayed at her father's house. Interestingly, her father had used these exact words when telling me about his reluctance to bring the child to the mother's apartment. However, the realities were that, although the father did live in a house, the mother's apartment complex was more a small city in that it had both indoor and outdoor swimming pools, a health spa, a basketball court, tennis courts, and a mini-mall, with video games, a triplex cinema, restaurants, and various organized child-oriented programs. The realities also were that the mother lived in the marital home and the child had many more friends at her mother's than she did at her father's house.

One nine-year-old girl's mother told me that her child has "separation anxiety" every time she has to leave her to visit with her father. When I asked further about the specific manifestations of this disorder the mother stated, "She hyperventilates every time she has to go off with him." On further inquiry I learned that this separation anxiety disorder was very specific in that it did not exhibit itself when the child had to separate from her mother to go to school, to visit with friends, or, as a matter of fact, to part with her mother to go with any other acceptable person. It was a very rare form of the disorder that confined itself only to separations that involved visits with her father. In my session with the girl, she told me that she did not want to visit with her father because she "hyperventilates" whenever she has to visit with him. When I asked her to be more specific, and to describe exactly what she meant by "hyperventilate," she stated, "I don't know. I just know that I hyperventilate." One four-year-old girl, who was programmed against her mother by her father, claimed that she did not want to visit with her mother because "she lacks discipline." It was indeed the case that the mother was somewhat lackadaisical when compared to her very compulsive ex-husband; however, she was a perfectly competent caretaker. When I asked the child exactly what she meant when she said that her mother "lacked discipline," she was unable to provide me with a meaningful answer and it was clear that she did not have the faintest idea what she was talking about. And this is one of the hallmarks of the borrowed scenario: When the child is asked to define the term, he (she) is generally unable to provide a satisfactory definition.

One father, who was successful in convincing the court that the children's mother was indeed defective in her child-rearing capacities, was awarded primary custody. He was also successful in inducing in his children a parental alienation syndrome. Their interviews with the judge had played a role in this transfer which, in my opinion, was completely unwarranted and significantly detrimental to the children. The father was rigid, domineering, and quite compulsive. When I asked the eight-year-old son why he did not want to visit with his mother, he replied: "She didn't make us study hard enough." Obviously, this is not a comment that was generated spontaneously by the child. Anyone who has had experience with children—whether it be as a parent, teacher, or in any other capacity—will agree that one would have to wait a long time before seeing a child who would spontaneously make such a complaint. It is a typical example of the borrowed scenario comments that become incorporated into the scenarios of denigration. This child's sister, when asked why she did not want to visit her mother, added, in addition to her brother's complaint, "She's always trying to bribe us with gifts and toys." Again, it is a rare child who will view gifts and toys as bribes, but children can easily be convinced that they are so in the context of a parental alienation syndrome.

When I asked one eight-year-old boy why he refused to visit with his father he stated, "He keeps harassing us with lawsuits." On inquiry I learned that these lawsuits were the result of the father's having been repeatedly unsuccessful in getting the mother to allow him to visit with the children. The child was completely oblivious to this element, and he had no appreciation that they were a strong manifestation of his father's ongoing affection. Rather, he joined in with the mother in viewing them as ongoing irritants. Another girl claimed that she did not ever want to see her father again because "he's a liar, he's a cheat, and he's always tricking us." I asked her if she could define specifically each of these terms and provide me with examples of why her father deserves these epithets. Although she had a good idea about the meaning of these terms, she was not able to provide one concrete example to support the allegations. Rather, they were all part of the litany of denigrations that she had learned from her mother. The inability to provide substantive examples of the allegations is another one of the hallmarks of the borrowed scenario.

Spread of the Animosity to the Extended Family of the Hated Parent

The hatred of the parent often extends to include that parent's complete extended family. Cousins, aunts, uncles, and grandparents—with whom the child previously may have had loving relationships—are now viewed as similarly obnoxious. Grandparents, who previously had a loving and tender relationship with the child, now find themselves suddenly and inexplicably rejected. The child has no guilt over such rejection, nor does the loved parent. Greeting cards are not reciprocated. Presents sent to the home are refused, remain unopened, or even destroyed (generally in the presence of the loved parent). When the hated parent's relatives call on the telephone, the child will respond with angry vilifications or quickly hang up on the caller. (These responses are more likely to occur if the loved parent is within hearing distance of the conversation.) With regard to the hatred of the relatives, the child is even less capable of providing justifications for the animosity. The rage of these children is so great that they become completely oblivious to the privations they are causing themselves. Again, the loved parent is typically unconcerned with the untoward psychological effects on the child of this rejection of the network of relatives who previously provided important psychological gratifications.

A common excuse that these children give for not wanting to have anything to do with members of the hated parent's extended family is that those people have been trying to influence the child to improve their relationships with their hated parent. Typical comments: "I don't want to see my Uncle Ted because he made me feel bad about not seeing my father," "I hate my Aunt Sarah. She's always bugging me to be nice to my father and she doesn't listen to me when I tell her that I hate him." Such comments, of course, place these relatives in a no-win situation. If they stand aside and do nothing, they feel they are contributing to a perpetuation of the alienation; if they step forth and try to encourage rapprochement, they may similarly be rejected and, worse, provide ammunition for the child to justify rejection. The feelings of impotence then suffered by the alienated parent become extended to the relatives.

Particularly pained in such situations are doting grandparents who become grieved over the sudden loss of their grandchildren. Previously, these grandchildren may have been their "pride and joy" and an enormous source of gratification. Now, suddenly, without warning, the child suddenly spurns them as if they were noxious and poisonous. Commonly, such alienation can go on for years, resulting in an important loss of psychological gratifications for all concerned. They frequently describe themselves as being "heartbroken" and "grief stricken." I have seen two situations in which grandmothers have literally died of heart attacks under these circumstances. Both were women in their sixties and were previously in good health. Neither smoked, had high blood pressure, suffered with diabetes, or had any of the illnesses that would predispose one to a heart attack. I am convinced that in both of these cases their deaths were the final culmination of the deep and prolonged grief (three and four years) they had suffered over the rejection of their beloved grandchildren. In both of these cases I believe that these women died of broken hearts. Obviously, I am not speaking literally here, only figuratively. The years of "heartbreak" contributed, I am sure, to their premature deaths by heart attacks. In one of these cases, the child's father (the son of the deceased grandmother) gave his daughter a picture of his recently deceased mother as a token of remembrance. The nine-year-old daughter's response was, "I don't want it. You're blaming me that grandma died and I had nothing to do with it." Clearly, this child had some guilt over the grandmother's death (and appropriately so) and, unfortunately, used this offering as a further excuse for totally refusing to see her father. Again, it is a no-win situation for the alienated parent. Incidentally, this vignette is a good example of the potential that children have for cruelty, a potential that is not given the attention it deserves. Elsewhere (Gardner, 1991a, 1992a) I have elaborated on this point.

Concluding Comments

Those who have never seen such children may consider this description a caricature. Those who have seen them will recognize the description immediately, although most children may not manifest all the symptoms. The parental alienation syndrome is becoming increasingly common, and there is good reason to predict that it will become even more prevalent if the recommendations presented in this book are not implemented. As mentioned, the parental alienation syndrome is primarily the result of injudicious legal criteria by which parental preference has been determined in recent years. As long as the misguided egalitarianism of these recent proposals remains in effect, we will continue to see children with this disorder.

THE PROGRAMMING MOTHER

Introduction

The parent's contributions and manifestations range from those that are entirely conscious to those that are deeply unconscious. These factors operate at all points on the continuum and tend to shift, over the passage of time, from the conscious to the unconscious level. In short, they become so automatic and so deeply incorporated into the programming parent's psychic structure that they are performed reflexively, without conscious appreciation of their detrimental effects. Accordingly, although I roughly divide these maneuvers into conscious and unconscious categories, it is important for the reader to appreciate that we are dealing here with various points on a continuum that is ever shifting in the direction of the automatic and unconscious.

Furthermore, many of these maneuvers may have both conscious and unconscious elements. Whereas I was able to divide the manifestations of the child's contributions into categories, with minimal overlap, this could not be easily accomplished with regard to the adult's contributions. There was so much overlap that I found it practically impossible to define "pure" categories of maneuvers. What one can say, however, is that practically all of these manipulations share in common certain basic factors, which include denigration of the hated spouse, the utilization of him (her) as a target for hostility, and exclusionary maneuvers. It is somewhat easier, therefore, to divide the maneuvers into the conscious and unconscious categories, but even here one has to appreciate the aforementioned continuum.

Programming ("Brainwashing")

I use the word *programming* to refer to those maneuvers by which a parent consciously seeks to alienate the child from the hated spouse. I will use the word *programming* synonymously with *brainwashing*. Although the latter is generally considered a lay term and not frequently found as an acceptable term in strictly scientific publications, I consider it to be a useful word because of its direct reference to a conscious process by which one individual attempts to change the thinking of another. Also implied is the repetition over time of the messages imparted to bring about this goal. The programming factor may be present to varying degrees. In some cases it may be minimal or even absent, and the disturbance results primarily from the child's contributions and possibly the situation (examples to be provided later in this chapter). Most often, the parental input is the predominant factor and the programming is overt and obvious to the sensitive and astute examiner. The loved parent embarks upon an unrelenting campaign of denigration that may last for years. A mother, for example, whose divorce was the result of marital problems that contributed to her husband's seeking the affection of another woman, may continually vilify the father to her children with such terms as "adulterer," "philanderer," and "abandoner." Similarly, she may refer to the father's new woman friend as a "slut," "whore," and "home breaker." No attention is given to the problems in the marriage, especially this mother's problem(s), that may have contributed to the new involvement.

At times the criticisms may even be delusional, but the child is brought to believe entirely the validity of the accusations. The child may thereby come to view the hated parent as the incarnation of evil. A father, for example, may develop the delusion that his wife has been unfaithful to him and may even divorce her without any specific evidence for an affair. Innocent conversations with strange men are viewed as proof of her infidelity, and the children may come to view their mother as an adulteress. Often the infrequency of visits or lack of contact with the hated parent facilitates the child's accepting completely the loved parent's criticisms. There is little or no opportunity to correct the distortions by actual experiences. Although the delusion (obviously) has its origins in unconscious factors (especially projection), the brainwashing of the child may very well be a conscious operation. (We see here, then, the complexity of these maneuvers and how the placement of them into categories of conscious and unconscious is somewhat artificial. However, I do try to make the differentiation because it has value with regard to the degree of responsibility and this, of course, has therapeutic implications for both psychiatric treatment and the legal process.)

There are mothers who, at the time of their husband's departure, will rampage through the house destroying every item that might bring about reminders of his existence. Clearly, one of the mechanisms operative here is that of displacement. The murderous rage she would like to vent on her husband is displaced onto these objects and by destroying them she symbolically destroys him. Although the fringe benefit of not being reminded of him may be salutary, and ultimately helpful in her working through her reactions to the divorce, this maneuver, like all psychopathological maneuvers, is not without its drawbacks. One of these is that it deprives the child of the opportunity for continuity of contact with the now-absent father. If the father were to have died in the course of a stable marriage, the mother probably would have kept many of these mementos around in order to serve as a link to the deceased father. She would recognize that these mementos are of psychological value in that they enable the child to have some continuity with the lost parent. In the divorce situation, however, this important factor is not given consideration.

The maneuver can contribute to the development of a parental alienation syndrome in that it communicates to the child that the father is so despicable an individual, so hateful, that any remnant of his existence somehow putrefies the household, and all evidence of his existence must be obliterated. Included may be photographs of pleasant and even joyful experiences, and this contributes to the child's previously described capacity to obliterate from conscious awareness all recollection of the "good old days." Destruction of pictures of the father's relatives may contribute to the process by which the hatred of the father is spread to his extended family. It is similar to the process sometimes utilized in certain totalitarian states in which individuals totally disappear from the face of the earth and any remnants of their existence are confiscated and destroyed.

A common form of criticism of the father is to complain about how little money he is giving. I am not referring here to situations in which the divorce has brought about some predictable privation. The healthy mother in such a situation recognizes that she and the children will not enjoy the same financial flexibility that they had prior to the separation. I am referring here to the use of financial restrictions in the service of deprecating the father. A mother may complain so much about her financial privations that she will lead the children to believe that they may actually go without food, clothing, shelter, and that they may very well freeze and/or starve to death. I have seen cases in which extremely wealthy women utilized this maneuver, women who have been left with so much money that they will be comfortable for the rest of their lives. They may be spending thousands of dollars on extravagances, and yet the children may come to believe that because of their father's stinginess they are constantly on the verge of starvation.

There are mothers who, when talking to the children about their husbands having left the home, will make such statements as, "Your father's abandoned us." In most cases the father has left the mother and has not lost any affection for the children. Lumping the children together with herself (by using the word "us" rather than "me") promulgates the notion that they too have been rejected. In this way the mother contributes to the children's view of the father as a cruel abandoner, insensitive to the feelings of those he has left behind. The father in such situations may attempt (often unsuccessfully) to reassure the children that he has left the mother and not them, that he no longer loves the mother, but he still loves them.

Another way of brainwashing is to exaggerate a parent's minor psychological problems. The parent who may have drunk a little extra alcohol on occasion will gradually become spoken of as "an alcoholic." And the parent who may have experimented occasionally with drugs comes to be viewed as "a drug addict." Even though the accusing parent may have joined with the former spouse in such experimentation with drugs, the vilified parent is given the epithet. The deprecated parent might then be described in quite "colorful" terms: "He was dead drunk that night and he was literally out cold on the floor. We had to drag him to the car and dump him in the back seat." "The man was so stoned that he didn't have the faintest idea where he was and what he was doing." Often denial by the accused parent proves futile, especially if the accuser can provide concrete evidence such as a pipe used to smoke pot or a collection of bottles of liquor (which may be no more than the average person has in one's home anyway).

A common maneuver is to require the visiting father to park his car in front of the house and blow the horn when he arrives. He is not permitted to come to the doorstep, let alone ring the doorbell. Although not stated, the implication here is that this very act might somehow contaminate the whole household. It is as if poisonous fumes would emanate from the tip of his finger, somehow get transmitted into the household, and thereby spread noxious fumes throughout the household. Although there are literally millions of other people who would be permitted to ring the doorbell with impunity, the father is singled out as a person who is strictly prohibited from engaging in this common everyday act. Rather, he must keep his distance, sit outside in the gutter (where lowlife types belong), honk his horn, and hope that he will be heard (and often he is not). There are mothers who have actually obtained court orders requiring the father to visit in this way. If the order has been obtained because of actual physical violence then, of course, it might be justified. But in many cases, such restraining orders are the result of fabricated and even delusional complaints about such violence. (It is important for the reader to remember, once again, that when there is actual physical abuse [of either mother or child], then it is less likely that the parental alienation syndrome concept is applicable.)

There are parents who are quite creative in their brainwashing maneuvers. A father calls the home to speak to his son. The mother answers the telephone and happens to be in the son's room at the time. The father simply asks if he can speak with his son. The mother (with the boy right next to her) says nothing. Again, the father asks to speak with his son. There is more silence (during which the son is unable to hear his father's pleas for a response). Finally, the mother responds: "I'm glad he can't hear what you're saying right now" or "If he heard what you just said, I'm sure he would never speak with you again." When the father finally speaks with the boy and explains that he had said absolutely nothing that was critical, the boy may be incredulous. The result is that the father becomes very fearful of calling his son, lest he again be trapped in this way. A related maneuver is for the mother to say to the calling father (after a long period of stony silence during which the boy is within earshot of the mother and the father has made an innocuous statement): "That's *your* opinion. In *my* opinion he's a *very fine* boy." The implication here is that the father has made some scathing criticism and that the mother is defending the child.

Another mother greets her husband at the front door while their daughter is upstairs awaiting her father's visitation. Although the conversation is calm and unemotional, the mother suddenly dashes to the corner of the room, buries her head in her arms, and while cowering in the corner screams out, "No, no, no. Don't hit me again." The girl comes running into the living room, and although she did not actually observe her father hit her mother, she believes her mother's claim that her father had just pulled himself back from beating her when he heard the girl coming down the stairs.

Another maneuver is to repeatedly tell the child that the father has referred to him (her) as "stupid," "a jerk," and " a moron." The father not only has never referred to the child in this way, but may not even be aware of the fact that this programming is contributing to the child's alienation. When he does learn that this has been going on, his denials may not be believed by the child, thus bringing about a sense of impotent frustration. If he tells the child that the mother is lying, he may find himself in the position of being called a liar and that this is one of the reasons why the child does not want to visit him. Another "creative" maneuver involves providing the child with a full meal on the morning just before the father picks up the child for a weekend visit. Unbeknownst to the child, the mother then informs the father that the child has not eaten and that he should be sure to give the child a *full* breakfast. The child will predictably thwart the father in such attempts, and this will bring about a predictable confrontation, thereby contributing to the "spoiling" of the visit. Anything the mother can do, both before and during the visit, that will predictably produce difficulties within the time frame of the visitation will be tried.

Another maneuver I have come across in this regard is to call the father's home at two or three in the morning, thus waking up the whole family. The ostensible purpose here might be the mother's reporting a "bad dream" in which "something terrible happened to the child," and she just wants to make sure that everything is okay. Somehow these bad dreams occur only during the times of visitation and, predictably, disrupt the smooth flow of the visit. They result in the child's being tired and irritable the next day and compromises, thereby, the father's and the children's opportunity to enjoy the visitation experience.

Another way of accomplishing this goal is to provide comments such as these prior to the child's leaving the house: "I feel so bad for you that you have to go," "I've done everything to protect you from these visits, but the court insists that you go," "You know I'll be thinking about you and praying for you," and "Don't worry, it's only a weekend. You'll be home before you realize it." Sometimes the mother will express such grief over the painful experience that the child is soon to be subjected to that she may actually cry as she bids the child goodbye. Obviously, all these histrionics have the effect of compromising the child's opportunity to have a good time. They have the effect of sabotaging the visit in advance.

In recent years, the answering machine has enjoyed widespread utilization. I personally consider it to be a wonderful invention, a very inexpensive and useful timesaver. However, what may be a boon to civilized society has become the bane of the existence of many separated and divorced fathers. The answering machine has become a very powerful weapon in the hands of parents who wish to alienate their children from their despised spouses. A typical scenario involves the machine being kept on 24 hours a day, whether or not anyone is at home. In this way calls are screened. All callers, then, can be divided into two categories, those who are acceptable and those who are not. When the phone rings, those in the house listen carefully to ascertain first who the caller is and then decide whether or not the phone will be picked up. A wide variety of friends and relatives are in the acceptable category. Number one on the list of the unacceptables is the father and possibly people who are trying to solicit sales. The children, then, are given firsthand lessons in maneuvers that exclude the father. Needless to say, in most situations in which a parental alienation syndrome is present, the calls to the hated spouse are not returned. And this is the case whether or not someone is at home to listen to the message being left. The aforementioned is a widespread practice. I have been involved in a number of cases in which the father has had to resort to obtaining a court order to require the mother to turn off the answering machine when she is at home and pick up the phone when he calls. Unfortunately, in many of these cases, such an order has been flaunted with impunity, which is often the case with regard to parental alienation syndrome parents and the courts.

Selected use of pictures can also be used in the brainwashing process. There is hardly a child who hasn't at some time or other refused to be included in a family picture. There is hardly a family who hasn't had the experience of having to cajole a child to join the others in a photograph. In many families a picture of the crying child will be taken, with a fond memory of the situation, the child's crying notwithstanding. Such a picture may be used by a brainwashing parent to convince the child that the other parent caused the child's grief and tears. The parent who is collecting evidence for litigation may be very quick to take pictures that could be interpreted as proof of the other parent's hostility toward the child. The healthy parent will argue with a child, scream once in a while, and make threatening gestures. If these can be preserved on film they are considered to be good evidence for the parent's sadistic behavior toward the child.

Typically, these mothers will consider a wide variety of other people preferable to serve as babysitters. Accordingly, in situations when they themselves are not available, and the former husband is, they will not allow him to see the child. Most often they use as their excuse the argument that the times he has requested to see the child are not within the confines of the visitation schedule. Other mothers recognize that being with the father is generally preferable to being with babysitters, relatives, and friends, because of their appreciation that now that the father is out of the house, any extra time spent with him could be salutary for the child. These mothers seem oblivious to this obvious fact. Any babysitters, even those who have previously been unknown to the child, are considered to be preferable individuals with whom the child should spend time. Although sometimes, in these situations, it may be a choice between the child's being with the father and playmates, the decision for these mothers always seems to be in favor of the playmates.

The visitation schedule is an important area of conflict in

which such parents may manifest their contributions. A mother, for example, will argue vigorously against mid-week visits and even long weekend visits with rationalizations such as: "He needs continuity." "The visits break up her routine." "The schedule disrupts his routine." Although the routine might involve visits to the homes of other friends, visits for music lessons, and a wide variety of other places to which the child travels, visits to the father's home are the only ones that appear to break up the routine.

These mothers are particularly rigid with regard to the schedule. Common manifestations of this are, "If you come up on this porch one minute early, I'll call the police," and, not entirely paradoxically, "If you come here one minute late, you can't have the children." Flexibility is not a word that is to be found in their vocabularies, at least when it applies to the father's visitation schedule. Obviously, makeups for missed visits are not permitted and the father may have to get a court order to obtain such. If there is any difference of opinion regarding the interpretation of the court order, these mothers will invariably argue for the most stringent and exclusionary interpretation. Unfortunately, visitation schedules—even those that are most meticulously and obsessively planned—are generally not perfect and there are certain unforeseen events that may require some flexibility and a willingness for modification. For example, I have seen numerous arguments around the question regarding when Christmas Eve begins. Some hold that it begins at 12:01 a.m. on December 24th, that is, one minute after midnight December 23rd. Others hold that it begins at sunup on December 24th; others that it begins at noon on December 24th; and others that it begins at sundown on December 24th. In two cases, I have seen parents actually go to court to get a definition of this term. Christmas is an especially active time in divorce courts because of the enormous amount of conflict over how the children should spend Christmas. One mother said to me, "I know that the court order says that we should alternate Christmases. I don't know where my head was when I signed that. I'll never let him have these children on Christmas. That's the one day of the year that's too important for me to allow him to have them. I'll go to court if I have to. I'll go to the Supreme Court if I have to. It's only *over my dead body* that he'll have these children on Christmas." We see here a good example of the effects of divorce animosity on the "Christian spirit."

Most parents recognize that as time progresses there may be important and necessary modifications of the visitation schedule. A common example is the schedule for infants. Most would agree that an infant who is breast-feeding is not a candidate for the traditional every-other-weekend visitation schedule. However, most would agree that as the child grows older he (she) does well to expand into that kind of arrangement. Typically, these mothers consider the pace of expansion much too rapid. No matter how slow and turtle-like the father's proposals, the mothers complain, "You're pushing things too fast," and will find a wide variety of excuses to contract the rate of expansion. I have been involved in situations in which I have served as court-appointed therapist for such families (I discuss this in detail in Chapter Five). When dealing with visitation expansion programs, I generally advise trial-and-error approaches to the problem. I inform all that I cannot know in advance exactly how much visitation a particular child can tolerate and what the effects of such expanded visitations will be. I recommend a program in which we try out various visitation programs in which I observe the children myself after each visit in order to ascertain what detrimental effects, if any, have resulted from the visits. One mother, after hearing my proposal, stated, "I won't subject my child to experiments." I was unsuccessful in getting her to appreciate that her child was not a guinea pig in a cage, to be slaughtered for scientific purposes, but rather was involved in an empirical program for determining what would be the optimum time to be spent with her former husband. Because of her intransigence I had to ask the judge to order her to comply with the various programs I was recommending. Another argument given to stall the expansion is, "When he's old enough, he'll be able to decide himself how much time he wants to visit." To such a statement, I invariably ask, "Well, how old do you think he has to be before he himself will be able to decide what his visitation schedule should be." The usual answer is somewhere in the range of 10 to 13. Although this may be a decade away, it is too soon for these mothers.

Visitation obstructionism is a very powerful vengeance maneuver. After all, the father is no longer in the house and the only direct contact with him may be at the times of visitation. And, withholding of the children is a very powerful vengeance maneuver. It is in this area that a cruel mother can wreak vengeance in a most effective way, and the longer the father has to travel in order to be with the children, the more powerful this weapon can be. I have been involved in a number of cases in which fathers have traveled to opposite ends of the continent in order to visit with their children, only to find that they were not there at the appointed time of pickup. In some cases the whereabouts of the mother was entirely unknown and the father had to return home without ever seeing his children. Unfortunately, in most of these cases the courts do little about such cruelty. Of relevance to the parental alienation syndrome is the message given to the children that the loss of a visit with their father is of no consequence and treating him sadistically should be of no concern to anyone.

Another common maneuver that contributes to the parental alienation syndrome is the mother's attitude regarding the father's capacity to take care of a sick child. A father calls to pick up his daughter for a weekend visit. The mother informs him that the child is sick and she cannot go. I am not referring here to a fabrication in which the mother knows quite well that the child is not sick, but is using this professed illness as an excuse for not allowing the child to visit. And I am not referring here to the situation in which the child joins in the collusion. Rather, I am referring here to one of the run-of-the-mill illnesses, which may or may not be associated with low fever and which may not be in any way affected by transportation of the child to the father's home. The general assumption is made that the mother is in a better position to care for this sick child than the father and that if the child were to be transported, some terrible calamity would befall her and that her care would be seriously compromised. Sick children need the support and even indulgence of a parent, regardless of the sex of that parent. When the same child becomes sick at the father's home, it is expected that he bring the child to the mother's home immediately. The idea that the father might be capable of caring for the child is not given serious consideration. Interestingly, that exposure to the outdoors (father's home to mother's home) is not considered to be detrimental. It is only in the opposite direction (mother's home to father's home) that the deleterious influences of outdoor travel are considered to affect the child. Again, the child is given the message that the father is unable to care for a sick child and may even be dangerous.

Sarcasm is another way of getting across the message that the father is an undesirable character. A mother might say, "Isn't that wonderful, he's taking you to a baseball game." Although the words themselves are innocent enough, and might very well apply in a benevolent or noncharged situation, the sarcastic tonal quality says just the opposite. It implies, "After all these years he's finally gotten around to taking you to a baseball game" or "He really considers himself a big sport for parting with the few bucks he's spending to take you to a ball game." Another mother says, in a singsong way, "Well, here he is again, your good ol' Daddy-O." Another says to her daughter, "So, the knight-in-shining-armor is taking his damsel to the movies." These comments are powerful forms of deprecation. If a therapist were to attempt to point out to such a mother how undermining these comments are, she might respond that she was "only kidding" and accuse the therapist of not having a good sense of humor.

A common maneuver used by these mothers is to instruct their children to tell the father that they are not at home when he calls. Or, these mothers will tell their children to give excuses for her not coming to the phone like "She's in the bathroom" or "She's in the shower." These children are not only being taught to be deceitful, but they are being used as accomplices in the war between the parents. Of pertinence here is the message that the father is not an individual who is worthy of being treated with honesty and respect. Furthermore, there is the implication that he has objectionable qualities that warrant his being lied to and rejected. One mother told her children not to reveal the name and location of the day camp they were attending, and the children dutifully submitted to their mother's demand. When questioned in family session as to why she gave her children these instructions, she could only come up with a series of weak rationalizations: "He'll go to the camp and make trouble," "He'll embarrass them when he visits," and "I just get the feeling that it's not good for them for their father to know where they're going to camp." I knew the husband well enough to know that there was absolutely no justification for these concerns. Clearly, this mother was using the children as accomplices in her war and they were submitting.

There are a wide variety of other ways in which a mother may contribute to the children's alienation against their father. She may not forward to him copies of school reports. The implication to the children here is that he is not interested in such material and that any comments he may make about school reports will be of little value to the child. Many go further and obstruct the father's attempt to obtain such material and may even inform the school that they, as the custodial parent, have every right to prevent the school from transmitting such material. She may refuse to allow the father to join with her in teachers' conferences, and this may require the teacher to set up two separate meetings. When asked why she refuses to allow him to join her, the mother will often provide weak answers such as, "He'll disrupt the meeting," "I need all the time for myself," and "I just don't want to be in the same room with that man and that should be enough of an explanation." Such mothers may inform school authorities that they are the primary custodial parent and prohibit completely any communication of information about the child to the father. These situations have reached a point where in many states laws have now been passed that require schools to provide information to both parents, regardless of their marital status.

A common maneuver is not giving the father copies of school photographs. When I have asked such mothers what possible harm could be done by the father's having school photographs of the children I am generally given such cop-out answers as, "What happens in her school is none of his business," "If you think that

I'm going to spend a penny on buying pictures for him you're crazy," and "If he wants school pictures, let him go there himself and take them." These exclusionary maneuvers may extend throughout the whole course of the child's education. When applying to college, one mother refused to tell the father which colleges the child was applying to (even though he was going to be required to pay for the school selected). When I asked the mother why she had not provided the father with this information, she replied, "I don't want to invade her privacy."

Of course, such mothers will have problems with school plays, concerts, and other presentations that are only given once. They may place the children in a very difficult position by stating that if the father attends she will not. Again, the implication is that even if the father is in the same auditorium with her, unpleasant and even terrible things are going to happen. And this position may be taken with regard to confirmations, Bar Mitzvahs, graduations, and family events to which both parents may be invited. These refusals also transmit the message that the father is somehow a noxious individual whose presence at any of these affairs is likely to ruin them. My experience has been that mothers who obstruct their husband's attendance at such school events are the ones who are more likely to engage in public demonstrations than their hated husbands. This is a good example of how the mechanism of projection operates for these mothers.

One exclusionary maneuver that I have seen on a few occasions relates to the child's name. Let us say, for example, that a child's name is Susan Smith and that the mother's maiden name was Anna Jones. Soon after the separation the child will suddenly acquire the name Susan Jones-Smith. This is a common practice in our society today, especially espoused by women who object to the tradition by which children automatically assume the surname of their fathers. However, this hyphenated name only serves as a transition and soon thereafter the child becomes known only as Susan Jones. The parents then start fighting over what name the child shall use and the school may even be brought into the conflict. When at the father's house the child will refer to herself as Susan Smith and at the mother's house, Susan Jones. A court order may become necessary in order to settle the problem. Of significance here is the message to the child that the father is so odious that the traditional bearing of his name is somehow undesirable, especially because it is viewed by the mother as an ongoing remnant of his existence.

The same mechanisms may operate in families in which the parents are of different religions. Although during the marriage the parents may have agreed to bring the child up in the father's religion, following the separation the mother suddenly becomes stringently committed to her earlier religion—even to the point of fanaticism. Once again, the child becomes used as a rope in this tug-of-war. In the mother's home the child espouses one religious belief and in the father's home another. It may take a court ruling to bring about a peace treaty in this religious war. And once again, the child is given the message that the earlier religion, which was that of the father, has now become undesirable as part of the larger programming against the father.

A common way in which a parent will contribute to the alienation is to label as "harassment" the attempts by the hated parent to make contact with the children. The alienated parent expresses interest by telephone calls, attempts at visitation, the sending of presents, etc. These are termed "harassment" by the mother, and the children themselves come to view such overtures in the same vein. In frustration the father increases efforts to communicate, thereby increasing the likelihood that his attempts will be viewed as nuisances. A vicious cycle ensues in which the denigrated father increases his efforts, thereby increasing the likelihood that the approaches will be viewed as harassments. When such fathers call, the mother may respond with a quick statement that seemingly justifies hanging up on him immediately, without giving him any chance to respond or communicate with the children. Some of the more common putoffs utilized are, "They're busy," "They're just ready to eat," "They're eating," "They're not done eating yet," "They're watching TV," "They're doing their homework and can't be disturbed," "They're playing with friends," and "They're getting ready to go to sleep." The father never seems to call at the right time. No matter what the children are doing, their activity serves as an excuse not to interrupt them. Every activity, no matter how mundane or inconsequential, takes priority over speaking with the father.

One mother who used this maneuver said, "Since the separation I've had to go back and live with my mother. She agrees with me that my ex-husband is despicable and she hangs up on him every time he calls. I can't control her." This too is a weak rationalization for the mother's support of the exclusionary maneuvers of the maternal grandmother. Related to this view of the calls as harassments, a mother may say to a calling father (with the child within earshot), "If you keep up this pressure to see him we're going to have one of those teen-age suicides on our hands." If this is said enough times the child then learns that this is a good way to avoid seeing his father. The next step then is for the child to threaten suicide if the father attempts to visit, to which the mother can then say to the father, "He keeps saying that he'll kill himself if he has to visit with you. Look what you've driven him to." The child's professions of suicidal intent, of course, are stated in the desire to comply with the mother's wishes that he make such professions and thereby fulfill her prophecy.

I have encountered a series of mothers who will bring their children to treatment for psychotherapy without the father's knowledge. They strictly prohibit the therapist from communicating with the father, and the treatment may go on for months and even years without his knowledge. Unfortunately, my experience has been that there are many therapists who go along with this program and thereby unwittingly contribute to the perpetuation of their patients' parental alienation syndrome. Confidentiality is used here in the service of perpetuating psychopathology. Astute and ethical therapists will have no part of this scheme. The result of such therapy is that it contributes to further alienation of the father.

There are parents who will lure their children into alienation one at a time, starting with the oldest and then moving down the line. In the process the oldest becomes the cohort of the mother in

Ricky followed Davis's to not want to Mom July 4 97

Lead in wanting

I have to love this

with not to, to

Filer oppose

subject.

S., fact.

influencing the one who is next in line. Operating under the principle that younger children are often the parrots of their older siblings, the scheme might very well work. Also, having an older sibling as one's cohort allows for "inside job" operations in the father's home during visitation. If the parent is successful in obtaining primary custody of the oldest (as a result of the child's professions of animosity that are part of the parental alienation syndrome), then it becomes more likely that the younger ones will follow because they want to live with the older sibling(s). This is also a technique that I have observed to be utilized by fathers who program children against their mothers.

Subtle and Often Unconscious Parental Programming

The aforementioned attempts to denigrate a parent are primarily conscious and deliberate. The brainwashing parent is well aware of what he (she) is doing. There are, however, other ways of programming children that can be equally if not more effective, but which do not involve the parent's actually recognizing what is going on. In this way the parent can profess innocence of brainwashing propensities. The motivations and mechanisms here are either unconscious (completely unavailable to conscious awareness) or subconscious (not easily available to conscious awareness). As mentioned, one should view these processes as a continuum with fully conscious operations at the one end and deeply unconscious maneuvers on the other, with most falling at some point between the two ends of the continuum. Also, one must recognize that as time passes, there is likely to be a gradual shift from the conscious to the unconscious end of the continuum.

There are many ways in which a parent may subtly and often unconsciously contribute to the alienation. A parent may profess to be a strong subscriber to the common advice, "Never criticize the other parent to the child." A mother may implement this advice with comments to the child such as, "There are things I could say about your father that would make your hair stand on end, but I'm not the kind of a person who criticizes a parent to his children." Such a comment engenders far more fear, distrust, and even hatred than would the presentation of an actual list of the father's alleged defects. A mother insists that the father park his car at a specific distance from the home and honk the horn, rather than ring the doorbell. She is implicitly saying to the child, "The person in that car is a dangerous and/or undesirable individual, someone whom I would not want to ring the doorbell of my house, let alone enter— even to say hello."

The parent who expresses neutrality regarding visitation ("I respect her decision regarding whether or not she wishes to visit with her father") is essentially communicating criticism of the father. The healthy parent appreciates how vital the children's ongoing involvement is with the noncustodial parent and encourages visitation, even when the child is "not in the mood." The healthy parent does not accept inconsequential and frivolous reasons for not visiting. Under the guise of neutrality, such a parent can engender and foster alienation. The "neutrality" essentially communicates to the child the message that the noncustodial parent cannot provide enough affection, attention, and other desirable input to make a missed visitation a loss of any consequence. Such a parent fails to appreciate that neutrality is as much a position in a conflict as overt support of either side.

Related to the neutrality maneuver is the parent who repeatedly insists that the child be the one to make the decision regarding visitation. Such a parent hammers away at the child with this principle. The child generally knows that the parent basically does not want the visitation, and so the child then professes the strong opinion that he (she) does not wish to visit. Such a mother might say, after the child refuses, "I respect your strength in standing up for your rights." I once saw a mother in this category who went further and said, "If you don't want to visit with him, you can count on my full support. If we have to go to court to defend you we'll do it. I'm not going to let him push you around. You have your *right* to say no, and you can count on me to defend you." In extreme cases I have seen mothers who will actually hire an attorney to "protect" the child from this so-called coercing father who is insisting on visitation. Such mothers will give their children the impression that they would go to the Supreme Court if necessary in order to support them in "their" decision not to visit. And the more vociferous and determined the mothers become, the more adamant the children become in their refusal—refusal based not on the genuine desire not to see the father, but refusal based on the fear of not complying with their mothers' wish that they not visit. The mother and children then build together a stone wall of resistance against the father's overtures for involvement with the children. These same mothers would not "respect" the child's refusal to go to school, keep a doctor's appointment, or assume other important obligations. There is only one category of refusal that is respected, and that is refusal to have anything to do with the father.

In one case, a separated father calls, the mother answers, exchanges a few amenities, and then, in a calm and relaxed manner, calls the child to the phone. Another mother answers and curtly says to the child, "It's your *father*" and stiffly gives the phone to the child—conveying the message that the caller is not a former husband, but a person who is so objectionable that the mother would not want in any way to be associated with him. The implication is that the caller is a possession of the child and is in no way related to her.

One mother encourages her child to visit with the father by saying, "You have to go see your father. If you don't he'll take us to court." Nothing is mentioned about the positive benefits to be derived by the child from seeing the father. The only reason to go is for them to protect *themselves* (". . .he'll take us to court") from the father's lawsuit. One mother, who had agreed to involve herself in court-appointed therapy in order to bring about a rapprochement between her two daughters and their father, told me early in the first session that her main purpose was to bring about such reconciliation. However, about ten minutes later she told me that she felt it was her obligation, as a good mother, to help support her daughters' decision not to see their father. In this case, there was absolutely no good reason for their not seeing their father, except that they were complying with their mother's subconscious wishes that they not do so.

While the child is visiting with the father, there are mothers who will use the telephone in the service of their manipulative and exclusionary maneuvers. They may spend significant periods on the telephone making detailed inquiry about everything the child has done, is doing, and will be doing. No detail is too small to focus on. The time devoted to these calls in itself serves to erode the child's time with the father. In the course of such telephone calls, the mother might say (in a somewhat ominous tone), "Is everything okay?" "Is everything all right?" or "I hope you're okay." The implication here is that dangers abound and the child is living ever on the brink of some catastrophic events taking place in the father's home. Such a maneuver is especially likely to be utilized by overprotective mothers whom I will discuss subsequently. The inquiry into every detail ostensibly serves to protect the child from these catastrophes and to become alerted to them in advance. Of course, more overt programming can take place during the course of these lengthy conversations, especially if the child is advised to make the calls when the father is sleeping or involved in other activities. Such children, when they arrive home, may be greeted with, "Are you all right?" or "Thank God you're here!" Here, the child is being given the message, "Thank God you have survived all these terrible dangers and you've been returned intact."

There are mothers who use the "guilt trip" approach to programming their children against their husbands. For example, when the child wants to visit with the father during the scheduled visitation period, the mother might say, "How can you leave your poor old mother?" Not only is the child made to feel guilty about abandoning the mother, but in the ensuing discussion the father is also portrayed as an individual with little or no sensitivity to the mother's feelings. He has not only abandoned this poor helpless mother, but is now luring the children away, thereby increasing her loneliness. He comes to be viewed by the children as insensitive and cruel. The children then, by exaggerating any of the father's weaknesses or deficiencies, can justify their not visiting with him and thereby lessen the guilt they feel over the abandonment of their mother.

Another subtle maneuver commonly utilized by brainwashing parents relates to the psychological mechanism of doing and undoing. An example of this would be an individual who makes a racial slur, recognizes that the other person has been offended, and then retracts the statement by saying, "Oh, I didn't really mean it" or "I was only fooling." In the vast majority of cases the person so criticized does not "get the joke," the smiles and acceptance of the apology notwithstanding. Doing and undoing is not the same as never having done anything at all. A mother might angrily say, "*What* do you *mean* you're going to your father's house?" This may then be followed immediately with the statement, "Oh, what am I saying? That's wrong. I shouldn't have said that. I shouldn't discourage you from seeing your father. Forget I said that. Of course, it's okay for you to go to your father's house." The initial statement and the retraction, all taken together, are not the same as undiluted and unambivalent encouragement. The child gets the message that a strong part of the mother does not want the visitation.

Some mothers may make such derogatory comments and then, when confronted with them later, claim that they were said at a time of extreme duress and that they were really not meant. One mother threatened her husband, as he left the home, "If you leave this marriage I vow to God that you'll never see your children again." She said this to her husband in front of their four children. In subsequent custody litigation she first denied to me that she had ever made the statement. When, however, in family session her husband and four children "refreshed her memory," she reluctantly admitted that she had made the statement. She then gave as her excuse that she was quite upset when her husband was leaving and she was thereby not responsible for her comment. She explained at length how, when people are upset, they will say all kinds of things that they don't really mean. Again, doing and undoing is not the same as never having done at all—and the children, at some level, recognize this.

There are other maneuvers that may be seen. One mother insisted that her daughter wear a bathing suit when the father would bathe her in order to protect her from being sexually abused. The thought that the father had to put on the bathing suit and take off the bathing suit did not deter her from pressuring him to submit to this demand. The message given to the child, of course, is that the father will potentially abuse her and that she needs to protect herself from sexual exploitation.

Some mothers have justified recalcitrance with regard to visitation with this rationalization: "He only wants the children to satisfy his own needs. He's not thinking about the child's needs." The father's insistence that he wants to see his child is viewed only as a pathological maneuver in which he is selfishly gratifying his own morbid desires; the notion that his insistence upon seeing the child may relate to his love and affection and his desire to gratify the child's needs (as well as his own *healthy* needs) is not given consideration.

And just about any excuse known to humanity may be utilized to justify obstructing the visitation program: "He lives in a bad neighborhood and I don't trust him to watch her properly," "There are very few trees where he lives and I know that she *loves* trees. She can't possibly be happy there." "He just doesn't have enough toys and things for her in his house. She's always complaining about how few toys he has."

There are some mothers who will remove every object in the home that is in any way reminiscent of the father, directly or indirectly. They want to create an atmosphere similar to the one that would prevail if he had never existed. In line with this they never speak of the father either. It is as if he has evaporated from the face of the earth. The children recognize that any mention of their father will be met with the mother's animosity and rejection. In order to protect themselves from this fate, they strictly avoid mentioning their father. Not only is this one part of the campaign of exclusion, but it also has the effect of communicating to the children that the father is an extremely evil person, even too terrible to talk about. This only increases the children's view of their father as noxious and dangerous. The situation is similar to the home in which sex is never spoken about. The effect of this is to produce sexual inhibitions. If a child has a choice between a parent who provides daily lectures on the evils and sins of sex and one who never speaks about sex at all, the former will produce less guilt and inhibition than the latter. In the former case, the subject is at least spoken about; in the latter, it is too terrible to mention.

The mother who moves to a distant city or state is essentially communicating to the children that distance from the father is not a consequential consideration. It is sometimes done with the implication that they are moving to bring about a cessation of the harassment and other indignities that they suffer while living close to the father. I am not referring here to situations in which such a move might be to the mother's benefit with regard to job opportunities or remarriage. Rather, I am referring to situations in which there is absolutely no good reason for the move, other than to put distance between the children and their father. Sometimes parents will even litigate in order to gain permission to leave the state. However, the ostensible reasons are often unconvincing; the basic reason is to bring about a cessation of the parent-child relationship.

Concluding Comments

As mentioned at the beginning of this section on the mother's programming, the wide variety of possible maneuvers resulted in a situation where I found it practically impossible to subdivide them into meaningful categories. Such inability is, in part, a testament to the versatility and creativity of the parents who have devised these maneuvers, many of which are indeed ingenious, their nefarious object notwithstanding. As I am sure the reader can appreciate, I have had a wealth of experience with such programming parents. Furthermore, the list of maneuvers continues to grow. As I write this, I have the feeling that next week there will be others that I would have liked to add because they provide yet further testament to the creativity of the human mind. I am reminded here of the ancient observation that scientific progress generally takes place more rapidly in wartime, because the new exigencies stimulate creativity and productivity. And the analogy to war goes further in that in both cases the products being created serve more destructive than constructive purposes.

THE PROGRAMMING FATHER

As mentioned, mothers, far more often than fathers, are the active contributors in a child's parental alienation syndrome. However, my experience has been that in about 10 percent of cases it is the father who is the primary programmer of the child. This had been my experience prior to the publication of my first article on the parental alienation syndrome (1985a) and this is still my experience at the time I write this (in late 1991). Less important than the consistency of the observation and any embarrassment I may have suffered by being wrong is the fact that this consistency lends weight to my theory regarding the etiology of the parental alienation syndrome, especially that aspect of the theory that lends understanding to this gender disparity. Here I focus on some experiences I have had with fathers who were the active contributors to their children's parental alienation syndrome.

I will discuss in detail in subsequent chapters my theory regarding the role of the child's psychological bond with a parent in the etiology of the parental alienation syndrome. I will elaborate then on the crucial importance of the parent-child psychological bond in the development of the parental alienation syndrome. In some cases in which the father is the preferred parent, he has been the primary custodial parent during the earliest years of the child's life and so has been the primary parent with whom the child has bonded. In such cases it is not surprising that the child creates scenarios that support his position in the child custody dispute. There are situations, however, in which the mother was indeed the primary custodial parent during the child's infancy; yet the father becomes the preferred parent in the child custodial dispute, the one with whom the child sides when a parental alienation syndrome develops. My experience has been that when this takes place the father has embarked on a long program—often over many months and even years—that is designed to lure the child away from the mother and has the effect of attenuating the previously strong psychological bond. In the child custody tug-of-war, the parent who was the primary caretaker in infancy is more likely to have developed a stronger psychological bond with the child and is more likely to draw the child over onto his (her) side. Yet, this does not necessarily mean that it will be a lost cause for the other parent. With time, energy, persistence, and cunning, that parent may ultimately prevail, but it is going to take a much longer time. Both parents must rely on children's malleability, suggestibility, and their desire to comply with adult authority. These factors, which may operate easily for the primarily bonded parent, can also operate, although with much greater difficulty and with much more programming, for the parent who starts with the weaker parent-child bond.

One father, the owner of a large trucking company, dealt effectively with tough and often brutal truckers, union chiefs, and even underworld Mafia figures. He considered carrying a gun to be crucial for his survival as well as that of his company. A gun was viewed as standard professional equipment, like a doctor's stethoscope. He described numerous encounters with violent gangland figures. His fearlessness in these situations was remarkable. Yet, this same man claimed total impotence with regard to convincing his somewhat underweight and scrawny ten-year-old daughter to visit his former wife. His professions of helplessness were often quite convincing to his friends and relatives, and even when I pointed out to him the disparity between his ability to impose his opinion on people at work as compared to his home, he still claimed that he had absolutely no power over his child: "Doctor, I can't do a thing with her!" Although this child's mother had been the primary caretaker during infancy, she was a woman who had poorly developed parenting skills, was often scatter-brained, and was therefore seriously compromised in caring for her children. The children found her unreliable and at times untruthful. The father was viewed as the far more stable person, even though he had spent less time in the home. We had here, then, a situation in which there was a weak bond with the mother and a much stronger one with the father. However, he too was not above utilizing maneuvers such as the aforementioned in the service of winning the day in his custody dispute.

I recall another case in which a father had been successful in overriding the stronger bond the child had with the mother. The mother had been the primary caretaker but the father, over a period of two years, was finally successful in luring his son over to his side. In this case, as is my usual practice, I made every attempt to serve the court as an impartial examiner but was unsuccessful in achieving this goal. The father's attorney fought vigorously against my appointment, recognizing, I believe, the weakness in the father's position. And the judge refused to order the father's involvement above his refusals. Furthermore, the judge even refused to order my seeing the child, so convincing were both the father and the child that it would be psychologically detrimental to the child for me to interview him. Accordingly, after seeing the mother and reviewing significant materials, I was convinced that the mother warranted my support in her custody dispute. Accordingly, I agreed to go to court and testify on her behalf. It is my practice in such situations to state clearly — both in my written report and in my testimony — that I only agree to serve as an advocate after I have exhausted all possibilities to serve as an impartial examiner *and* only when I am convinced — beyond a reasonable doubt — that my advocacy is warranted and ethical.

When I entered the court waiting room, I was greeted by the mother and her attorney, and I sat down next to them. The mother pointed out to me the father and child, who were sitting at the opposite end of the waiting room. We could only see their backs, and the father had his arm around the child, as if protecting him from the mother. He would periodically and furtively glance backward, as if to assure himself that she was not stepping forth. And they maintained this position consistently — as if the danger were omnipresent. After about a half hour, during which time the mother, her attorney, and I discussed other matters relative to the litigation, I asked the mother if she would introduce me to her son. She readily agreed to do so. Accordingly, we walked up to the boy. When the father saw us approaching him from the side, he immediately clutched the boy as if to protect him from some dangerous act that might be perpetrated at that point. He said to the boy, "Don't worry. I'll protect you. You have nothing to worry about." I extended my hand to say hello to the boy and he absolutely refused to shake it. The father said to the both of us, "If you don't get away from here, I'm going to call the guard." This last comment, as well, communicated to the child that there were imminent dangers if we were to remain close to him any longer. Accordingly, we went back to our seats. I would not have been surprised if the father, on observing us to be approaching, had fled with the boy in terror or hid with him under the bench, as if we were ready to machine gun him down.

When I testified in court, I described in detail the aforementioned experience. It added significant weight to my earlier conclusions that this father was programming this child against the mother and that he was contributing thereby to the child's parental alienation syndrome. I subsequently learned that the judge ordered that the child be returned to the mother, and things went well.

Another father embarked upon a program of denigration of the mother in an attempt to lure his children away from her. As part of this package he concocted a sex-abuse allegation in which he claimed that the mother's live-in man friend had performed anal sex on his four-year-old son, the youngest of his four children. (There were three older sisters.) As a result of the allegation he was granted temporary custody of the four-year-old pending a trial. One Sunday while the three older girls were visiting, they all went to church. In the course of the services the father walked up to the alter and publicly requested that the congregation pray to Christ for the soul of his four-year-old son, who had been sexually molested by his former wife's live-in friend. He was successful in obtaining the active support of the church community, and this played no small role in the other three girls becoming convinced of the validity of the accusation. This man was operating on the aforementioned principle of starting with one and then gradually luring the others over seriatim.

Another father against whom I testified had also been successful in overriding the earlier bonding with the mother. His primary tack was one of wide-eyed innocence regarding the accusations that he was programming his two girls against their mother. He elaborated his program over a four-year period. When I asked him why he was not allowing the children to call their mother during visitation, he denied that he was preventing them but said, "I don't understand why they need to talk with her when they're with me. We have so little time together when they're with me. They don't have much of a chance to talk with her, the week is so filled with activities. I don't understand why it's necessary." He professed no understanding of the importance of the bonding between the children and their mother and was puzzled by her preoccupation with communicating with the girls during visits. He himself had had significant difficulties in his relationship with his own mother, and this probably played a role in his blind spot for the importance of this bond. This father utilized primarily seductive maneuvers, kept referring to the girls as his "little girl friends," and was ever cuddling and hugging them. He bribed them with presents and convinced them that their mother's family were despicable human beings, pointing as justification to their anger over what they saw to be the progressive erosion of the children from their mother.

As is true for mothers, the borrowed scenario phenomenon can also be seen in situations in which the father is programming the children. In one case, one of the children's primary criticisms of the mother was that "she never worked a day in her life." The father did not consider the enormous labors of raising three children to be "work," and the children reflexively agreed with him on this point. They had, of course, the support of society in which this delusion is commonly promulgated (often in subtle ways). The mother had interrupted her education in order to marry, and the father flaunted his superior educational background. This resulted in the children often referring to her as "stupid," again an epithet derived from the father's programming. In actuality, it was the father who was the stupid one here (his superior education notwithstanding) because he did not appreciate the importance of the mother-child bond in the development of his children. One five-year-old child, when asked why he no longer wanted to see his mother, answered, "She feeds us junk food and junk food is no good for us." Obviously, five-year-old children are not famous for stringently restricting themselves from eating "junk food." Obviously, he learned this from someone, and in this case someone was his father. Another child claimed that he did not want to visit with his mother because "she just doesn't feed us." This was obviously not the case, and at some level I believe the child knew it but was mouthing one of the absurd complaints made by the father against his despised wife.

I have seen a few cases in which the father's campaign to lure the children away from the mother incorporated macho techniques, which are especially attractive to boys. And I am not referring here simply to sports, but even more macho activities. One such father involved the boys in an extremely strenuous exercise program, which included jogging, calisthenics, and the martial arts. He hired a private instructor who came daily. Whenever possible, the father joined the children (three boys and one girl) in this program. All five wore the same uniforms and, when jogging, gave the appearance of a very tight-knit and well-disciplined family in which the "team spirit" prevailed. The private instructor not only imbued the children with military discipline, including martial arts, but lectured them on the importance of the development of honesty, respect of one's parents, reliability, and other noble principles. They were required to keep a daily diary in which they recorded all the events of the day. Both the father and the instructor reviewed the diary each evening and graded the children, especially with regard to their adherence to their exercise program, homework assignments, and subscription to the aforementioned ideals. The diary was graded on a scale of 0 - 100 and when a score below 90 was obtained, punishments and restrictions were imposed. Interestingly, in the course of marking these diaries, both the military instructor and the father marked points off for transgressions against the father, but absolutely none for transgressions against the mother. Even the most vile profanities were not considered justification for deficiency marks.

Another father embarked on a program in which there was a military theme, particularly World War II. They sang old war songs, bought World War II khakis, boots, and other insignia. They did calisthenics and even military exercises. The father practiced secret code words with the children that were used in the service of hurting the mother. For example, he told the boys that he would like them to assault their mother during visitation. Predictably, the mother would call the father to get him to prevail upon the boys to stop their sadistic treatment of her. The father told the boys that when such calls were made (which they predictably were), they were to ignore his overt pleas to cease and desist no matter how convincingly they were professed. However, they were instructed to listen carefully to certain "secret code words" like "do me a favor" and "do it for my sake." *Only* when these phrases were used were they to stop their assaults. In both of these cases many exclusionary maneuvers were being utilized together, all for the purpose of establishing a separate, coherent unit as a replacement for the original family. Boys are much more likely to gravitate toward such programs than girls. And when girls are brought in (as they may very well be), they are encouraged to abrogate traditional feminine activities.

Fortunately, in both of these cases the mothers had been the primary caretakers during the earliest years of the children's lives, and I considered them to be the preferable parents. But the fathers had indeed been successful in alienating the children. In both of these cases, as well, the fathers had devoted themselves assiduously and consciously to the goal of alienation. For different reasons, I did not have the opportunity in either of these cases to go to court and provide my recommendations, which would have included return of the children to the mothers. I am convinced that in each of these cases such disposition would have been accomplished without significant difficulty for the children because the bonding with the mother was still formidable and the fathers' efforts had not been completely successful in attenuating the earlier bonding to the point where it was inconsequential. As I will discuss subsequently, such bonding can only withstand a certain amount of attenuation, after which the programming parent may be completely successful in destroying it permanently. On the basis of my experiences up to this writing, I believe that the mother-child bond in such children is capable of withstanding much longer attenuation than the father-child bond and that such children, when programmed by their fathers, are less likely to become permanently estranged. Furthermore, again on the basis of my experiences to date, I believe that fathers who program under such circumstances have a much harder uphill fight and that the macho-sport-militaristic-group program must be utilized over a significant period if it is to work.

One father, who was successful in luring the children away from their mother and inducing in them a parental alienation syndrome, was quite creative in the maneuvers he utilized to alienate the children from their mother. He had been successful in convincing the court that the mother was indeed the neglectful wretch that he viewed her to be, and he was awarded primary custody of the children. This court "victory" notwithstanding, the children still craved to see the mother. Accordingly, in order to maintain his advantage, he would periodically set up situations designed to convince the children that their mother was indeed a despicable individual. It was as if they needed "booster shots" to maintain their "immunity" to their mother. On one occasion, during an altercation with his six-year-old son, the boy insisted that he wanted to go back and live with his mother. Much to the boy's surprise, the father agreed and packed his luggage. He then went to the telephone and ostensibly dialed the mother's telephone number. The boy did not appreciate that the father had punched only six of the seven numbers and so was not really talking to anyone during this feigned conversation. What the boy heard was the father telling the mother that the youngster wished to return to live with her and the father's agreement to effect the transfer immediately. The bags were packed and the mother,

from what the boy could appreciate from this feigned conversation, would be at her door waiting to receive the child. The father
knew that the mother was working at that time and would not be
home for at least three hours. He dropped the boy off at the house
and drove away as the youngster walked up the path to the door
of the mother's house. The boy became panic stricken when he
found that his mother was not home, and he went to the home of
neighbors (which the father knew he would do). When the
mother came home three hours later, the boy was still in a state of
agitated rage and repeatedly called her a "liar." As the father had
predicted, the boy asked once again to return to the home of his
father. The mother had no choice but to allow the return because
the court had designated the father the primary custodial parent
and this event did not take place during a scheduled visitation
time.

One alienating father, who had convinced the court that he
was indeed the better parent (which he was not), strictly withheld
from the mother school information, both curricular and extracurricular. When she attempted to obtain this information from
her children, she was told, "We're too old to have our mothers
come to school" and "You should feel embarrassed coming to
school for children our age." The children were seven and nine
and were clearly mouthing the father's words. One such father
repeatedly told the children that they were staying exclusively in
his home and were not going to be able to visit their mother's
home because she had "sold" them to him. As proof of this
transaction, he showed them the weekly alimony checks he
claimed were part of the agreed-upon payoff. He equated them to
the property that he was indeed buying off in installments as part
of the divorce settlement. Not surprisingly, when the mother
would try to gain contact with the children, she was angrily told,
"You're no longer our mother. You sold us to our father." We see
here yet another example of how cruel and deceptive a parent can
be to children in the service of alienating them from the other
parent.

One father, whose wife was of a different religious denom-
ination (but still worshiping under the general rubric of Christi-

anity) repeatedly told his children, "Your mother's not a Christian" and "Your mother's not a *real* Christian." A mother who brought her husband to court because of nonpayment of support and alimony obligations ultimately lost primary custody because of her husband's success in convincing the court that she was indeed a deficient mother. The children exhibited typical manifestations of a parental alienation syndrome. When the mother asked them why they would not visit with her, their most common reply was, "You sued our father."

THE CHILD'S UNDERLYING
PSYCHODYNAMICS

I focus here on the factors that initially involved no active contribution on the part of the loved parent, conscious or unconscious, blatant or subtle. These are factors that originate within the child. Of course, a parent may use the child's contribution to promote the alienation, but it originates from psychopathological factors within the child.

Maintenance of the Primary
Psychological Bond

The most important contributing factor relates to the fact that the child's basic psychological bond with the loved parent is stronger than with the hated parent. Actually, the child is psychologically bonded to both parents, but there is generally a stronger bonding with the parent who was the primary caretaker in the earliest years of the child's life. It is this primary psychological bond that the child wishes to preserve. The campaign, then, is an attempt to maintain that tie, the disruption of which is threatened by the litigation. The aforementioned maneuvers utilized by mothers (the more common "loved" parent) are also an attempt to maintain the integrity of this bond. (This point will be discussed in greater detail subsequently.)

It is important also for the reader to appreciate that the weapons children use to support the mother's position are often naive and simplistic. Children lack the adult sophistication to provide themselves with credible and meaningful ammunition. Accordingly, to the outside observer the reasons given for the alienation will often seem frivolous. Unfortunately, the mother who welcomes the expression of such resentments and complaints will be gullible and accept with relish the most preposterous complaints. Also, unfortunately, attorneys and even judges are sometimes taken in by these children and do not frequently ask themselves the question, "Is this a justifiable reason for the child's *never* wanting to see the father again?" The inconsequential nature of the complaints and their absurdity are the hallmarks of the child's contribution to the development of the parental alienation syndrome.

Fear of Disruption of the Primary Psychological Bond

Related to the aforementioned desire of the child to maintain the psychological bond with the preferred parent (usually the mother) is the *fear* of disruption of that bond. And there is also the fear of alienating the preferred parent. The hated parent is only ostensibly hated; there is still much love. But the loved parent is sometimes feared much more than loved. And it is this factor, sometimes more than any other, that contributes to the various symptoms discussed in this section. Generally, the fear is that of losing the love of the preferred parent. In the usual situation it is the father who has left the home. He has thereby created for himself the reputation of being the rejecter and abandoner. No matter how justified his leaving the home, the children will generally view him as an abandoner. Most often the children subscribe to the dictum, "If you (father) really loved us you would tolerate the indignities and pains you suffer in your relationship with our mother." Having already been abandoned by one parent, the children are not going to risk abandonment by the second. Accordingly, they fear expressing resentment to the remaining parent (usually the mother) and will often automatically take her position in any conflict with the father. This fear of the loss of mother's love may be the most important factor in the development of the symptoms that I describe in this chapter. The parental alienation syndrome, however, provides a vehicle for expression of the anger felt toward the father because of his abandonment. This expression of resentment is supported by the mother, both overtly and covertly. It is part of the maneuver by which the children become willing weapons in the mother's hands, weapons that enable her to gratify her hostility through them.

Reaction Formation

A common factor that contributes to the obsessive hatred of the father is the utilization of the reaction formation mechanism. Obsessive hatred is often a thin disguise for deep love. This is especially the case when there is absolutely no reason to justify the preoccupation with the hated person's defects. True rejection is neutrality, when there is little if any thought of the person. The opposite of love is not hate, but indifference. Each time these children think about how much they hate their fathers, they are still thinking about them. Although the visual imagery may involve hostile fantasies, their fathers are still very much on their minds. The love, however, is expressed as hate in order to assuage the guilt they would feel over overt expression of affection for their fathers, especially in their mothers' presence. This guilt is often coupled with the aforementioned fear of their mothers' rejection if such expressions of affection for their fathers were to be overtly expressed. One boy, when alone with me, stated, "I'm bad for wanting to visit with my father." This was a clear statement of guilt over his wish to visit with his father, his professions of hatred notwithstanding. This child was not born with the idea that it is bad to want to spend time with his father. Rather, he was programmed by his mother to feel guilty about such thoughts and feelings.

Identification with the Aggressor

The identification with the aggressor phenomenon may be operative. This phenomenon manifests itself when a person who is in a weak or impotent position in relation to a more overpowering, threatening individual may deal with the situation by taking on the characteristics of the stronger person. In this way the individual compensates for the feelings of insecurity and the sense of impotency attendant to being weak and vulnerable. The child whose raging mother is incessantly denigrating his father may join forces with her in an attempt to protect himself from being the target of her enormous hostility. He does this from the fear that if he were to join in with his father, he too would be the target of such violent outbursts. The mechanism is operative in the old principle, "If you can't fight 'em, join 'em." Also operative here is the "There-but-for-the-grace-of-God-go-I" mechanism. By joining the mother, the child can say to himself (herself), "If I did not do so I might be in father's position." Also operative here is the mechanism of jumping on the bandwagon of the stronger party in order to share in the joys of victory. A paranoid mother may be so successful in programming her child against the father that the child will take on her paranoid delusions. In such cases the child may exhibit morbid fear at the prospect of the father's coming to the home — lest the terrible consequences predicted by the mother be realized. Such children may even hide in closets and under beds when the father comes to the home, and visitation under such circumstances may be extremely difficult if not impossible. In this case the bonding with the mother is unhealthy, a situation that should lead the examiner to strongly consider recommending that primary custody be transferred to the father. I will have more to say about this in Chapters Six and Seven.

Identification with an Idealized Person

Related to the identification-with-the-aggressor phenomenon is the process of identification with an idealized person. In the course of the mother's deprecation, the father becomes viewed as loathsome, worthless, and an individual with few if any admirable qualities. Identification with and emulation of such

E's live I person
strong me
no bad person

a person becomes compromised. Deprived of an admirable father for identification, the child may then switch to the mother as the only person to emulate. At the same time that she denigrates the father, she is likely to whitewash herself. The identification, then, is with a perfect individual and this is viewed as a way of attaining the state of perfection oneself. The psychological fusion that takes place here contributes to the development of the folie-à-deux relationship so commonly seen in the parental alien-ation syndrome. This contributes to the child's exaggerated reactions to any criticisms the father may have about the mother. Such a child operates on the principle, "I'm like her. When he criticizes her, it's the same as criticizing me."

Release of Hostility

The development of a parental alienation syndrome can serve as a vehicle for the release of anger, which may have a variety of sources. It is as if it allows for the "sucking in" of a wide variety of anger-evoking experiences and allows for a sanctioned release of them, at least by the mother. If not for the presence of the parental alienation syndrome, such anger might have been suppressed, repressed, or channeled into other modes of release, both healthy and pathological. Mention has already been made of the anger engendered by the father's leaving the home, an act that is viewed as an abandonment. There may be anger at the father for the financial compromises that are most often attendant to divorce—especially a litigated divorce. When parents are swept up in their divorce and custody dispute hostilities, they pay less attention to their children, and this produces frustration and anger in them. Not only are the children deprived of attention, but even when they are focused on, the parents have little leftover emotion for their children, so drained have they been by the divorce hostilities. There may be anger over the presence of new partners in their parents' lives. These strangers were rarely invited and, in most circumstances, are viewed as unwelcome intruders. However, the children have no power over their presence and are most often resentful of them. There may be anger over the thwarting of reconciliation preoccupations that, as time goes on, become ever more futile—especially if new persons appear on the scene. Elsewhere (Gardner, 1976, 1977, 1986a, 1991b, 1991c), I have discussed in detail these and other sources of anger for children of divorce, especially those involved in custody disputes.

Infectiousness of Emotions

Then there is what I refer to as the vibrating-tuning-fork principle. This relates to the infectiousness of emotions. Emotions have a way of transmitting themselves from one individual to another, often in very rapid fashion. Walk into a room in which people are grieving for the death of a loved one. The visitor may not even know the deceased but, in a few minutes, may find himself (herself) crying or at least depressed. Comedians know well that they are far less likely to be successful with small audiences than large audiences. The large audience provides them the opportunity for spreading the laughter to those who might not have initially been swept up. The same phenomenon is operative in mass hysteria (1991a). All of these examples operate like vibrating tuning forks: Take two tuning forks of the same fixed intrinsic frequency of vibration. Strike one and hold the second (unstruck) close by. Almost immediately the second one will start to vibrate in unison with the first. Children living in a home with an enraged parent who is preoccupied with anger and who may in addition have hysterical outbursts of rage are likely to "vibrate" with such a parent and join in with similar emotions. Without knowing the exact reasons why they are so swept up, they may provide the kinds of rationalizations that result in the preposterous scenarios already described.

Sexual Rivalry

Sexual and sexual rivalry factors are sometimes operative in the alienation. A girl who has a seductive and romanticized relationship with her father (sometimes abetted by the father himself) may find his involvement with a new woman particularly painful. Whereas visitations may have gone somewhat smoothly prior to the father's new relationship, following the new involvement there may be a rapid deterioration in the girl's relationship with her father. Such a girl may say to her father, "You've got to choose between me and her." In such situations there may be no hope for a warm and meaningful relationship between the father's new woman friend and his daughter. Sometimes the mothers of such girls will support the animosity in that it serves well their desire for vengeance.

THE MOTHER'S UNDERLYING PSYCHODYNAMICS

Maintenance of the Primary Psychological Bond

The primary psychodynamic factor operative for most of these mothers is the desire to maintain the psychological bond with the child. Obviously, the custody dispute threatens this bond and there is the omnipresent risk of its interruption, attenuation, and possibly even its ultimate obliteration. Fueling the program of vilification is the proverbial "maternal instinct" (an instinct that I believe exists, as does a paternal instinct [although I believe it to be somewhat weaker]). Throughout the animal kingdom it is well known that mothers will literally fight to the death in order to safeguard their progeny, and the women I am talking about here are operating with the same genetic programming. Under these circumstances, fair play is viewed as a nicety that can be reserved for less important conflicts, but it has no place in a battle for one's children. Judicial restraints and threats are ignored (often with impunity), and the name of the game here is to get away with as much as one can. Many of these mothers rely on judges' passivity to enforce their orders, threats of meaningful sanctions notwithstanding. With such high stakes, threats of imprisonment, fines, and even loss of the children will be risked—so important is this cause.

It would be an error for the reader to consider me completely unsympathetic to these women. I am sympathetic to many of them, especially those who are in the mild and slightly moderate categories (to be defined more precisely later in this chapter). They indeed have been "shortchanged" by the recent egalitarianism of the criteria for assigning primary custodial status. With regard to those who are in the more moderate and severe categories, I have less sympathy because of the psychopathic elements that are often incorporated into their maneuvers. To the degree that they are sadistic and to the degree that they strive toward total elimination of the father, to that degree they lose my sympathy. Their cruel maneuvers are often derivatives of psychopathological processes that become incorporated into their programming and exclusionary procedures.

The Fury of the Scorned Woman

Another psychodynamic factor relates to the old saying, "Hell hath no fury like a woman scorned." Actually, the original statement of William Congreve was, "Heaven has no rage, like love to hatred turned. Nor hell a fury, like a woman scorn'd" (*The Mourning Bride*, III, viii). Because these mothers are separated, and cannot retaliate directly against their husbands, they may wreak vengeance by attempting to deprive their former spouses of their most treasured possessions, the children. And the brainwashing program is an attempt to achieve this goal. One of the reasons why such brainwashing is less common in fathers is that they, more often than mothers, have the opportunity to find new partners. Less frustrated, they are less angry and less in need of getting revenge and, if the husband has become involved with a new woman friend—either before or after the separation—the rage so engendered may be even greater. And this is especially the case if the abandoned woman has not been provided with the compensatory gratifications attendant to a new involvement herself.

Economic Disparity

The fury may be fueled by the economic disparity between the two spouses following the separation. With rare exception, divorce causes economic privation for both spouses. Only the wealthy avoid this frequent result of the separation. And, with rare exception, the woman suffers more economic privation than the man. These frustrations and the attendant anger may fuel the parental alienation syndrome. Furthermore, the woman may be less capable of affording more competent lawyers and may therefore find herself in a more vulnerable position in the courtroom. As a result of this legal disadvantage, she may resort to programming the children against the father as a way of prevailing in the courtroom. Moreover, the inevitable frustrations that most litigating parents suffer in their experiences with their lawyers may fuel the anger that becomes directed toward the husband via maneuvers that may deprive him of his children.

[handwritten margin notes: No not an example for E]

Reaction Formation

The reaction formation element may also be operative. As mentioned, the opposite of love is not hate but indifference. Love and hate are better viewed as opposite sides of the same coin. One boy breaks up with his girlfriend and has no subsequent thoughts about her and goes on his way. Another boy breaks up with his girlfriend and writes her a 30-page letter detailing all the reasons why he no longer wants to see her. The girl in the first situation has far less hope for rapprochement than the girl in the second. At some level she probably appreciates that the long letter writer is still "hooked" and "hanging in there" and therefore is a better candidate for reconciliation. Just as romantic loving feelings can serve to suppress anger—and this can be especially useful during the courting period when denial mechanisms may be necessary to call into play if one is to overcome the tensions and anxieties attendant to getting married—angry feelings at the time of divorce can be used to suppress residual loving feelings. The exaggerated angry feelings energize the steps necessary to bring about the severance of the relationship.

As a psychiatrist, I have access to information about people that is not readily available to others (including lawyers). My experience has been that about 10 percent of people who are involved in vicious divorce and custody litigation still occasionally have sexual relations. They might not reveal this to their attorneys because of the potential compromise of their legal position, and they might not even reveal this to their friends because of embarrassment. I do not believe that my sample is atypical and, when one considers the reaction formation factor, such manifestations of residual affection are not surprising. With these people it is almost as if they are saying, "Well, now that we've gotten the orgasms out of the way, let's get back to the battlefield."

The aforementioned examples of reaction formation refer to the mother's feelings about her husband and the need to use anger as a mechanism to cover up affection. I focus now on the role of the reaction formation element in the relationship of these mothers to their children. It is important for the reader to appreciate that many of these mothers are far less loving toward their children than their actions would suggest to the naive observer. Ostensibly, all their attempts to protect the child from harm by the dreaded parent are made in the service of their love for their children. Actually, the truly loving parent appreciates the importance of the noncustodial parent in the lives of the children and, with the exception of the genuinely abusing parent, facilitates meaningful contact between the children and their estranged spouse. The campaigns of denigration that these mothers embark upon when they engender a parental alienation syndrome in their children are not in the children's best interests and are in themselves manifestations of parental deficiency. Their obsessive love of their children is often a cover-up for their underlying hostility. People who need to prove to themselves continuously that they *love* are often fighting underlying feelings of hate. On a few occasions, I have observed dramatic examples of this in my custody evaluations. In the midst of what could only be considered to be violent custodial conflicts—in which both parties were swept up in all-consuming anger—the mother would suddenly state that she was giving up the custody conflict and handing the child over to the father.

In one such case, in the middle of a very heated session, the mother suddenly stated to the father, "Okay, if you want him that bad, take him." When I asked the mother if she was certain that this was her decision, she replied in the affirmative. I reemphasized that the implication of her statement was that the custody litigation should be discontinued and that I would therefore be writing a letter to the judge informing him that my services were no longer being enlisted because the mother had decided voluntarily to turn primary custody over to the father. At this point the mother's second husband leaned over and asked her if she appreciated the implications of what she was saying. After two or three "jolts" by her new husband, the mother appeared to "sober up again" and stated, "Oh, I guess I didn't realize what I was saying. Of course, I love him very much." She then turned to her son and hugged him closely, but without any genuine expression of affection on her face. I believe that what happened here was an inexplicable relaxation of internal censorship that keeps unconscious processes relegated out of conscious awareness. My statement and that of her new husband served to "put things back in place," and she then proceeded with the litigation as viciously as ever. In short, we see another motivation for the obsessive affection that these mothers exhibit toward their children, namely, to suppress and repress continually unconscious impulses to reject, abandon, and otherwise harm the child. And when these mothers "win," they not only win custody, but they win total alienation of their children from the hated spouse. The victory here results in psychological destruction of the children that, I believe, is what they may basically want anyway. And they are dimly aware that their unrelenting litigation, indoctrination, and alienation will bring this about.

Projection

The mechanism of projection is often operative for many of these mothers. They will attribute to their husbands tendencies and practices that are unlikely if not impossible and are products of their own imaginations. These expectations and dire predictions result from their own inclinations in these areas projected out and attributed to their husbands. They can then consider themselves to be free of such odious practices. This mechanism, of course, is central to paranoia, which is the ultimate and extreme result of this mechanism. Projections, however, are not necessarily paranoid. If the individual is able to correct the distorted thinking by logic and confrontation with reality, then the process should not be considered paranoid, but merely a manifestation of the utilization of the mechanism of projection. When the belief becomes fixed and unswerving, in spite of confrontations with disproving logic and reality, then the term *paranoid* is warranted.

I have already given the example of the mother who expects the father to "make a scene" if he were permitted to attend a school recital or summer camp. It is more often the case that it is these mothers themselves who can be relied upon to make such scenes. A very good example is the sex-abuse allegation. As mentioned elsewhere (Gardner, 1987, 1991b, 1991c, 1992a), bona fide sex abuse can certainly take place at the same time that there is a custody dispute. However, the frequency of false accusations under these circumstances is quite high, especially because of the vengeance and exclusionary benefits to be derived from such an accusation. Not surprisingly, then, a sex-abuse allegation has been a common addition to the parental alienation syndrome. However, it is beyond the purposes of this book to discuss this factor in detail. It is, however, discussed in great detail elsewhere (Gardner, 1991a, 1992a). Many of these accusations are conscious and deliberate, and the accuser knows quite well that the spouse did not in any way sexually molest the child. In other cases, however, subconscious and unconscious factors are operative, especially projection. The mother's own suppressed and re-pressed sexual fantasies are projected onto the child and father. By visualizing the father having a sexual experience with the child, the mother is satisfying vicariously her own desires to be the recipient of such overtures and activities. It is also a manifes-tation of the lingering love that is on the other side of the hate coin. The reader does well to consider this factor to be operative in any sex-abuse accusation about the husband that is absurd, ludicrous, has no basis in reality, and is extremely unlikely to have even been thought about by the husband. Such an accusation, then, must be viewed as a product of the mother's own mind—having no basis in reality—and is therefore likely to have within it an element of projection.

Elaboration of Preseparation Exclusionary Tactics

Sometimes the exclusionary maneuvers do not begin at the time of the custody dispute. Rather, they may have antedated significantly the custody conflict and may be merely an extension of previous exclusionary tactics. And sometimes these exclusionary maneuvers date to the time of the birth of the child. I recall one mother in this category, who refused to allow her husband into the delivery room because she considered it a "private matter" between her and the child. When the husband, contrary to her "orders," entered the delivery room during the final few minutes, she diverted herself from the matters under consideration and screamed out hysterically that he should leave the delivery room. Accordingly, he was rapidly ushered out. She held this "invasion of privacy" over his head for many years thereafter, claiming that she will never forget how unsympathetic he was to her and the child's needs. One father described his wife as having been exclusionary from the earliest weeks of the child's life, not simply at the time of the initiation of the child custody dispute. He claimed that when he and his former wife first brought their child back home from the hospital, she refused to let him hold his new daughter for fear that he might drop her. She never left him alone with the child and even considered babysitters more reliable than he. When he would take the child out to the park, she invariably came along in order to ensure that nothing terrible would happen. He often complained that he had served merely as a sperm donor and that after the birth of the child his services were no longer considered necessary.

One mother suffered with a severe germ phobia. Although she herself was constantly cleaning and disinfecting the home, she considered her husband to be a much greater danger to the child because he was not as fastidious as she with regard to avoiding germ contamination. This reached a point where she would not permit the husband to touch the child because, as everyone knows, newborn infants are susceptible to infection. She allowed herself to touch the child because she had taken the proper sanitary precautions. However, no matter what precautions the husband took, no matter how many times he washed his hands, he never reached that proper level of antiseptic purity to allow him to involve himself in the daily care of the child. Another mother never felt that the father was competent enough to take care of the children when they were sick and that only she and the housekeeper could be trusted in this capacity. Although fathers, in general, may be less available and committed to such activities, this father was in no way compromised in his ability to take care of the children during these periods, and his job situation made him easily available for such involvement. Another mother took the child for psychiatric treatment without the father's knowing. And she convinced the therapist that the father's involvement in the therapy could only be detrimental. The father only learned of the treatment after the separation and was only successful in learning about what was going on therein by court order.

As is true of many forms of human behavior, such maneuvers have multiple psychodynamic determinants. One possible factor is competition. By viewing her husband as an incompetent, such mothers thereby enhance their feelings of competence. And this can be especially useful as a mechanism for compensating for low feelings of self-worth. It can also serve as a mechanism for dealing with one's own unconscious desires to inflict harm on the baby. By projecting these desires outward, the mother exonerates herself from thoughts and feelings that would otherwise produce guilt. All human relationships are ambivalent and mother-child relationships are no exception to this principle. The frustrations, privations, and sacrifices inevitably attendant to child rearing will invariably cause frustrations and resentments. And these may even result in thoughts of inflicting harm on the child. The healthier mother can tolerate these unpleasant thoughts and feelings without significant guilt or self-recrimination. A person who is too inhibited to tolerate them may need to project them outward and attribute them to someone else nearby. And a husband may be a convenient repository for such projected thoughts and feelings. Hostility may also be operative. Viewing the husband as a dangerous incompetent is certainly a form of deprecation and can be especially effective at the time of the birth of a baby, when the father's paternal instincts are likely to be operating at full capacity. In some of these exclusionary mothers it is clear that the jealousy factor is operative. They cannot tolerate the child's showing affection to the father because they interpret it to mean that there will be less left over for them. It is almost as if the child is being viewed as a mistress or lover, a rival for the mother's affection. All these preexisting factors can then become incorporated into the exclusionary tactics of the mother who is promulgating a parental alienation syndrome in her children.

Overprotectiveness

I have recently come to appreciate the overlap between maternal overprotection and the development of the parental alienation syndrome. Although the two phenomena can certainly exist independently, there is no question that mothers who are overprotective during the course of the marriage may incorporate the same mechanisms into the programming of their children in the course of producing a parental alienation syndrome. The overprotective mother is essentially communicating to her child the following message: "The world is a dangerous place and calamity may befall you at any time. Stick ever by my side and I will protect you from these catastrophes. Separate from me and venture forth and you may die at any time, before you even appreciate what has happened to you." It is not my purpose here to discuss in detail the complex psychodynamic patterns that are operative in maternal overprotection and the separation anxiety disorder that often results from it. I have discussed these in greater detail elsewhere (Gardner, 1985b, 1992b). I will, however, focus here on those psychodynamic factors that relate to the parental alienation syndrome.

One factor operative in maternal overprotection is anger. The mother is always anticipating violent catastrophes to befall the child. These images, which go above and beyond reality, relate to her own hostile thoughts and feelings, expressed in primitive fashion and dealt with by the mechanisms of projection and reaction formation. Prior to the separation she may have viewed a wide variety of other individuals as potential sources of danger, e.g., reckless drivers, insensitive teachers, people who might have allowed the child's food to be contaminated, nonvigilant lifeguards, etc. Following the separation her husband, who might have served as an assistant to her in protecting the child from these omnipresent dangers, now becomes added to the list of those who might neglect and even harm the child. Excluding him, then, not only serves the purposes of the earlier overprotective maneuvers, but now has the additional fringe benefit of fueling the development of a parental alienation syndrome in the child.

Another factor operative in the development of maternal overprotection is the mother's need for gratification of her own infantile dependency needs. She may have been frustrated in the gratification of these in her own childhood and cannot overtly satisfy these now that she is an adult, especially as a mother herself. However, these can be gratified vicariously through the child. It is as if each time she ministers to the child she is providing for her projected self. She thereby vicariously gratifies her own desires to obtain these infantile satisfactions. The need to keep the child ever by her side and indulge it is, in part, a derivative of this need to feed and minister to her projected self. This pattern, also, easily becomes incorporated into a parental alienation syndrome. A marital separation is going to jeopardize the symbiotic relationship that the overprotective mother has with her overdependent child. A visitation schedule with the father has no place in such a mother's scheme of things. Her need for continual vicarious gratification of her own infantile dependency needs via the baby is so great that she cannot tolerate such removal of her children. Whereas for other mothers the exclusionary maneuvers serve to preserve a healthy or possibly mildly pathological parent-child psychological bond, for these mothers the exclusionary maneuvers serve to protect the more pathological symbiotic bond.

Overprotection of children can also serve to compensate for feelings of low self-worth. Such mothers often view themselves as "super mothers" and will look down with disdain on other mothers who are viewed as uncaring and neglectful. They pride themselves on their knowledge of which foods are healthy and which are unhealthy, which are nutritious and which are "junk." They pride themselves on how many precautions they take to protect their children from germs, illnesses, accidents, etc. Mothering may become their primary (if not exclusive) source of ego-enhancement. For such mothers a visitation schedule is extremely threatening. Once again, these same factors may operate in bringing about a parental alienation syndrome.

It is because of these considerations that I believe the overprotective mother is a high-risk candidate for providing the kind of programming that may result in a parental alienation syndrome. Overprotectiveness is much more common in mothers than fathers. Programming children to develop parental alienation syndromes is much more commonly done by mothers than fathers. This gender difference is probably also playing a role in the overlap of the two disorders. Examiners, therefore, do well to be alert to this and, when in doubt about the diagnosis, do well to ascertain whether there is a past history of maternal overprotectiveness. It would be an error for the reader to equate overprotectiveness and the parental alienation syndrome because of their overlap. Although maternal overprotectiveness may contribute to the formation of a parental alienation syndrome, and may continue to fuel it, there is no question that much more is going on in the parental alienation syndrome than simple maternal overprotectiveness. These additional factors are described in detail throughout the course of this book.

Additional Psychodynamic Factors

There are certainly other factors that may contribute to a mother's programming her children in order to produce a parental alienation syndrome. There may be significant anger that antedated the marriage, anger that found release in marital squabbles and conflicts and is now fueling the parental alienation syndrome. And a wide variety of factors may have been operative in producing such anger, e.g., deprivations in her own childhood, death of a parent, substance abuse, physical illness, etc. Separation and divorce, in themselves, produce significant anger. And, if the parents are litigating, especially litigating over custody of their children, the anger generated is likely to be enormous. And inducing a parental alienation syndrome in one's children can serve as a predictable vehicle for releasing such rage. One does not simply induce the disorder and then sit back; rather, it requires constant attention. Accordingly, the fires need continual fueling if the program of denigration is to prove successful.

Preexisting anxieties and phobias can become intensified at the time of separation and these symptoms, as well, can contribute to the mother's exaggerated need for the child for companionship and even protection. Depression, stemming from sources that antedated the marriage, may become intensified at the time of the separation with the result that the mother's need for the child becomes greater. Examiners do well to understand these factors when trying to determine the causes of the mother's contribution to the child's parental alienation syndrome and, even more importantly, to understand them in depth if one is to effectively treat such patients. It is my hope here that the examiner will be somewhat overwhelmed by the complexity of these factors and therefore will be somewhat modest about attributing the behavior to one or two simple causes.

THE FATHER'S UNDERLYING PSYCHODYNAMICS

Because I have seen fewer fathers than mothers who have programmed their children, I have less knowledge and experience about the underlying psychodynamics of such fathers. As mentioned, they represent about 10 per cent of the cases I have seen, and colleagues of mine are in agreement that this figure appears to be reasonable. There are, however, certain statements I can make about such fathers at this point. I will use as my guidelines the same categories of psychodynamic patterns applicable to the mother and comment regarding the applicability of each of them for the father.

Maintenance of the Primary Psychological Bond

There are some fathers who have indeed been more involved with their children than their wives and the children's psychological bond with them is stronger than the mothers'. In some cases the mother may have initially been the primary parent, but over the years the children have gradually gravitated toward their father, so much so that at the time of the custody dispute they are indeed more bonded to him than they are to the mother. The current popularity of gender egalitarianism notwithstanding, many judges still subscribe to the tender-years presumption. Accordingly, in many custody cases defective mothers are still awarded primary custody, much to the detriment of the children. In such cases, the father may attempt to enhance his cause by programming the children against the mother. The weaker the psychological bond the children have with the mother, the greater the likelihood of the father's success in this campaign.

Kopetski (1988) points out that the legal system is gender-biased with regard to its reactions to the complaining parent. If a male parent is the focus of the child's denigration, then it is far more likely that that parent's visitation will be restricted and even suspended (especially if there is a sex-abuse allegation) than if the female parent is so accused. In the latter case, the children are usually allowed to remain with the mother until the court is convinced either of her innocence or her guilt. I myself have had the same experiences. We see here a good example of the court's bias and, hence, a reason why some fathers might resort to the programming of their children.

The Fury of the Scorned Man

Although we do not say, "Hell hath no fury like that of a man scorned," there are still many angry men who have been spurned by their wives. Although it is probably true that women are more likely to be enraged following a marital abandonment than a man, this still does not preclude men reacting with intense anger when they are rejected. A woman's lot is generally worse than that of a man's following a separation, especially if she has children. The financial disparity is still prevalent, attempts at rectification of this inegalitarianism notwithstanding. Accordingly, the frustrations for women are greater and the likelihood of rage more. However, there are sources of anger other than financial privation, and loss of self-esteem is one of them. A man in such a situation may wish to wreak vengeance upon a woman who has rejected him; taking away her children will predictably be the most effective way of achieving this goal. Accordingly, the vengeance motivation may very well operate in men who program their children against their wives—in a manner similar to rejected women who program their children to be alienated from their husbands. Just as the woman is likely to be angry if her husband has a new involvement, a man is likely to be angry if his wife has a new involvement, especially if the new involvement antedated and was the cause of the separation.

Economic Disparity

The economic disparity following a separation works differently for men and women with regard to the induction of a parental alienation syndrome in their children. The woman's more vulnerable position makes it less likely that she will be able to afford the same kind of legal counsel as her husband. Accordingly, she may resort to the induction of symptoms of alienation in the children in order to increase the likelihood that she will be successful in the courtroom. For the father, more costly and effective lawyers may enable him to obtain primary custody without the necessity of inducing in his children a parental alienation syndrome. He may, however, be able to win them over with the lure of his superior financial position. And this is especially the case when he is well off. A larger house (especially one with a pool), a better neighborhood, roomier quarters, more toys, a bigger backyard, play equipment, etc., can all contribute to the children's viewing the father's home as a more desirable place to live. I am not claiming that these lures are as powerful as a mother's bonding with the children. I am only claiming that they can play a role in tipping the balance in the father's direction. Evaluators do well to put such factors in proper perspective and not give inordinate weight to them. A father may use his economic advantage in another way, a way that may contribute to the development of a parental alienation syndrome against the mother. He may threaten to withhold payment for private and higher education if the children do not support his position. Obviously, this threat is more likely to work with older children than younger ones.

Reaction Formation

Just as the mother's residual love of her husband may be dealt with by reaction formation—resulting in hatred as the main manifestation of her affection, the husband may react similarly. And this hatred may manifest itself by programming the children against her. Furthermore, just as the mother's obsessive love of the children may serve as reaction formation to underlying deficiencies in maternal capacity, the father is not immune from these mechanisms as well. In both cases, the reaction formation element may contribute to the development of a parental alienation syndrome in them.

I have seen many fathers who were uninvolved with their families prior to the separation. Some have been workaholics and were minimally involved with their families. Then, at the time of the separation, there is a sudden transformation. Suddenly, they become "fathers of the year!" The children and the mother all recognize this. Astute evaluators, as well, appreciate this phenomenon and are not going to give great weight to it. The campaign proving to the world that they are "super fathers" serves to compensate such fathers for the feelings of paternal inadequacy with which they basically suffer. It may also serve to assuage the guilt they have over their past neglect of their children. Inducing a parental alienation syndrome in their children, then, can serve these mechanisms by enabling them to convince themselves that they are superior to the mothers with regard to parenting capacity. As is true of such mothers, such fathers do not seem to appreciate that alienating the children from a parent is in no way a manifestation of affection for them.

Projection

I have not found the projective mechanism to be as common in men as it is in women with regard to the production of parental alienation syndromes in their children. I am not talking about the utilization of this mechanism in general, only insofar as it relates to the induction of the parental alienation syndrome. I have seen many more women who are paranoid with regard to their husband's involvement with their children, than men who are paranoid with regard to their wife's involvement with their children. Perhaps this is a derivative of the biological differences between men and women, especially with regard to parental commitment. Women are more vulnerable to the effects of disruption of the parent-child psychological bond, are more likely to be angry over the threat of such disruption, and are more likely, then, to project such anger in periods of stress.

In my discussion of the projective element in the section on the mother's psychodynamics, I made reference to the sex-abuse accusation, so commonly incorporated into the parental alienation syndrome in recent years. One factor operative in such projection is the woman's sexual inhibition. It is as if she is saying, "It is not I who have these dirty sexual thoughts and feelings, it is he (my husband)." Because men in our society are less likely to be sexually inhibited (I did not say that they are immune from this disorder), they are less likely to need to project their sexual impulses onto others. Accordingly, they are less likely to develop the delusion that a child has been sexually abused. However, men have used the sex-abuse allegation. My experience has been that this is more likely to be a conscious fabrication than a product of projection. It is a manifestation of the "backlash" that men have utilized in recent years in response to the rash of false sex-abuse accusations that are commonly incorporated into the parental alienation syndrome.

Exclusionary Tactics

In the section on women's psychodynamics, I describe the parental alienation syndrome to be an outgrowth of exclusionary maneuvers that may have for years antedated the marital separation. Certainly exclusionary maneuvers are to be seen in full-blown form in the parental alienation syndrome. But this is a post-separation phenomenon. Because fathers are generally less involved with their children than mothers, and because their bonding in the traditional home is less, they are less likely to have been exclusionary prior to the marital separation. The exclusionary tactic seen in fathers in the process of the development of the parental alienation syndrome is more a strategic tactic that serves the goal of depriving the children of the opportunity to be with their mother. It serves, thereby, to attenuate the psychological bond that they have developed with her.

Overprotectiveness

What I have said about exclusionary maneuvers is also true of overprotectiveness. Prior to the separation, mothers are generally far more likely to be overprotective than fathers. But even after the separation and even when a parental alienation syndrome is being programmed into children, fathers are less likely to use overprotectiveness as one of the maneuvers.

Power

Few would doubt that men have much more power than women in our society, and this has been the case throughout the history of the human race. Even though women may subtly wield power over men, there is no question that the balance is tipped in favor of men. Men not only have more power, but serve as a symbol for it. Children especially are likely to view the father as the more powerful figure, their stronger bonding with their mothers notwithstanding. When I attended grade school, unruly children would often be threatened that if they continued misbehaving, their mothers would be called to school. If, however, things really got bad, then their father might be brought in as well. If the school authorities had to resort to calling in one's father, it meant that the situation had indeed deteriorated to a very low level. Heavyweight action then had to be taken, action that involved the father—the symbol of power and strength.

Although not as clearcut today, I believe the situation still prevails. The father earns more money, has the power to purchase more things, has the greater power to decide whether or not he wants to remarry, and is more likely to employ people than the mother. From a young age, children appreciate this. And this may play a role in the children's gravitating toward the father in parental conflict and contributes to their being willing subjects to the manipulations that are designed to induce in them a parental alienation syndrome. Every man of wealth and power recognizes that there are a sea of women out there who view him as a primary "turn-on." These men may be stupid, ugly, and crude—their wealth notwithstanding. Yet, their wealth and power causes their admirers to blind themselves to these obvious defects. And the same principal may be operative in children who favor their fathers and develop parental alienation syndromes against their mothers. Although, as mentioned, my experience with mothers inducing the disorder is greater than my experience with fathers, my preliminary observations have been that rich men are more likely to be successful in inducing this disorder in their children than poor men.

The Father's New Woman Involvement

My experience has been that a mother's new male involvement is not as likely to play as formidable a role in the development of the children's parental alienation syndrome as a father's new woman involvement. A father's new woman friend is more likely to try to win the children over to the father's side, in order to entrench her relationship with the father, than a mother's new man friend. I believe that this phenomenon is related to the greater vulnerability of women in the marital situation. Encouraging the children to join forces with their father against his former wife will enhance the likelihood of the new woman's establishing a more solid family in the father's home and increase, thereby, the likelihood of this new arrangement becoming permanent. As described elsewhere (1991b, 1991c), stepmothers are more likely to be rivalrous with biological mothers than stepfathers with biological fathers. This rivalry stems, in part, from women's vulnerabilities and insecurities in their relationships with men. In some cases, the new woman's contribution to the parental alienation syndrome began with her attempts to ingratiate herself with the children when first meeting them. This may have been one of the maneuvers designed to attract their father to her. The parental alienation syndrome, then, developed as an outgrowth of this earlier seductive stratagem. Then, if her new husband has a need to program the children against their mother (for one or more of the variety of reasons described here), she becomes his willing cohort—now in the attempt to strengthen her relationship with him. I am not claiming that all these maneuvers are conscious designs; many are unconscious. In either case they have the effect of enhancing the likelihood that the children will become alienated from their mother.

Additional Psychodynamic Factors

As mentioned in the section on mothers, there may be a wide variety of other psychological processes that contribute to the need to develop a parental alienation syndrome in one's children. Mention was made in that section of anger that existed in the marriage, anger that antedated the separation, and anger that is now fueling a parental alienation syndrome. The wide variety of anger-related symptoms that antedated the separation may become intensified as a result of the divorce trauma, especially if litigation is present. And this anger can be released via the generation and maintenance of a parental alienation syndrome in the children. The anger generated by litigation can, in itself, find release through the development of a parental alienation syndrome. Examiners do well to appreciate the complexity of the factors that contribute to the development of the disorder and to determine which particular factors are operative in any particular father. The factors that I have described in this section are some of the more common, but there are certainly others. One cannot predict in advance which ones will be operative in any particular parent. It is only through detailed investigation that one can delineate the psychodynamics of any particular patient.

SITUATIONAL FACTORS

Often situational factors are conducive to the development of the disorder. By situational factors, I refer to external events that contribute to the development of the parental alienation syndrome—factors that abet the internal psychological processes in the parents and in the child. Most parents in a custody conflict know that time is on the side of the custodial parent. They appreciate that the longer the child remains with a particular parent, the greater the likelihood the child will resist moving to the home of the other. Furthermore, the longer a child remains with a particular parent the greater the opportunity that parent will have for brainwashing the child to provide professions of support and allegiance in the custody dispute. Even adults find change of domicile to be anxiety provoking. One way for a child to deal with this fear is to denigrate the noncustodial parent with criticisms that justify the child's remaining in the custodial home. For example, a mother dies and the maternal grandparents take over care of the child. Although at first the father may welcome their involvement, there are many cases in which the maternal grandparents subsequently litigate for the custody of the child. The child may then develop formidable resentments against the father in order to ensure that he (she) will remain with the grandparents, the people whom the child has come to view as the preferable parents. And this is especially likely to be the case if the grandparents program the child into developing a parental alienation syndrome.

In one case I was involved with, two girls developed this disorder after their mother, with whom they were living in New Jersey, met a man who lived in Colorado. The mother then decided to move there with the two girls. The father brought the mother to court in an attempt to restrain her from moving out of the state of New Jersey with the children. Whereas previously there had been a good relationship with their father, the girls gradually developed increasing hatred of him, as their mother became progressively more deeply embroiled in the litigation. It was clear that the disorder would not have arisen had the mother not met a man who lived in Colorado, a man whom she wished to marry.

A common situation in which the child will develop complaints about the hated parent is one in which the child has observed a sibling being treated harshly and even being rejected for expressing affection for the hated parent. One boy I treated repeatedly observed his mother castigating his sister for her expressions of affection for their father. The sister was older and could better withstand the mother's vociferous denigration of her. The boy, however, was frightened by his mother's outbursts of rage toward his sister and was adamant in his refusal to see his father, claiming that he hated him, but only giving inconsequential reasons for his hostility. In this way he protected himself from his mother's turning her animosity toward him. This child was utilizing the previously described identification-with-the-aggressor mechanism. He chose to identify with his mother rather than become the target of his mother's hostility. He could not fight her so he chose to join her. We see here clearly how his hatred of his father stemmed not so much from alienating qualities within the father, but from fear of the loss of his mother's affection. We see here also the situation creating an atmosphere conducive to the utilization of the identification-with-the-aggressor mechanism.

One girl observed her mother making terrible threats to her

older brother: "If you go to court and tell the judge that you want to live with your father, I'll have you put away as a psychotic. I'll have the child authorities put you away. You're crazy if you want to live with him." In this case the father was an unusually good parent, and the mother suffered with a moderately severe psychiatric disturbance. The older brother was strong enough to overtly express his preference for living with the father and appreciated that the mother had no power to unilaterally and perfunctorily have him committed to a mental hospital. The younger sister, however, believed that such placement was a possibility and therefore told the judge that she wanted to live with her mother. Again, it was fear, not love, of the mother that brought about the child's professions of preference.

One boy repeatedly observed his father sadistically and mercilessly beating his mother. In order to protect himself from similar maltreatment, the boy professed deep affection for his father and hatred of his mother. The professions of love here stemmed from fear rather than from genuine feelings of affection. This boy, also, was operating on the identification-with-the-aggressor principle. Those who were knowledgeable about the father's brutal treatment of the mother expressed amazement that the child was obsessed with hatred of his mother and love of his father, and they were unable to understand why the boy kept pleading for the opportunity to live with his father. Another factor that may be operative in such situations is the child's model of what a loving relationship should be like. Love is viewed as manifesting itself by hostile interaction. Father demonstrates his "affection" for mother by beating her. In order to be sure of obtaining this "love," the child opted to live with the hostile parent. This mechanism, of course, is central to *masochism*.

I have repeatedly emphasized throughout this book that the parental alienation syndrome is separate from physical, emotional, and sexual abuse. Although this is certainly the case, this does not mean that one may not find parallel abuses and even abuse that may affect or become incorporated into the parental alienation syndrome. Cancer and pneumonia are two separate diseases, but this does mean that a person with cancer cannot also get pneumonia. Nor does it mean that the presence of one cannot affect the other. I have already mentioned the incorporation of a sex-abuse allegation into a parental alienation syndrome. They are still separate entities and one can certainly exist without the other. In the case mentioned here, there was physical abuse of the mother by the father. If the boy developed animosity toward his father (the expected response), then I would not consider the parental alienation syndrome explanation to be applicable. There was genuine abuse that warranted his rejection and animosity. In this case, the boy reacted in an entirely unexpected way, namely, he joined with his abusing father against his mother. Primary here was the identification-with-the-aggressor mechanism, which, as mentioned, is one of the factors operative in bringing about a parental alienation syndrome. In this case, if any label of emotional abuse was to be utilized, it would be the father's inducing the parental alienation syndrome in his son. In general, the parent who is inducing a parental alienation syndrome is perpetrating a kind of emotional abuse. However, the child's anger at the "hated" parent is not the result of that parent's abuse of the child, but of the programmer's abuse, namely, the induction of a parental alienation syndrome.

One father was attending law school at the time of the birth of his first child. When his second was born, he was employed by a major law firm that required 14 hours a day of work, 6-1/2 days a week. Although he was paid very well for this servitude, he saw very little of his family. The paternal grandfather, however, spent significant periods in the home helping the wife with the children. Subsequently, the family moved to another part of the United States, leaving behind the paternal grandfather, to whom both children had become significantly attached. Five years later, the parents separated. At the time of the separation the father accused the mother of sex abuse and was successful in convincing the court that the children should be transferred immediately to his home. At that point the paternal grandfather suddenly appeared on the scene.

Through the next year, while the lawsuit was dragging along, the father and the grandfather were successful in program ming the children to become alienated from their mother. The children's siding with their father became easier for the father to accomplish because of their earlier experiences—in the crucial bonding period of infancy—with the paternal grandfather. Accordingly, the grandfather facilitated the father's attenuating the earlier strong bonding that the children also had with their mother. The father, although he began the programming process with a weaker bond (and, therefore, should have been unsuccessful), had combined forces with the paternal grandfather, whose bonding with the children enhanced their lure toward the two men. During the year's time that these two men "worked over" these children, they were successful in bringing about what appeared to be a typical parental alienation syndrome in which the mother was the object of their hostility. In this case I found no evidence for sex abuse and recommended that the children be returned immediately to the mother's primary care.

Although the children's parental alienation syndrome ostensibly suggested that bonding now was stronger with the father, I believed that his one year of indoctrination was not enough to override the earlier maternal contributions. Furthermore, although the grandfather had some bonding with the children as well, I considered the mother's bonding with the children to be stronger, the children's professions of "hatred" notwithstanding. Fortunately, the court considered my recommendation judicious, ordered immediate return of the children to their mother, and within a week or two they were "cured." We see here a good example of how transfer of the children could bring about results that might never have been accomplished with psychotherapy, no matter how skilled or talented the therapist. (I will elaborate further on this point in Chapter Five.)

In one case in which I was involved, two boys, ages 11 and 13, became alienated from their mother (who had been the primary caretaker throughout the course of their lives) by the situation they found themselves in following the parental separation. The family lived on one patch of a large segment of land, which had been owned originally by their paternal grandfather (whom, I will refer to as Mr. Sanders). He was quite wealthy and, over the years, arranged to have all six of his children and their families live on segments of his property. He viewed all his children, stepchildren, and grandchildren as part of a large family of which he was the grand patriarch. All of his direct descendants were extremely dependent on him, both financially and psychologically. As the two boys grew up, there was a whole network of cousins, uncles, and aunts with whom they involved themselves, and all members of the extended family flowed smoothly and naturally from one home to the other. When the boys' parents divorced, the father moved out of the marital home back into the home of the paternal grandparents (who certainly had many spare rooms in their mansion). Although the mother recognized that it would be better for her and the boys to move elsewhere, the father was successful in convincing the judge to rule that the mother could have the family home if she remained residing in it with the boys, but would lose it if she moved elsewhere. Not surprisingly, following the separation, the mother became alienated from the grandparents and the other members of the father's extended family. Basically, when it came to the boys' loyalties, she was no match for the clan, even though she had been the primary parent throughout their lives. It took only minimal programming by the father to lure the boys to him. He told them, "You boys are Sanders and you'll always be Sanders, no matter what happens to your mother." The boys recognized that loyalty to their mother would result in the alienation of all other members of the extended family. Within a few months of the separation they began refusing to return to their mother's home at the end of visitation and, two years later, when I was first consulted in this case, the bonds with their mother had been significantly attenuated. I was convinced that the situational factors here were the most important in bringing about their alienation from their mother.

One 13-year-old girl's mother died in an automobile accident during the course of her parents' custody litigation. Specifically, she was killed en route home from a visit to her lawyer. Even prior to her mother's death, the girl had identified with and supported her mother's position and viewed her father as an abandoner. Her mother was supported in this regard by the maternal grandmother as well. At the time of the mother's death the girl manifested what I have described elsewhere (Gardner, 1979) as an "instantaneous identification" with her dead mother. This is one of the ways in which children (and even adults) may deal with the death of a parent. It is as if they are saying, "My parent isn't dead; he (she) now resides within my own body." In the context of such immediate identification the child takes on many of the dead parent's personality traits, often almost overnight. And this is what occurred in this case. There was a very rapid maturational process in which the girl acquired many of the mannerisms of her mother. As part of this process she intensified her hatred of her father and even accused him of having caused the death of her mother: "If you hadn't treated my mother so badly, there wouldn't have been a breakup of the marriage, she wouldn't have had to go visit with her lawyer, and she wouldn't have been killed on the way home from his office." Although there were many other factors involved in her obsessive hatred and rejection of her father, this identification factor was an important one. Prior to her mother's death she had grudgingly and intermittently seen her father; after the death there was a total cessation of visitation. Interestingly, this identification process was supported by the maternal grandmother, who began to view the girl as the reincarnation of her dead daughter. And in the service of this process she supported the girl in her rejection of her father.

THE PARENTAL ALIENATION SYNDROME, AN EXAMPLE OF *FOLIE À DEUX*

The parental alienation syndrome is an excellent example of *folie à deux* (French: "folly for two" or "double insanity"). *Folie à deux* is a form of psychiatric disorder in which one party (usually the more domineering and authoritative) creates in another party (usually the more passive and suggestible) a psychiatric disturbance. By this process the first party transmits his (her) pathology to the second. Although not a form of insanity in the strictest sense, the parental alienation syndrome is very much a *folie-à-deux* form of psychiatric disturbance. Campbell's Psychiatric Dictionary (1989) states, "Suggestibility plays a part, among other factors, in the genesis of *folie à deux*." I have already mentioned how children's suggestibility and their need to ingratiate themselves to adult authority play an important role in the development of the parental alienation syndrome. This is one of the reasons why the older the child, the less the likelihood of the syndrome's development, although, as I will describe below, older children are by no means immune. Campbell also states, "The condition is not necessarily confined to two persons, and may involve three and even more (*folie à trois, folie à quatre,* etc.)." In the parental alienation syndrome with two children who join with the mother, we have a *folie-à-trois* situation, and when three children do so we have a *folie à quatre,* etc.

Another kind of *folie-à-trois* relationship seen in the parental alienation syndrome is one in which the mother, the child, and the psychotherapist are the participants. I suspect that this statement may come as a surprise for some readers, but I am convinced that this is a widespread phenomenon and that my own experiences with this kind of arrangement are not atypical. Parental alienation syndrome mothers have a way of finding therapists (almost invariably women) who reflexly join with them in their campaign of denigration of the father. In some cases they even join in with the mother's paranoid delusional system. Typically, these therapists see no need to interview the father, let alone work with him. Accordingly, they get no alternative opinions regarding what is going on. I have seen such therapists come to court and testify on the mother's behalf, and even provide testimony that the father sexually abused the child—again, without having even offered to interview him. Some of these therapists are paranoid themselves. Others harbor deep-seated hostility toward men, hostility so strong that they will seize upon every opportunity to vent their rage on them. A parental alienation syndrome provides them with just such an opportunity. I have no problem labeling such a therapist as being one of the participants in a *folie-à-trois* form of psychopathology.

There are some who consider the parental alienation syndrome to be nothing more than a disorder known as "Münchausen syndrome by proxy." The Münchausen syndrome derives its name from the mythical 18th-century Baron von Münchausen, who was famous for his elaborate fabrications (Kolb and Brodie, 1982). These patients wander from hospital to hospital feigning medical and/or surgical illnesses and provide false and fanciful information about their medical history. The diagnostic triad of symptoms is comprised of *pseudologia fantastica* (pathological fabrication of fantastic stories), *perigrination* (wandering from hospital to hospital), and *disease simulation* (feigning the symptoms of a wide variety of medical and surgical diseases) (Campbell, 1989). Münchausen syndrome by proxy is a term first introduced by Money (1986). Money and Werlwas (1976, 1980) refer to a *folie à deux* in which the parents describe physical illness in the child and the child concurs. Epstein et al. (1987) also use the term to refer to the induction by parents of a factitious illness in their child. More recently Rand (1989) uses the term to refer to the parental induction of an abuse fabrication in the child. Although this description is closer to the parental alienation syndrome in that psychological rather than physical symptoms are being induced, Rand's description is confined to parent and child complaints of abuse, but does not give proper attention to the child's own contribution to the scenario. In other reports as well (Libow and Scherier, 1986), the term is used to refer to the child's fabricating physical abuse, but these reporters, as well, do not give proper attention to the child's own contributions and view the child as merely the passive recipient of the parental induction and as a parrot-like repeater of the parentally induced litanies. Accordingly, I do not believe that Münchausen syndrome by proxy is exactly the same as the parental alienation syndrome, although there is certainly the factor of inducement.

I am certain that there were others who observed the same parent-child phenomena as I did when I first defined the disorder in the early 1980s. I do not believe that I have discovered anything here; rather, I believe that I have provided a name for the disorder and provided understanding of its etiology, pathogenesis, a detailed description of its manifestations, psychodynamics, and therapeutic and legal approaches to its alleviation. I would not be surprised if others, as well, have described what I have; however, their work has not yet come to my attention.

THE THREE TYPES OF
PARENTAL ALIENATION SYNDROME

The history of medicine, in a sense, is the history of our capacity to make increasingly finer discriminations. In fact, this is one of the reasons why Hippocrates (or his school if, in fact, he did not exist) is recognized as the Father of Medicine. Prior to his time people were observed to have "fits," that is, episodes in which their bodies would writhe and move, seemingly in an uncontrollable fashion. It was Hippocrates who recognized that all these fits were the same. Some began after the individual had traveled in marshy climates where the air was stagnant. These were called *malaria*, because they were considered to be caused by the bad air found in such places. (We know now that it had less to do with the air than it had to do with certain types of mosquitoes.) Others, primarily women, were considered to be suffering from looseness of the uterus (hysteros) which resulted in a wandering of the uterus throughout their body, thus the name *hysteria*. Still others' fits seem to come from without as if they were seized from above, a phenomenon which, if expressed in Greek, is termed *epilepsy*. Obviously, each of these three types of "fit" requires a different kind of treatment. Yet, without such differentiation one is ill equipped to provide the specific proper treatment. There was a time when it was recognized that certain symptoms resulted from diseases of the heart; yet, the multiplicity of heart diseases was far from being understood. Now we know of many different kinds of heart disease and it is reasonable to predict that each one of these types may become parent to various subtypes in future generations, subtypes that will be delineated as our knowledge increases.

And this is what has occurred in my understanding of the parental alienation syndrome. I now consider there to be three types, each of which requires a separate approach—both by mental health and legal professionals. Failure to make this differentiation may result in injudicious and even detrimental therapy as well as incorrect and probably detrimental placement of the child. Although there is actually a continuum, and many cases do not fit neatly into one of these categories, the differentiation is still useful—especially with regard to the therapeutic approaches. In each of the three categories, not only are the children different, but the mothers as well. It is extremely important that evaluators determine the proper category if they are to provide the most judicious recommendations. In each category I will discuss the mothers, the children, and the appropriate therapeutic approaches. I will use the mother as the example of the preferred parent, as this is so in the majority of cases; however, the same considerations apply to the father when he is the favored parent. I will describe here the three types one sees clinically. In Chapter Six I will discuss the psychotherapeutic approaches to each of these three types and in Chapter Seven I will discuss the recommendations that I have to the legal and judicial community regarding how to deal with each of them.

I wish to emphasize at this point that in many cases the therapy of these families is not possible without court support. Only the court has the power to order these mothers to stop their manipulations and maneuvering. And it is only the court that has the power to place the children in whichever home would best suit their needs at the particular time. Therapists who embark upon the treatment of such families without such court backing are not likely to be successful. I cannot emphasize this point strongly enough.

Severe Cases of the
Parental Alienation Syndrome

The *mothers* of these children are often fanatic. They will use every mechanism at their disposal (legal and illegal) to prevent visitation. They are obsessed with antagonism toward their husbands. In many cases they are paranoid. Sometimes the paranoid thoughts and feelings about the husband are isolated to him alone; in other cases this paranoia is just one example of many types of paranoid thinking. Often the paranoia did not exhibit itself prior to the breakup of the marriage and may be a manifestation of the psychiatric deterioration that frequently is seen in the context of divorce disputes, especially custody disputes (Gardner, 1986a). Central to the paranoid mechanism is projection. These mothers see in their husbands many noxious qualities that actually exist within themselves. By projecting these unacceptable qualities onto their husbands they can consider themselves innocent victims of their husband's persecutions. When a sex-abuse allegation becomes part of the package (Gardner, 1987, 1989a, 1991a, 1992a), they may be projecting their own sexual inclinations onto him. In the service of this goal they exaggerate and distort any comment the child makes that might justify the accusation. And this is not difficult to do because children normally will entertain sexual fantasies, often of the most bizarre form. I am in agreement with Freud (1905) that children are "polymorphous perverse" and they thereby provide these mothers with an ample supply of material to serve as nuclei for their projections and accusations.

Such mothers do not respond to logic, confrontations with reality, or appeals to reason. They will readily believe the most preposterous scenarios. Skilled mental health examiners who claim that there is no evidence for the accusation are dismissed as being against them or as being paid off by the husband. And this is typical of paranoid thinking: it does not respond to logic, and any confrontation that might shake the system is rationalized by incorporation into the paranoid scenario. Even a court decision that the father is not guilty of the abominations alleged by the mother does not alter her beliefs or reduce her commitment to her campaign of denigration. Energizing the rage is the "hell-hath-no-fury-like-a-woman-scorned" phenomenon. Of course, many of the other psychodynamic factors described previously for the mother may also be contributing.

The *children* of these mothers are similarly fanatic. They have joined together with her in a *folie-à-deux* relationship in which they share her paranoid fantasies about the father. They may become panic-stricken over the prospect of visiting with their father. Their blood-curdling shrieks, panicked states, and hostility may be so severe that visitation is impossible. If placed in the father's home they may run away, become paralyzed with morbid fear, or be so destructive that removal becomes warranted. Unlike children in the moderate and mild categories, their panic and hostility may not be reduced in the father's home, even when separated from the mother for significant periods.

Moderate Cases of the Parental Alienation Syndrome

The *mothers* of children in this category are not as fanatic as those in the more severe category; but are more disturbed than those in the mild category (who may not have a psychiatric disturbance). In these cases the rage-of-the-rejected-woman factor is more important than the paranoid projection contribution. They are able to make some differentiation between allegations that are preposterous and those that are not. There is still, however, a campaign of denigration and a significant desire to withhold the children from the father as a vengeance maneuver. Here too, other psychodynamic factors described previously may be operative. These mothers will find a wide variety of excuses to interfere with or circumvent visitation. They may be unreceptive to complying with court orders; however, they will often comply under great pressure, threats of sanctions, transfer of custody, etc. These mothers are less likely to be paranoid than those in the severe category. When a sex-abuse allegation is brought into the parental alienation syndrome, they will be able to differentiate between the children's preposterous claims and those that may have some validity.

Whereas the mothers in the severe category have a sick psychological bond with the children (often a paranoid one), the mothers of children in this category are more likely to have a healthy psychological bond that is being compromised by their rage. The mothers in this category are more likely to have been good child rearers prior to the divorce. In contrast, the mothers in the severe category, even though not significantly disturbed prior to the separation, often have exhibited formidable impairments in child-rearing capacity prior to the separation. It is for these reasons that the mothers in the moderate category can most often be allowed to remain the primary custodial parent, and the combined efforts of the court and the therapist may be successful in enabling the children to resume normal visitation with the father.

The *children* in this category are less fanatic in their vilification of the father than those in the severe category, but more than those in the mild category. They, too, have their campaigns of depreciation of the father, but are much more likely to give up their scenarios when alone with him, especially for long periods. Once removed entirely from their mother's purview, the children generally quiet down, relax their guard, and involve themselves benevolently with their father. A younger child may often need the support of an older one to keep the campaign going. Under such circumstances the older child is serving as a mother surrogate during visitation. The primary motive for the children's scenarios is to maintain the healthy psychological bond with the mother.

Mild Cases of the
Parental Alienation Syndrome

The *mothers* of children in this category generally have a healthy psychological bond with the children. These mothers may recognize that gender egalitarianism in custody disputes is a disservice to children, but are healthy enough not to involve themselves in significant degrees of courtroom litigation in order to gain primary custody. These mothers recognize that alienation from the father is not in the best interests of their children and are willing to take a more conciliatory approach to the father's requests. They either go along with a joint custodial compromise or even allow (albeit reluctantly) the father to have sole custody with their having a liberal visitation program. Although these mothers believe it would be in the best interests of the children to remain with them, they recognize that protracted litigation is going to cause all family members to suffer more grief than an injudicious custody arrangement, namely one in which the father has more involvement (either sole or joint custody) than they consider warranted. However, we may still see some manifestations of programming in these mothers in order to strengthen their positions. There is no paranoia here, but there is anger and there may be some desire for vengeance. The motive for programming the children, however, is less likely to be vengeance than it is merely to entrench their positions in an unequal situation. Here again, any of the other psychodynamic factors described previously for such mothers may be operative. Of the three categories of mothers, these mothers have generally been the most dedicated ones during the earliest years of their children's lives and have thereby developed the strongest and healthiest psychological bonds with them.

The *children* in this category also develop their own scenarios, again with the slight prodding of the mother. Here the children's primary motive is to strengthen the mother's position in the custody dispute in order to maintain the stronger healthy psychological bond that they have with their mothers. These are the children who are most likely to be ambivalent about visitation and are most free to express affection for their fathers, even in their mothers' presence.

CONCLUDING COMMENTS

One could argue that the programming described above for mothers and fathers is extremely common in the divorce situation. One could argue, also, that children in the divorce situation invariably exhibit loyalty conflicts and may play one parent against the other. I myself have certainly described this phenomenon in previous publications (Gardner, 1976, 1977, 1991b, 1991c). I cannot deny this. However, in the parental alienation syndrome the child is *obsessed* with resentment above and beyond what might be expected in the usual divorce. It is the extent and depth of the alienation that differentiates the parental alienation syndrome from the mild alienation that is engendered in many divorces. In addition, there are other factors operative in producing the parental alienation syndrome that are not present in the common type of divorce programming—the most important of which are the *presence of custody litigation* and the threat of disruption of a strong parent-child (usually mother-child) bond.

Lawyers and judges often ask examiners involved in custody evaluations whether a particular child has or has not been "brainwashed." Frequently, under cross-examination, they will request a yes or no answer. Under these circumstances I generally respond, "I cannot answer yes or no." To answer simply yes, I would only be providing a partially correct response and this would be a disservice to the programming mother. The yes-or-no response does not give me the opportunity to describe the more complex factors, especially those originating within the child as well as the environmental situation.

Examiners are sometimes asked, "With which parent does the child have a psychological bond?" Again, I usually refuse to answer this question. If I am given an opportunity to elaborate, I state that there is rarely a situation in which a child has a psychological bond with one parent and not with the other. Generally, the child has psychological bonds with *both* parents. What one really wants to know in custody evaluations is which is the parent with whom the child has the *stronger and/or healthier* psychological bond. And, if a stepparent is under consideration, one wants to know about the strength and nature of the psychological bond with the stepparent, as compared with each of the natural parents. The psychological bond consideration will be discussed in greater detail in subsequent chapters.

I have sometimes been asked about whether or not there is an age limit beyond which children will not develop a parental alienation syndrome. I have always been dubious about age cutoff points and prefer to view things as being points along a continuum. As mentioned, I believe that the younger the child, the greater the suggestibility, the greater the need for ingratiation with adult authority, and the greater the likelihood the child will become a participant in the parental alienation syndrome *folie à deux*. Furthermore, the younger the child, the greater will be the dependency of that child on the primary parent and the greater will be the likelihood that the child will provide his (her) own contributions to the disorder. But what about the upper age limit? My views (once again) may come as a surprise to the reader: there is none. I believe that adult children of divorced parents may not be immune. Of course, one does not see here the full-blown picture, but one may see manifestations of the syndrome nevertheless. The psychological bonds that we form with our parents in infancy remain strong in most families, especially when there is ongoing contact between parents and children during the adult years. Such bonds are stronger with mothers than fathers, and such bonds continue no matter how independent and old we become. Even when we are old ourselves and even when our parents are long deceased, we still maintain these bonds in our psychic structure. When people talk about their deceased parents, one will often see evidence for the continuation of this bond, which only dies when we die. I believe, however, that in those situations in which a person is cut off entirely—for many years—from a parent, the bond may indeed disintegrate to the zero level. For such adults there may be no parental alienation syndrome when their parents divorce.

As might be expected, the adult children usually, and often reflexively, side with the mother. Although they are old enough to understand what has gone on and they may have even sat down with the divorcing parents and heard them out, and although there may have been absolutely no programming on the part of either parent, the adult children tend to gravitate toward the mother's side and see her as the one who was abandoned, victimized, or otherwise maltreated. They will often deny evidence to the contrary and provide elaborate rationalizations in support of the mother's position. Although these do not have the fantastic and absurd quality one sees in young children, the adult children's arguments in support of the mother are not free from distortion and exaggeration. Once again, the fathers feel impotent and victimized. Although the loss of the children is no longer a factor, a sense of alienation still prevails.

FOUR
DIAGNOSTIC CONSIDERATIONS FOR THE MENTAL HEALTH PROFESSIONAL

INTRODUCTORY COMMENTS

An evaluation of a family embroiled in a child custody dispute is quite complex. *Family Evaluation in Child Custody Mediation, Arbitration, and Litigation* (Gardner, 1989a), in which I discuss in detail the techniques I utilize for such evaluations, is quite lengthy (670 pages), and the reader who is serious about doing such evaluations does well to refer to that text. Here I will focus on certain aspects of that evaluation that are particularly pertinent to ascertaining whether or not a parental alienation syndrome is present. The examiner must keep in mind that all children of divorce will exhibit loyalty conflicts, will play one parent against the other, and exhibit other symptoms that can be directly traced to the parental conflict. The parental alienation syndrome, however, should be viewed as one subcategory of children's divorce psychopathology, namely, a disorder that arises in the context of a child custody dispute, and such disputes certainly are not necessarily a part of the divorce dispute. Moreover, in this subcategory of divorce dispute psychopathology there is a special kind of *folie-à-deux* relationship in which a parent is programming the child against the other and the child contributes his (her) own

157

contributions to the scenario of deprecation. The material presented in Chapter Three should provide the examiner with good guidelines for what to look for in order to make the diagnosis. In this chapter I focus primarily on technical issues; issues related to the structuring of the evaluative process. Examiners who follow these guidelines are more likely to elicit the kinds of information that will enable them to determine whether the disorder is present.

STRUCTURE OF THE EVALUATION

Readers who are familiar with my work know well how stringent I am with regard to my requirement that I do everything possible to serve as an impartial examiner, rather than as an advocate, in child custody litigation. And this requirement is particularly applicable when one is evaluating for the presence of a parental alienation syndrome. When one says, "Mother and father are litigating for custody of the children," one is making reference to three people involved (in one way or another) in the conflict. The examiner who does not evaluate all three people is likely to be seriously compromised with regard to obtaining an optimum amount of pertinent information. Furthermore, when one says, "The mother is programming the children against the father," one is also talking about three people involved in a particular kind of interaction. Again, it is crucial that all three parties be interviewed if one is to get an accurate assessment of what is really going on, especially with regard to whether or not a parental alienation syndrome is present.

In order to achieve this goal I refuse to accept an invitation to do such an evaluation until every reasonable step has been taken to have me appointed by the court as its impartial examiner. The reader should note here that I do not simply accept an informal invitation, loosely arrived at by the parties, to conduct an evaluation. Rather, I require that I be ordered by the court to conduct such an evaluation and be viewed by the court as its representative. This is not only important when conducting all child custody evaluations, but is even more important when conducting an evaluation for the presence of the parental alienation syndrome.

First, examiners who are foolish enough to conduct an evaluation as a result of a loose agreement between the parties will predictably find themselves serving as an advocate of the side whose position they support and will be viewed as a nonexistent person by the party who is not supported. That side is likely to conveniently forget the previous verbal agreement, even to the point of denying that it ever took place. A court order in which the examiner's role as impartial examiner is clearly spelled out protects against this inevitable deterioration of the verbal contract. Furthermore, a court order requiring the participation of all members of the family lessens the likelihood of obstructionism, lack of cooperation, and manipulation of the examiner—maneuvers that are typically utilized by programming parents.

Before interviewing anyone, I require both parents to sign a document that outlines in detail the provisions that I require to be satisfied before agreeing to conduct a child custody evaluation (Addendum). I only agree to embark upon the evaluation after receiving signed copies of this document from *both* parents, as well as a copy of the court order specifically mentioning my name as the court's appointee and specifically directing me to conduct a child custody evaluation. Stated therein there may be other requests of the court, such as enlisting my opinion on whether or not the child has been abused or what visitation program I might recommend. As can be seen from that document, I do not automatically refuse to involve myself if the other parent refuses to participate. I am willing to conduct the evaluation if the reluctant party is ordered by the court to participate, above the party's protestations. This is a common procedure in some jurisdictions in which each party is permitted to bring in its own adversary mental health evaluator, but each evaluator is ordered by the court to interview both parents. I do not approve of this arrangement, especially because it places the visiting parent in a very vulnerable position—especially if the mental health examiner is committed to supporting the position of the inviting party at the outset. I routinely make it quite clear to the visitor that I made no promises of support beforehand to the initially inviting party, and that I will implement the same procedures utilized when I am serving as a court-appointed impartial examiner. I inform both parties, as well, that on a number of occasions I have actually testified in court on behalf of the visitor. And these are not empty promises. My guess would be that in about 20 percent of cases, I concluded that I could not support with conviction the parent who initially enlisted my services, but favored the parent who refused initially to involve me as an impartial examiner and only reluctantly participated in the evaluation.

If the second proposed arrangement, as well, is not realized because the court still refuses to order the reluctant party to be interviewed by me, I will not automatically remove myself from the case. Rather, I am willing to interview the inviting party, review materials, and then make a decision regarding whether or not I can support with conviction the inviting party's position. If I choose to do so, I come to court, again recognized as that party's advocate. However, I state clearly at the outset (both in my report and in my testimony) that I have made every reasonable attempt to serve as a court-appointed impartial examiner, to evaluate both sides, and that such efforts were thwarted. Attached to my report is the written documentation of these efforts. (In fact, I require such written documentation before agreeing to serve as the advocate of the inviting party.)

Even at this point, before the documents have been signed and before either party has been seen, I may have already obtained some information useful in making the parental alienation syndrome diagnosis. Typically, the programming parent (here again more commonly the mother, and so I will refer to her as the programmer) is very reluctant to engage the services of an impartial examiner, mine or anyone else's. Rather, she will fight vigorously to prevent such an appointment. I believe this relates to her recognition, at some level, that she is being deceitful. She recognizes that an adversary evaluator—especially one who does not see her husband—is less likely to "smoke out the truth." A history of such reluctance then provides support for the diagnosis. However, as is obvious, this is only one small bit of datum among dozens and it by no means "clinches the diagnosis."

My experience has been that judges vary with regard to their receptivity to ordering reluctant parties to participate in custody evaluations with impartials. Some will do so with impunity and others will never do so. Those in the latter category, I believe, are making a serious error. Their refusal results in a parade of mental health advocates, each of whom is supporting one of the parents, and none of whom is likely to evaluate both parents. These tend to cancel one another out and may not provide the court with the vital information that can only be derived from joint interviews and the other investigative techniques that can be utilized by the impartial examiner.

Another advantage of the court order is that it provides examiners with powers that they would not otherwise have. This is especially important when conducting evaluations for the presence of the parental alienation syndrome because of the recalcitrance and lack of cooperation by the programming parent. The court order enables the examiner to require people to "fall into line" and cooperate. If they do not, the examiner can make it known that the court will be advised of the obstructionism, and this cannot but compromise that parent's position in the subsequent litigation. Evaluators who are comfortable with taking an authoritarian role are more likely to be successful when conducting such evaluations. Evaluators who take a more laid-back approach to their evaluations, who tend to be passive in the data collection process, are not as likely to obtain the information necessary if one is to make the diagnosis.

As mentioned in detail elsewhere (Gardner, 1989a), examiners who work with parents who are litigating over child custody must have a "thick skin" and be able to tolerate frustrations that examiners in other areas are not subjected to as predictably. I have had situations in which both attorneys, both clients, and the judge are all in agreement that I be appointed the impartial examiner. However, I have then been informed that the mother, although willing to participate (sometimes with her arm being twisted), has informed everyone that she absolutely refuses to be in the same room with her husband. This is presented as a nonnegotiable proviso. In response I inform the parties that they should not consider me a candidate for such an evaluation because I will thereby be deprived of my most valuable source of information, namely, the joint interview. Any examiner who agrees to conduct the evaluation with that omission is like a surgeon who agrees to operate on a patient without using a scalpel. People generally do not impose such restrictions and provisos with other physicians; somehow, they feel comfortable imposing them in their relationships with psychiatrists. When the patient starts dictating the diagnostic procedures and the tests to be utilized, the diagnostic process is likely to suffer considerably. I have never submitted to this restriction, and I cannot imagine myself doing so.

On a few occasions, however, I have been told that the mother is in fear of her physical well-being and refuses to go into the room with the father because she anticipates that she will be physically assaulted, even in the context of a joint interview with the examiner. Although I am aware that there are certainly husbands who beat their wives, I consider it highly unlikely that such abuse will take place in my office, under my very nose—especially when I am the court-appointed impartial examiner and can directly relate my observations to the judge. Most often, this is part of the programming process in which the mother is trying to convince me (before she even sees me) that her husband is dangerous. In such situations I may agree to see the mother alone first, hear her out, and then make a decision regarding whether or not I think there is sufficient danger to preclude my conducting joint interviews. I may see the husband alone, as well, if I decide that information from him is necessary to obtain to make my decision about the danger of the joint interviews. In such situations, I let it be known that I am not committing myself to the evaluation beyond these first interviews. Then, if I conclude that the danger to the mother is so negligible, for all practical purposes nonexistent, then the mother has to decide whether she is going to participate. If she removes herself, then I at least am not placed in the position of conducting a compromised evaluation. To date I have never had the experience that, following these individual interviews, I have concluded that separate interviews are indeed warranted because of the dangers to the mother. Rather, after these initial interviews I have been successful in conducting the joint interviews because the mother's fears have either been assuaged or she has come to recognize that the manipulation just won't work.

In some situations like this I have told the mother that she can bring along a third party, even a private policeman, who can accompany her to the office, sit in the waiting room, or even join her in all joint sessions if that will make her more comfortable. (I advise her that I will encourage the husband to allow this.) Interestingly, at no point has this invitation ever been accepted. On occasion, I have told the mother that she can bring along a friend to sit in the waiting room and "protect her" if she anticipates that she will be assaulted either before or after the interview. Again, what usually happens is that the protecting party will be present at one or two visits (outside the consultation room) and then will no longer be seen. In short, the whole scenario of danger tends to fizzle out when it no longer serves the purpose of manipulating this examiner into believing that the joint interviews will be dangerous. Last, it is important for the reader to appreciate that I am talking here about families in which a parental alienation syndrome is being evaluated and not families in which there has been genuine abuse. When there *is* genuine abuse, then such private interviews may be warranted; but then we are not talking about an evaluation for the presence of the parental alienation syndrome. The mothers I am talking about here have not been subjected to genuine abuse, and their claims that there is such a danger is at some point on the continuum between fabrication and delusion. We see here yet another important distinction between the parental alienation syndrome (where the abuse is fantasized by both the parent and child) and situations in which there is genuine abuse (and there is no fantasy operative).

My purpose in this section has been to comment briefly on some preliminary considerations before agreeing to conduct an evaluation for the presence of a parental alienation syndrome. In

my book on child custody evaluations (Gardner, 1989a), I describe in great detail the exact procedures I utilize when conducting a child custody evaluation, the kind of evaluation in
which a parental alienation syndrome can be most predictably
evaluated.

THE STRONGER HEALTHY PSYCHOLOGICAL
BOND AND "GRANDMA'S CRITERIA"

Mention has been made in Chapter Three of the parent-child
psychological bond and its relevance to the development of the
parental alienation syndrome. Not only is this concept crucial to
the understanding of the disorder, but its determination is vital,
as well, to considerations of primary parental placement (the
home in which the children shall live primarily) and other legal
rulings (such as visitation). Furthermore, it is central to the
guidelines for custody determination that I will be elaborating
upon in subsequent chapters. I have not yet, in this volume, been
more specific with regard to exactly what I mean when I use the
term *psychological bond*. Accordingly, I will try to provide here a
more accurate definition of this term, but the reader should
recognize that the concept does not lend itself well to a very
rigorous definition or objective measurement.

I use this term to refer to the psychological bonding that a
parent has with a child. Obviously, this cannot be measured
directly in any objective way by any known procedure. One must
get a sense of its strength via relatively peripheral observations. If
one could get a computer printout of all the thoughts and feelings
involving the child that each parent has over a specific period,
one might then be able to count the number of such psychic
events that related to the child. And if one could do this, as well,
with regard to the child's thoughts and feelings that relate to
either of the parents, one might then have some objective
measurement of this bonding. However, this would be merely a
quantitative figure. One would also have to have a *qualitative*
measure related to the content of these thoughts and feelings,
especially with regard to where they fall on the continuum

between benevolence and malevolence. Obviously, we have no such instrument and so we must resort to less objective measurements of this bonding.

In each of the sections below in which I focus on the interview structure I recommend for each of the parties, I will address myself to procedures for obtaining information about this bonding. I focus here on the general concept of such assessment, which I refer to as "grandma's criteria," for determining the strength of this bond. These are the parent-child experiences that grandma would have considered to be manifestations of parental capacity if her ghost were free to roam the house and then report her findings to the examiner. Most grandmas do not have Ph.D.s in child psychology or the equivalent advanced training and therefore have not been contaminated by the presumably more sophisticated and sensitive criteria that we professionals pride ourselves on utilizing. Grandma would focus on the parental behaviors that indicate affection, behaviors that manifest themselves throughout the course of the day (and night at times). These are the solid, commonplace events of the day, events that are often experienced together between parent and child and are the building blocks of the parent-child bond. Her criteria would also utilize willingness to inconvenience oneself and even sacrifice for the sake of the children. In the subsequent sections I will be more specific about these details. By the end of this chapter I hope that the reader will have a better understanding of what I mean when I refer to this somewhat nebulous concept of the psychological bond.

THE INITIAL INTERVIEW

The aforementioned insistence by the mother to see me alone, rather than in joint interview with her husband, is relatively uncommon. Most often, I see both parents together at the outset. I do not see the children during this initial interview because it is generally devoted to basic administrative issues related to the aforementioned provisions document as well as to the details of the ways in which I will conduct the evaluation. The interview usually lasts two hours, one-and-a-half hours of which is spent on these administrative and financial details. I do, generally, have about a half hour in which I can start to collect substantive data.

Pertinent to the question of whether a parental alienation syndrome is present, I will ask about the reasons for the separation. Here I may obtain information from the mother about the husband's alleged maltreatment of the children, especially her quotations from them regarding his maltreatment. I will also obtain from the husband his version of what is going on. From both I may obtain information similar to that which is described in Chapter Three and may, in the first interview, already have an inkling of the diagnosis.

I may in this interview, if time permits, obtain information about who the primary caretaker was during each child's infancy period. This is important information to obtain because the parent who was the primary caretaker during the infancy period is the one who is more likely to have developed the stronger bond with the children. Starting with birth, I may delineate the amount of time each parent spent with the child during successive time frames of the child's early life. However, I also want to know whether it was a healthy or unhealthy bond, and I may obtain such information in this early interview. Sometimes, this information is not easily acquired during the first interview because of the numerous transitions and fluctuations in child care. Or there may be vast differences of opinion regarding who was primarily with the child at various points in the children's growth and development. I may then have to reserve the more detailed inquiry for the subsequent joint sessions with both parents together again.

I am particularly interested in learning at this point when the symptoms of the possible parental alienation syndrome began. This is an extremely important area of inquiry. As mentioned, the parental alienation syndrome generally begins *after* the child becomes aware of the fact that a custody dispute is taking place. It is very much a disorder that is a derivative of such a dispute. It is then that the children are likely to begin creating their scenarios of denigration and exclusion. Of course, a parent can start to "work over" a child before the child becomes aware of the dispute and induce thereby early manifestations of the syndrome. In such cases the symptoms in the child are likely to be less formidable. In either case, the examiner does well to learn from each parent when he (she) first became aware that a child custody dispute was going to take place. If possible, one does well to attempt to pinpoint the day in which this became known to each of the parents. That day can serve as a point of departure for one's inquiries regarding the development of this disorder. This is an important diagnostic consideration and I cannot emphasize this point strongly enough.

One wants to begin, in this initial interview, to look for evidences of fabrication—separate from their presence in the parental alienation syndrome programming. There is an ancient legal principle: *Falsus in uno, falsus in omnibus* (Latin: False in one, false in all). Essentially this means that a person who lies in one area is also likely to lie in other areas. Because we are dealing here with courtroom litigation, examiners should be particularly interested in lies that they have directly observed themselves in the course of their interviews (either to themselves directly or to others involved in the evaluation) so that these can be testified to directly in the courtroom without resorting to hearsay (which may not be admissible). The more lies one directly observes oneself, the greater the likelihood that fabrication is present and the greater the likelihood a parental alienation syndrome is being programmed into the child. Accordingly, throughout the course of the evaluation (and starting with the initial interview), the examiner should be alerted to the presence of such deceits, regardless of which parent manifests them. This may be a tricky criterion, at times, because all parents typically lie in custody evaluations. The stakes are high and considerations of honesty may be secondary to considerations of "winning." Accordingly, the examiner does well to try to determine which parent lies more or which parent lies more easily and egregiously.

Also in this interview one should observe the nature of the relationship between the parents. Obviously, it is rarely going to be an amicable one, especially when a parental alienation syndrome is present. A mother who is inducing the disorder in her children is likely to be continually scornful of her husband, even when the children are not present. The presence of this ongoing state of contempt is one of the diagnostic signs. If it takes place in front of the examiner, it is likely to be taking place in the presence of the children. I generally make the assumption that behavior I observe in my office is not initiated for my benefit in my office, but is just one manifestation of an ongoing pattern. This is a good assumption for therapists to make, whether it be for evaluating for the presence of a parental alienation syndrome or for any other psychiatric examination. (It is even a valuable point to keep in mind in the process of treatment of children and adults.)

THE INDIVIDUAL INTERVIEWS
WITH THE PARENTS

Again there are many things that I could say about these interviews. I will focus here only on those items of particular interest when ascertaining whether a parental alienation syndrome is present. When obtaining each parent's background information, it is important to inquire into the nature of the bonding that each parent had with his (her) own parents (that is, the children's grandparents) during their own childhood. We tend to implement with our children the same patterns utilized by our own parents with us in childhood, our professions and resolutions to the contrary notwithstanding. Even though we may recognize such patterns to have caused us significant psychological distress, they still tend to be transmitted down to the next generation, often in ways beyond our control. These patterns of parenting become deeply embedded in our psychic structures and are not likely to be altered significantly, even though we may gain significant insight (through therapy or otherwise) about the pathological types of parenting that we may have been exposed to in childhood. Clearly, this inquiry has relevance to the parent-child bonding under consideration here.

During these individual interviews, one has more time to get an exact chronology of the time each parent spent with the children during the early years of life. Discrepancies here can be discussed in the subsequent joint interviews. In many families a surrogate parent may have been significantly involved in the children's upbringing, e.g., housekeepers, neighbors, grandparents, and day-care center personnel. Not only should the time frames of such care be delineated, but the quality of the care provided as well.

One wants to ascertain the emotional attitudes the parent exhibits toward the partner when alone, as opposed to those that were exhibited in the previous joint interview. All of us modify our behavior somewhat in accordance with who is in the room with us. A mother who is inducing a parental alienation syndrome in her children is likely to persist in her disdain of her husband, even when he is not present. It is another argument for the presence of the disorder. If, during the course of this interview, one learns that she is invoking a series of vengeful maneuvers, then this argues for the presence of the parental alienation syndrome in that the disorder is, in part, a derivative of such vengeance. She might be trying to wreak vengeance on him in the financial realm or, on occasion, by accusing him of sex abuse in order to bring about his social, financial, and professional destruction and even incarceration. As mentioned, a sex-abuse accusation can be a derivative of a parental alienation syndrome, especially when the initial maneuvers do not prove as effective as the programmer would have hoped.

One should also be alerted to the presence of paranoia. As mentioned, maternal paranoia is often present in the severe type of parental alienation syndrome as well as in the sex-abuse allegations that may be derived from it. In some cases, there were no manifestations of paranoia prior to the onset of the divorce dispute and the stresses of the divorce precipitated paranoid decompensation. In such cases the mother's paranoia may simply be confined to the alleged persecutions of the husband. In other cases, the individual exhibited manifestations of paranoia prior to the divorce and the stresses of the divorce intensified them. In such cases the husband may only be one of many individuals about whom the wife is paranoid. In the latter situation, it is likely that the examiner will soon become incorporated into the paranoid system. Clues of this may be obtained with comments such as, " I know my husband is paying you to testify for him." Although there may be truth to this in that husbands, more often than wives, are paying most if not all of my bills, it is not true regarding what he is paying me for. He is paying me for my time and for my services. I am not receiving the money with the understanding that I will support his position and that if I did not promise to do so he would not be paying me. This stretching of the truth may be a paranoid sign. It may be extended to the wife's belief that her husband is paying off the judge or that he has special influence with him.

The nature of the accusations against the husband may have a paranoid flavor. The wife may accuse him of having damaged her car, when there is absolutely no evidence that he was the perpetrator. She may accuse him of repeated marital infidelities, when there is little if any indication of such. In more severe cases of paranoia she may accuse him of controlling her mind or attempting to poison her food, either by himself or through agents. These manifestations are relatively easy to detect; the more subtle ones may not be. The examiner does well to appreciate that paranoia is more widespread than is generally recognized, and it is especially likely to be a contributing factor in severe cases of parental alienation syndrome. When assessing for paranoia, one does well to inquire about the therapy that each parent and the children may be involved in. Mention has already been made of therapists (almost invariably women) who will treat mothers without ever attempting to interview the fathers. They join in and support the mother's denigration of the father, whether or not it is paranoid. These therapists too, as mentioned, are sometimes paranoid themselves.

In the individual interviews one should get more information about grandma's criteria, that is, the details of the day-to-day interactions with each of the parents — starting in the morning and ending late at night. One should not only get this information about the parent being interviewed, but that parent's rendition of what goes on throughout the course of the day with the other parent. Also, one wants to get information about each parent's involvement in school (both curricular and extracurricular) as well as the children's other extradomestic activities. (I will be providing more substantive details about this inquiry in the section devoted to the interviews with the children.)

In this interview examiners should carefully write down exactly what the children have been telling each of the parents. When the parents provide details of the children's deprecations, one does well to listen for the presence of phrases that may have been borrowed from the programming parent. Of course, it is only when the children are interviewed, and it is only when the examiner has the opportunity to listen to their litanies directly, that one will be in the best position to know whether the "borrowed scenario" factor is operative. Here one does well to write down precisely what the children are saying and then to compare these statements with those the children profess directly to the examiner. In the course of the individual interviews with each of the parents, one wants to learn about exclusionary maneuvers, especially those that may have antedated the separation. As mentioned, there is often a history of such maneuvers that has predisposed the alienating parent to contribute toward the development of a parental alienation syndrome in the children.

INDIVIDUAL INTERVIEWS WITH THE CHILDREN

First, each of the children should be seen separately. There are examiners who will interview all the children together and entirely omit separate interviews. This is a grave error. It contributes to the cross-fertilization process that invariably is present in children with parental alienation syndrome. Generally, one of the children (usually the older) will transmit the disorder down to the younger ones. It spreads very much like an infectious disease. Seeing the children together exposes the younger and more suggestible ones to the litanies of the older ones and directly provides them with the opportunity to learn new scenarios. Seeing them separately also provides the examiner with the opportunity to assess for the presence of discrepancies about important events to which all the children have presumably been witness. For example, if the children are angry at their mother because their father is alleged to have beaten her, one wants to get detailed information about what each child actually saw, when they saw it, and where. The greater the number of discrepancies, the greater the likelihood this allegation is false and part of a parental alienation syndrome. Obviously, seeing them together lessens the likelihood of obtaining such comparative data.

It is important for examiners to appreciate that the child is likely to provide that particular scenario that is consistent with the position of the parent who is in the waiting room. And this is especially the case when a parental alienation syndrome is present. Unfortunately, judges seem to be unaware of this important phenomenon. I have not yet seen one case in which the judge has conducted an interview with the child when the mother brings him (her) and compares it to an interview when the father brings the youngster. Accordingly, the examiner does well to interview the children when they are brought by the father and to repeat the interview when they are brought by the mother. And, as will be mentioned below, there will be a third interview in which both parents are present in the waiting room while the child is being seen alone. For obvious logistical purposes, this third experience is most conveniently done during the same visit as the family interview.

When asking the child direct questions regarding the parents, my aim is to obtain concrete descriptions of parental assets and liabilities, without asking specifically which parent the child would prefer to live with. Of course, the information obtained relates directly to parental bonding. Again, I start with general questions before proceeding to more specific ones. I might say, "Tell me about your mother" or "Describe your father." These are far better than, "Do you love your mother?" "Does your father love you?" or "Who loves you more, your mother or your father?" The latter group of questions will provide yes or no answers or one-word responses. The former will generally elicit descriptive, concrete information that is much more valuable for the purposes of the custody evaluation. One should get the child to try to provide elaborations and examples in order to elicit as much information as possible. One can then proceed with statements like, "Everybody is a mixture of both good and bad parts. No one is perfect. Tell me some *good* things about your mother." When one has exhausted this line of inquiry, the evaluator should go on with questions like, "As I have said before, everybody is a mixture of both good and bad parts. Tell me some *bad* things about your mother. What things about your mother don't you like?" A similar inquiry should then be pursued with regard to the father. Another question in this category might be, "What's the best thing you can say about your mother (father)?" "What's the worst thing you can say about your mother (father)?" One must try to get the child to elaborate upon simple, short answers in order to get as much mileage as possible out of the responses.

The evaluator must appreciate that what the child may consider a "bad" quality on a parent's part may indeed be an asset. For example, if a child says, "My father makes me turn off the television set in order to go to sleep," and if the sleep time is a reasonable one, this "criticism" is actually an asset and a point of credit to the father in the evaluation. Obviously, the father who lets a child stay up late watching television (especially on school nights) is compromising his paternal capacity.

Children, especially older ones, are likely to provide important information relevant to grandma's criteria for assessing the strength of the psychological bond. One can lead the child along here and ask specific questions; however, it is preferable to start with a general statement like, "I'd like you to tell me about your *whole* day, from the time you get up in the morning until the time you go to bed at night. I'd like you to start at the time that you get up in the morning and continue to tell me about what happens each day, and who you do the various things with, until you go to sleep at night." After the child has given this description, the evaluator should then proceed with more specific questions. The spontaneous responses, unsolicited by the evaluator, are the more meaningful. For example, in answer to the original general question one boy stated, "Before my daddy left the house, he always used to wake me up because my mommy slept late. He always gave me my breakfast because my mommy didn't want to be waked up in the morning. Now that he's gone my mommy sometimes forgets and I've been late for school a lot." Such a response obviously gives much meaningful information about this mother's maternal capacity. However, if such specifics were not provided in the child's general description, the examiner might ask questions like, "Do you wake up yourself in the morning or does someone wake you up?" "Who wakes you up?" "Who helps you get dressed?" The main purpose of these questions is to learn about the child's depth of involvement with each of the parents and each parent's commitment to the child's rearing.

The questions should cover the wide variety of experiences the child has during the day. Because the question will usually be posed at a time when the parents are already separated, the examiner should direct the child to the time *prior* to the parents' separation. It is important to appreciate that a parent who was involved in a particular activity is not automatically the one who was most desirous of such involvement. It may be that the other parent was reasonably not available. For example, if a father's job required him to leave the home before the children awakened, it is unreasonable to consider this a manifestation of weak bonding if the mother was always the one to wake up the children. In fact, in the traditional household, the mother will generally have been the one involved in many of the daily activities with the child. Therefore, it may always have been the mother, for example, who greeted the children when they returned home from school, simply because the father was, with rare exception, working. At the same time the father may have been working diligently to provide for the family's food, clothing, shelter, and other necessities of life.

It is in the evening, however, when both parents are generally available that one can make the best comparisons. One might ask about the homework situation: "When both of your parents were living together, who helped you with your homework at night?" One should determine not only which parent was more involved, but the children's feelings about the *nature* of the parent's involvement. One wants to know whether doing homework with the child was accomplished smoothly or whether there were typically power struggles, tears, fits, tantrums, threats, and other manifestations of a poor relationship. One child stated, "I never wanted my father to help me with my homework because he was always screaming at me. My mother had much more patience." Such a statement may indeed be true. However, it also may be false and the kind of distortion one sees in a parental alienation syndrome. It is only through multiple interviews and obtaining data from various parties that the examiner is in a position to find out what really went on. In the inquiry one tries to determine whether a parent is doing the homework in an overprotective way, i.e., doing it *for* the child, rather than *helping* the child learn *how* to do the homework. Besides homework, one wants to inquire about recreational activities with the child during the evening. The working father who rarely spends such evening time with the child is generally compromised. Similarly, if such a father spends every evening with paperwork, this is also a parental deficiency, even though his work or business may have warranted such extra obligations. The healthy father knows his priorities with regard to profession vs. child rearing.

A particularly useful area to explore is the bedtime scene. The strongly involved parent enjoys sitting with the child at bedtime and reading bedtime stories. I am not claiming that *all* healthy parents will invariably *love* reading these stories endlessly, only that they will derive enough pleasure from them to make it a common activity. In addition, the examiner should try to determine whether the parent enjoys cuddling with the child while engaged in reading such stories. The strongly involved parent will also enjoy lying down with the child and cuddling as well. There are parents who will refrain from such cuddling practices (especially with opposite-sexed children) because they have been told that this will give the child an "Oedipus complex." The parent who follows such advice (often given by professionals such as psychiatrists and psychologists) may be complying with it to rationalize noninvolvement. The healthy parent does not take such advice seriously, the qualifications of the "expert" notwithstanding. The wise parent appreciates the difference between occasional cuddling and sexual stimulation—the former need not be associated with the latter.

The examiner should also inquire about what happens when the child wakes up in the middle of the night with nightmares. Who comes to console the child? To which parent does the child turn for reassurance and consolation? Which parent has traditionally taken the child to the emergency room or the doctor's office when there have been nighttime accidents and/or other medical emergencies? One should inquire about typical weekends prior to the separation. What was done? Who initiated recreational activities with the children? Who went with them? Who was more patient with the children while engaged in these activities? Who was willing to go to more inconvenience in order to involve the children in them?

One should inquire about each parent's involvement with the child's friends. Does the parent welcome the friends or view them as a nuisance? Is the parent more worried about the potential damage and mess that invariably accompany such visits than the value of the friendships? Is the parent more concerned with the status of the grass than the importance of children's playing in the backyard? Inquiries about each parent's sense of commitment to the child's involvement with members of the extended family can also provide information about bonding.

A most important area of inquiry relates to each parent's participation in school activities, both curricular and extracurricular. In fact, I would consider this an area of highest priority in ascertaining the strength of the psychological bond between the parent and child. Parents who are strongly bonded not only recognize the importance of these activities to children but derive enormous pleasure from such involvement. Healthy parents experience enormous pride and joy when observing a child at a school recital, playing in the school orchestra, dancing, singing, or otherwise involved in these performances. The parent who is bored by them, falls asleep during them, or finds excuses for routinely not attending is not only depriving the child of important input, but being deprived himself (herself) of one of the great joys of child rearing. Similarly, the strongly bonded parent considers parent-teacher meetings of the highest priority, will attend to every detail, and discuss these at great length with the children. Weakly bonded parents may find such meetings a boring or an absolute chore. Most often, the children will be able to detail each parent's involvement in these activities.

During these interviews with the children one does well to note carefully the exact wording of the children's scenarios of denigration, with special attention to the presence of borrowed scenario phraseology. Their presence is an important argument for the existence of a parental alienation syndrome. One wants to focus especially on terms that are way beyond the child's developmental level, that is, terms that are more traditionally utilized by much older children and even adults. Sometimes a child will make a statement such as, "My mother told me that my father touched my 'gina when he gave me a bath." Comments like these help "clinch the diagnosis."

Mention has been made of the typical lack of cooperation of parents who are inducing a parental alienation syndrome in their children. Failure to cooperate in the appointment of an impartial examiner is just one manifestation of such lack of cooperation. As mentioned, the main purpose of the recalcitrance is to lessen the likelihood that the examiner will learn the truth. Such obstructionism may become particularly apparent in situations when the mother brings the child for an individual interview. Although asked to sit in the waiting room, one may find her eavesdropping at the door. This is not only an example of deceit (and therefore should be placed on one's list of the deceits manifested by each parent) but a manifestation of a lack of cooperation. Sometimes the parent wants to be sure that the child is providing the "right" answers and wants to have the opportunity to correct any distortions that may have crept into the child's litany. In such cases the mother may have informed the child, prior to the interview, that she will be standing right outside the door. The purpose here is to ensure that the child will present her view of the situation. I recall one mother who repeatedly ignored my requests that she remain in the waiting room and not stand outside my door. I finally said to her, "It's important for you to know that I have made careful notes of your failure to cooperate during this evaluation. I will bring these to the attention of the judge, who I'm sure will take this into consideration when making his decision." I had no power to control this woman's body with regard to where it was placed. I did, however, have the power to confront her with the aforementioned threat, which, interestingly, did not prove effective in that she still continued to eavesdrop.

Readers who are familiar with my work know that I take a dim view of the use of projective tests in the evaluation of children embroiled in child custody disputes. Although I use these instruments significantly in my diagnostic work in other areas and in my therapeutic endeavors, I use them only to a limited degree in child custody litigation because they do not hold up well in court. Whatever interpretation the examiner may give to a patient's projection, there is likely to be another examiner who will provide a different one. All these tend to cancel one another out and are often a waste of time and money. Examiners do far better to testify about exact statements made by the child and exact observations that were made in the consultation room. These are less likely to be refuted in courtroom examination.

JOINT INTERVIEWS

As mentioned, the joint interviews provide the most important information in a child custody dispute, whether or not the focus is on the presence of a parental alienation syndrome. Even in the waiting room one can often obtain information that would not be obtained by individual interviews, no matter how astute and sensitive the examiner. This is a situation in which the whole is indeed greater than the sum of its parts. When I use the term *joint interviews*, I refer to any combination of family members whether it be two, three, four, or more.

Mother and Child Together

Of course, as is true for all other interviews, there are many things that I do in this interview. Of pertinence to my focus on the parental alienation syndrome, I am particularly interested in the disparagement of the father that the child provides when with the mother. These are to be compared to those provided when the child is seen alone with the father (see below). Typically, when a parental alienation syndrome is present, these are stated vociferously and directly when the mother is present; this is less likely to be the case in the joint interview with the father. I am particularly interested in the child's checking with the mother to make sure that the rendition is correct. Such checking is an important sign of the parental alienation syndrome. At times this is done overtly, at other times via side glances. The mother herself may be providing both verbal and nonverbal input in order to ensure that the correct scenarios are being provided. Not uncommonly, and this is especially the case for younger children, the child may ask the parent directly for help in recall. Obviously, this is strong confirmation for the presence of the parental alienation syndrome.

Father and Child Together

Children suffering with a parental alienation syndrome are often very reluctant to involve themselves in this particular interview. The most common reason for this is embarrassment. They recognize that their scenarios of denigration are false and they anticipate (justifiably) that their father will be very angry at them. In severe cases, such fear and embarrassment is often not present, so angry and vociferous are these children. In the mild and moderate types of parental alienation syndrome, the child may deny completely any professions of anger toward the father. Or, if they are admitted, they will be watered down significantly.

Fathers here have the opportunity to directly confront their children with regard to the allegations. I often say that the best person to cross-examine an accuser is the accused person himself (herself). These fathers are in a far better position than even the most astute and sensitive examiner to "smoke out the truth." There are some examiners who believe that such an interview must necessarily be psychologically traumatic to the child. I am not denying that this interview may be stressful at times. However, one must weigh this disadvantage against the more formidable disadvantages of the examiner's being deprived of this important information. Considering the fact that the child's whole future life may be at stake, because the custody decision rests on a proper evaluation, I consider this a small price to pay for the enormous benefits to be derived from joint interviews of this kind. And, when it is being conducted as part of a sex-abuse allegation, the consequences to the father may be even more formidable. Here, we are comparing the transient stress of the child's interview against the lifelong stress of the father associated with the destruction of his family, career, and even years of incarceration. I certainly consider myself a person who is respectful of children. However, one must not take this concept too far or interpret it too narrowly. One must also consider respect for the needs of other family members involved in the evaluation.

On a few occasions, when the father and the child have entered the consultation room, the child has whispered in my ear that he (she) wishes to see me "privately." Attempts to get the child to speak to me and the father regarding the reasons for this request have generally proved futile. Accordingly, I will ask the father to leave the room but make it clear to the child that this compliance with the request is only temporary. Once alone, the child generally will provide me with the litany of inconsequential and frivolous complaints and add that he (she) is in morbid terror of revealing them to the father lest he (she) suffer the most dire retaliatory consequences. This is only a thin rationalization. The father generally already knows what these complaints are usually, and he is not the kind of a person who would inflict draconian punishment on the child for making these statements. What is really going on is that the child is embarrassed over the duplicity and expects, justifiably, the father to be angry about their being professed. Such children are generally not aware that the very act of requesting the "private interview," and then providing inconsequential reasons for the request, is one of the symptoms of the parental alienation syndrome. Accordingly, even before the joint interview has begun, the child has provided corroborative data that contribute to the validation of the diagnosis. Furthermore, when the child's comments in the private interview are compared with what is said with the mother present, and/or with the father present, all provide confirmation for the diagnosis.

The Family Interview

The family interview generally provides important information when one is assessing the presence of a parental alienation syndrome. And one may start to gather the information in the waiting room, even before the family members enter the consultation room. Most often, they seat themselves in accordance with the family subsystems created by the disorder. Typically, the father is seated alone and the mother and children opposite him, as far away from him as possible. The children may be staring into space, as if the father did not exist. Or, if they are talking, they are huddling among themselves and with the mother. And the same arrangement will automatically take place when the family enters the consultation room. If, in the course of the interview, the mother is asked to leave (and I reserve my right to utilize any combination that may prove useful), the children may then warm up and relate more comfortably with the father. In severe cases, they cannot even allow themselves to relax their guard when the mother is not present (especially if she is only in the waiting room).

It is in the family interview, especially, that the children's loyalty conflicts are most likely to manifest themselves. It may be the first time in many months (and even years) that the family has sat down together for a discussion of the allegations. Such an interview becomes especially anxiety-provoking for children suffering with a parental alienation syndrome because they recognize, at the outset, that whatever they say will result in difficulties with one of the parents. If they profess directly the scenarios being programmed by their mother, they risk further alienation by their father. If, however, in an attempt to preserve whatever relationship is left with the father, they modify the allegations in a downward direction, they risk the alienation of the mother. Some children deal with this problem by saying nothing at all and claiming total forgetfulness. It is as if that part of the brain devoted to the storage of these particular memories has been obliterated. Again, I recognize that such confrontations may be stressful and I generally do not insist upon long interviews under these circumstances. A few minutes of observation of this phenomenon is enough to provide me with important information regarding whether or not a parental alienation syndrome is present.

For the child who is more comfortable expressing the scenarios of deprecation directly to the father (more commonly the case), one sees another phenomenon. Specifically, in any discussion in which the mother and father have a difference of opinion, the child reflexly supports the mother's position. This is done with a minimum of information and may often involve the child's supporting a preposterous and even impossible position by the mother. In many cases, throughout the whole course of the evaluation, the child has not once sided with the father. This is an important diagnostic sign for the presence of a parental alienation syndrome. When it is pointed out to these children that they are invariably accepting their mother's renditions on disputed issues, they typically will state, "My mother never lies to me, but my father's a big liar. He's always lying." When I then ask for specific examples of the father's lying, I generally receive none or am given such vague statements as, "I just know he lies. I can't give you any examples right now. I just know he's lying now when he says that this (the issue under consideration) didn't happen."

INTERVIEWING HOUSEKEEPERS

Housekeepers can be an extremely important source of information when evaluating families in child custody disputes. Unfortunately, they are rarely utilized in such evaluations. They live in the home, are party to what goes on, and may spend more of their time thinking about what happens between their employers than many other aspects of their lives. They are often surrogate parents and play an important role in the children's growth and development. If this is the case, the question as to whether or not they will be involved in the children's upbringing is an important one, and the kind of people they are—especially with regard to their maternal capacity—is an important consideration for the examiner.

Unfortunately, housekeepers may be very hesitant to divulge information about the families, fearing they may compromise their relationship with one or both employers. In addition, they may never have been in a psychiatrist's (or other mental health professional's) office before. They may be petrified over the prospect of seeing such an evaluator, may believe that their minds can be read, or they may just be generally fearful of authority. It is likely that the examiner has become an even more formidable figure to them because of what they have heard regarding the evaluation. Also, they may appreciate that each parent has placed the examiner in a position of great power. Furthermore, they may fear that if they criticize the parent with whom they are currently employed (usually the mother), they may compromise their position, even to the point of being fired. Accordingly, the examiner who interviews housekeepers may have formidable resistances to their being completely candid. Elsewhere (Gardner, 1989a), I provide guidelines for interviewing housekeepers. Of significance here is their ability to provide information regarding grandma's criteria. They live in the home for significant periods, observe the day-to-day activities between the children and the parents, and can provide a significant amount of "inside information"— especially with regard to time spent in child care and factors operative in the development of the parent-child psychological bond. Evaluators who are successful in obviating or circumventing their resistances may obtain valuable information indeed.

Concluding Comments
(Added for the Second Printing—1995)

It is important to appreciate that the sole determinant as to whether a parental alienation syndrome is categorized as mild, moderate, or severe is its manifestations in the *child*. In the vast majority of custody disputes, each parent attempts to induce in the child loyalty toward him (her). When such indoctrinations become strong, parental-alienation-syndrome symptoms may develop in the child. The stronger the programming, the greater the likelihood the child will create contributions of his (her) own, which then justify a diagnosis of parental alienation syndrome. It is important to appreciate that there are parents who might be designated as moderate and even severe programmers who are unsuccessful in producing significant symptoms of alienation in the child. For example, a mother in the severe category of indoctrinator might only be successful in bringing about a mild parental alienation syndrome in her child and may even fail entirely to induce such symptoms.

In some cases her failure is related to the fact that the bonding with the father has been so strong that her indoctrinations are unsuccessful in overriding the strong paternal ties the child has developed. Another factor is the age of the child: the younger the child, the greater the gullibility, and the greater the likelihood the programmer will be successful. Intelligence is also a factor, brighter children being less likely to believe some of the patently absurd criticisms. Personality factors are also operative. Some children are independent thinkers and extremely self-sufficient. They are far less likely to believe preposterous indoctrinations than children who are more passive characterologically.

FIVE
EVIDENCE-GATHERING PROCEDURES FOR LEGAL PROFESSIONALS

INTRODUCTION

Legal professionals do well to appreciate the drawbacks of the adversary system as a method for finding out "the truth." The system is based on the assumption that the best way to learn the truth is for each party to present its position before an impartial body (judge, tribunal, or jury) in such a manner that only its position is presented. Presumably, the presentation of the conflicting positions places the impartial body in the best position for ascertaining the truth. The disadvantages and the self-imposed handicaps that the participants place upon themselves with such a method is elaborated upon in other sections of this book. It is crucial that legal professionals be aware of these drawbacks when operating within the system.

It is important for legal professionals to have a thorough understanding of the parental alienation syndrome if they are to adequately serve families in which the children exhibit manifestations of this disorder. Without such understanding legal professionals are seriously compromised in their ability to make judicious recommendations for their clients that will truly serve the best interests of children. These professionals should under-

185

stand, as well, how recent changes in the criteria for determining custodial preference have played a role in bringing about the parental alienation syndrome. They should recognize that the legal system, especially because of its commitment to the adversarial approach to dispute resolution, has served as a powerful weapon for parents who wish to wreak vengeance on or exclude a hated spouse. Unfortunately, there are many legal professionals who are committed so deeply to adversarial proceedings that they do not allow themselves to even give consideration to the aforementioned issues. I believe that the clients of these people have suffered inordinately and unnecessarily from their failure to recognize these points.

The three roles that legal professionals traditionally play in child custody disputes with regard to the parental alienation syndrome are those of lawyers, judges, and guardians ad litem. I will focus in this chapter on evidence-gathering considerations ("diagnosis," as we refer to it in the mental health professions) and in Chapter Seven on legal implementation of court rulings that can be useful in dealing with these families ("treatment," as we call it in the mental health professions).

LAWYERS

Lawyers who work with these families may be presented with an important ethical dilemma. Attorneys who are of the persuasion that it is their ethical obligation to support zealously their client's position—even though they may have no conviction for it—may be satisfying the dictates of their profession, but they may not be providing what is in the best interests of children with parental alienation syndrome. This is especially the case if the client is the programmer. It is here that ignorance of the parental alienation syndrome can free such an attorney of any conflict. Such attorneys blindly accept as valid the statements made by their clients and the children and then forge ahead without guilt of internal conflict. Those, however, who are sensitive to what is going on, who are familiar with the parental alienation syndrome, may recognize that they are doing the children (whom they are indirectly representing) a terrible disservice. And this is especially the case if the client falls into the severe category of parental alienation syndrome. Lawyers with defects in their sense of morality do not have this dilemma. Those who recognize that what they are doing when supporting such a client may wreak havoc with the children (their professions of hatred of the despised parent notwithstanding) are the ones who will truly have this dilemma.

I believe that the most ethical thing for such a lawyer to do is not to agree to represent a programming client and explain exactly the reasons for the rejection. Unfortunately, my experience has been that there are few attorneys who are so noble. They readily recognize that if they reject the client there will be another attorney down the hall who will be happy to accept the client and take his (her) money. It is my hope that law schools will ultimately become truly moral when they educate students. This morality, however, will shake the adversary system at its very foundations because, in many cases, it is basically immoral. An important reason for the perpetuation of the system is that it predictably earns much more money for lawyers than most other forms of dispute resolution, such as mediation and arbitration. It is my hope that my publications may play a role (admittedly small) in revising this system and bringing to the attention of all concerned its intrinsic weaknesses and, in many situations, depravity.

Because my advice to attorneys who represent a programming parent is to remove themselves from the case, there is obviously little else I have to say to such attorneys. Thus, the brevity of this section. With regard to attorneys who represent the vilified parent, everything must be done to bring to the attention of the court information about the parental alienation syndrome. My experiences have been varied in this regard. Some judges have been receptive to reading material about it, even though it is not formally introduced as evidence during the course of the litigation. And, when introduced formally, judges have varied with regard to their receptivity to reading the material. Such attorneys, also, do well to bring in mental health professionals who are familiar with the disorder and provide them with the opportunity to educate the court during the course of their testimony. I myself have been brought in on many cases in which my primary role has been to testify—at the hypothetical level—on the parental alienation syndrome.

All attorneys, regardless of their morality or immorality, commitment or lack of commitment to adversarial proceedings, do well to appreciate the value of the court-appointed impartial examiner as opposed to an advocate. If one finds that one's client is very resistant to the idea of appointing an impartial examiner, then one should be suspicious about the presence of a parental alienation syndrome. It is crucial that the examiner (whether impartial or adversarial) be someone who is familiar with the parental alienation syndrome. To be avoided are examiners who consider themselves particularly sympathetic to children, especially with regard to their professed wishes and statements. All examiners, of course, claim sympathy with children. There are, however, examiners who equate sympathy with children with compliance with their requests, no matter how outlandish or preposterous. More recently, a new phenomenon has emerged. I am referring to the emergence of people who refer to themselves as "child advocates." These individuals come from various disciplines, and my experience has been that they are less competent than the average mental health professional. Waving the banner that they are going to protect the rights of children, they accept as gospel the most inane dribblings of their child clients. This can be particularly dangerous when we are dealing with the parental alienation syndrome.

If an attorney is unsuccessful in getting his (her) adversary to join in asking the court to appoint an impartial examiner, approved by both parties, then the attorney's second step should be to ask the court to order the reluctant side to participate in such an evaluation. Often this is most easily accomplished if both sides are given the opportunity for such parallel evaluations. I deplore this practice, especially because it places the reluctant party in "enemy territory," and the individual who is ordered to be interviewed by the adversarial evaluator cannot but have the feeling that everything said will be held against him (her). When I am appointed in this manner (a position I accept only after attempts to serve as an impartial examiner have proven futile), I make it clear at the outset (even at the point when my name is first proposed to the judge) that I will conduct the evaluation as if I were indeed an impartial examiner and might even come to court and testify on behalf of the originally reluctant party. (And this has happened in about 20 percent of the cases in which I was so engaged.)

Lawyers who are genuinely interested in engaging evaluators who will truly serve the best interests of children will do everything possible to be sure that the evaluator truly works in this way. However, attorneys should recognize that most evaluators will profess commitment to this position. Direct knowledge of a case or cases in which this turned out to be the situation, i.e., the evaluator actually went to court and testified on behalf of the initially reluctant party, can be reassuring that such a profession will actually be translated into practice. If the evaluator's policy is that the initiator must assume the obligation for payment for all services rendered *including* the preparation of the final report and courtroom testimony—regardless of whether the payer's position is supported—then the likelihood that this examiner is being truly impartial is strong. This policy lessens the likelihood that the evaluation will be compromised by the fear that one will not be paid if one testifies against the original inviting party. All these are spelled out in my provisions document (Addendum). If the examiner has a similar contract, then the attorney is in a better position to determine whether or not the aforementioned practice will be instituted.

Attorneys must recognize that they, like anyone else who only hears one side of the story directly, is likely to get fooled by one's client. Although the majority of attorneys will claim that they are astute enough not to be so fooled, this has not been my experience. I myself, in many cases, have been "taken in" over a period of many sessions, and I cannot say that I have never been duped. Because the adversary system does not provide what I consider to be reliable access to the other side (the other side's attorney's letters including selective material and the usual hyperbole are not sources of accurate information about the other side), the attorney must appreciate that the risk for being so duped is high. And this is especially the case if one is swept up in the fray and the proceedings degenerate into a situation in which "the name of the game is to win."

JUDGES

Introduction

Judges are increasingly interviewing children in the course of adversary litigation. In fact, in many states they are required to do so. As mentioned, my comments in this chapter regarding evidence gathering were brief as they pertain to lawyers because adversarial lawyers, in my opinion, are not in a good position to collect evidence in an optimum way due to their entrenchment in an adversary track. In contrast, judges are in a far better position to gather accurate evidence, not only in the courtroom but, more importantly, in their interviews with the child. However, even for judges, there are drawbacks and weaknesses intrinsic to the system within which they are operating. They still do not have the flexibility that mental health professionals have, especially with regard to in-depth interviews with the parents and joint interviews, which, as mentioned, are the most powerful source of information for finding out whether a parental alienation syndrome is present.

Intrinsic Weaknesses of
In-camera Interviews with Children

It is important for judges to appreciate that when they interview children in their chambers, they are doing so under significantly compromised circumstances. An appreciation of these compromises can help the judge to place in proper perspective the information so gained.

Absence of Family Interviews The court's primary question in custody/visitation litigation is this: Who would be a better parent for this *child* to live with, the *mother* or the *father?* This question is not likely to be answered reasonably unless data is collected from *all three parties* referred to in the question. Furthermore, the data-collection process will also be compromised if the parties are seen only alone and not in various combinations. Restricting oneself to interviewing only the child compromises the process significantly because it deprives the evaluator of obtaining data in joint interviews, which are often the most valuable part of the data-collection process. Family interviews also enable the interviewer to "smoke out" fabrications in which children traditionally say to each parent what they think that parent wants to hear at the moment. In custody evaluations, observing the parent-child relationship is the best source of information for ascertaining parental bonding, especially with regard to the question of to which parent the child is more strongly bonded. The present structure of courtroom proceedings generally precludes the court's conducting such parent-child and family interviews. It must rely on the information provided by mental health professionals who conduct these interviews elsewhere.

Absence of Multiple Interviews Another compromise relates to the fact that interviewees, regardless of age and circumstances, are more likely to reveal themselves to known parties than to strangers. And the longer and deeper the relationship with the interviewer, the greater the likelihood the interviewee will provide disclosures. The greater the "dangers" of such revelations, the greater the likelihood that valid information will not be obtained in a short period. And the younger the interviewee, the greater the likelihood that these impediments to obtaining valid data will be operative. Interviewing a child only once does not provide the court with the opportunity to develop the kind of relationship in which such divulgences are likely to be obtained. Judges rarely have the time for multiple interviews, the optimum setting for the kinds of revelations the court is hoping to obtain. Furthermore, the child generally enters the judge's chambers in a state of fear. Although *in-camera* interviews are less frightening than courtroom testimony, the judge is still held in awesome regard by most children and many adults. The fear element is likely to compromise significantly the data-gathering process, and this cannot but make the information so obtained of dubious value. Furthermore, without a series of interviews the judge is not in a position to observe the changes in the child's comments and preferences that are often observed in the course of intensive custody evaluations.

The Child's Cognitive Immaturity The child's level of cognitive development is also an important consideration. Obviously, the younger the child, the less meaningful his (her) verbalizations will be. In the individual interview, the court does not have the opportunity to get "translations" from a parent who better understands the child's terminology, innuendoes, and gestures. Accordingly, judges must appreciate that the person they are interviewing is the one of the three who is least capable cognitively to provide data pertinent to the court's considerations.

The Child's Impaired Capacity to Differentiate Fact from Fantasy The younger the child, the less the capability of differentiating fact from fantasy—a differentiation to which courts pay particular attention. Many states now require that the interviewer establish—preferably early in the interview—whether the child can differentiate fact from fantasy, or put more simply, "the truth from a lie." The child is usually asked some very simple questions that allegedly assess such differentiation, e.g., "If I said this table [in reality brown] was green, would that be the truth or a lie?" "If I said your dress [in reality yellow] was yellow, would that be the truth or a lie?" In a recent case in Florida in which I was involved, during the *in-camera* interview (with the attorneys present), Florida law required that the interviewers first establish whether the four-year-old girl being questioned could "tell the difference between the truth and a lie." This interview was conducted with a child whose parents were litigating over her custody and whose father was brought up on charges of sexual abuse because the child had told her mother that "Daddy killed Santa Claus. . . Daddy killed the Easter bunny. . .and Daddy put his finger in my 'gina.'" No one sent an expedition to the North Pole to see if Santa Claus was dead. No one sent out a search party to find out whether the body of the dead Easter bunny could be produced. But a horde of individuals descended upon this family in reaction to the third allegation. A four- year-old child who believes in the existence of Santa Claus and the Easter bunny *ipso facto* does not differentiate well between fact and fantasy. On the basis of the child's responses here, all interviewers agreed that she could do so for the purpose of the sexual-abuse investigation and the inquiry continued. (Incidentally, I concluded that the third allegation was as much a fantasy as the first two.) What is not taken into consideration in the course of such inquiry is that answering these simple questions does not preclude the development of fantasies and delusions in other areas, sex abuse being only one example. Nor does the ability to differentiate between the truth and the lie preclude conscious and deliberate lying, even for four-year-olds. These are naive and misguided laws indeed, their ostensible benevolence notwithstanding.

Learning "The Truth" from a Child The purpose of the judge's interview is to find out what the truth is with regard to various aspects of the custody dispute. The assumption is made that the child knows what the truth is regarding a variety of issues pertinent to the allegation. All of us distort the truth somewhat in accordance with what our wishes and fears are, and children even more so. Time generally blurs one's recollection of reality, and the younger the person is when an event occurs, the greater the likelihood time will distort its recollection. By the time a judge sees a child in chambers, the events under consideration may have taken place months or even years previously. It is reasonable to say that for many of the events being discussed with the judge, many children no longer know the truth and could not tell what the truth was, no matter how honest they were trying to be. The truth-versus-lie problem is further compounded when one considers that the child may indeed know the truth regarding certain simple issues, but not regarding more complex ones. For example, judges are traditionally instructed to ascertain whether or not the child knows the truth by asking simple questions designed to assess the child's capacity to make the differentiation. For example, while pointing to something red, the child is told, "This is green. Is that the truth or a lie?" Most children by the age of three, or the latest four, will be able to say that the judge is lying. Similarly, the judge may point to the picture of a girl and say, "This is a girl. Is this a truth or a lie?" Again, most children, even in this low age range, will have little difficulty responding that the judge's statement is true. However, if the child is asked to talk about whether Mother sleeps too much, Father drinks too much, or Mother spends too much time on the telephone and is thereby neglectful, the child is not likely to provide reasonable answers even though the child is being honest.

Next, the ability to differentiate the truth from a lie should by no means lead the judge to conclude that the child will not lie. Criminals (many of whom are sociopathic) know quite well the difference between a truth and a lie, yet they have little if any hesitation lying (even under oath on the witness stand). Courts are well aware of this. Yet, an assumption is sometimes made that merely because a child is able to differentiate between the truth and a lie that the child will therefore be honest. Some jurisdictions require the judge to proceed from the phase of establishing the child's ability to differentiate between the truth and a lie to extracting from the child the promise that he (she) will tell the truth. This, I presume, is the equivalent of the oath an adult takes just prior to testimony.

I have never been involved in a custody case in which I have not directly observed libel, slander, and perjury. (Incidentally, I have also never observed anyone's being prosecuted for these crimes.) Courts certainly recognize that adults will most often and almost predictably lie in the context of custody disputes (after all, the stakes are high and this is indeed a situation in which most parents take the position that the end justifies the means).

However, the assumption is somehow made that a child is more likely to adhere to the promise. For the court to believe this is an expression of naiveté.

Many studies demonstrate well how prone children are to lying. In fact, most people familiar with children consider it normal. Goleman (1988) describes a study conducted by Lewis, a psychiatrist at Rutgers Medical School. Goleman quotes Lewis: "In one study we just completed with three-year-olds, we set up an attractive toy behind the child's back and tell him not to look at it while we leave the room." (The children are then observed through a one-way mirror.) "About ten percent don't peek while we're gone. Of the rest, a third will admit they peeked, a third will lie and say that they did not peek, and a third will refuse to say." With regard to the third group, Lewis states, "Those who won't answer seem to represent a transition group, who are in the process of learning to lie, but don't do it well yet. They are visibly the most nervous. Those who say they did not look—who lie— looked the most relaxed. They've learned to lie well. There seems to be a certain relief in knowing how to lie effectively." It is reasonable to conclude that the third who refuse to say (who invoke the Fifth Amendment or will not respond until consultation with their attorneys) are also consciously aware of the fact that they are lying. In short, two-thirds of the children in this group lie and are consciously aware that they are lying.

As far back as 1911, Varendock demonstrated this point quite well in two classroom experiments. In one, a group of 19 seven-year-olds were asked a question about a familiar teacher, namely, "What color is Mr. B.'s beard? " Sixteen replied that his beard was black and two did not provide an answer. The facts were that Mr. B. had no beard. In another classroom experiment, 27 eight-year-olds listened to a male teacher talk to the class for five minutes, after which he left. Each child was then asked, "In which hand did Mr. A. hold his hat?" Seventeen children said that he held his hat in the right hand. Four stated that it was the left hand. And three stated that he wore no hat. The fact was that he wore no hat. In short, the vast majority of these seven- and eight-year-old children lied. The explanation is not difficult to understand.

Children do not enter the world with knowledge of what is going on within it. They are constantly making speculations and guesses in an attempt to understand elements in their environment. They are constantly looking to adult authority to correct their distortions. When the seven-year-olds were asked, "What color is Mr. B.'s beard?" it is reasonable to assume that many of their thought processes went along these lines: "I don't remember his having a beard. However, the question indicates that he had a beard. So I must have forgotten. I'm always distorting the real world anyway. I don't want to look stupid to the questioner. Therefore I'll guess and I hope that I'll get the right answer. Black is the most common color for a beard, so I might as well guess black. I hope I'm right." I would speculate also that a similar line of reasoning went through the minds of those who guessed in which hand Mr. A. held his hat.

Children are constantly trying to ingratiate themselves to adults, especially to adults in authority like parents, teachers, and professionals such as physicians, lawyers, and judges. Like all of us, they want to be liked. If lying will serve this end, they are likely to do so. They also lie to avoid punishment. When caught fighting, the vast majority of children under nine or ten are going to claim that the other child started it. They lie also to make excuses for themselves; to rationalize inappropriate or unacceptable behavior. In divorce situations they predictably lie and say to each parent what that parent wants to hear, especially regarding criticisms of the other. This is the most common way they deal with the loyalty conflicts that emerge from divorce, especially from custody disputes. Children embroiled in a custody dispute know where their "bread is buttered." They know that if they express affection for parent B when with parent A, they may alienate parent A. In contrast, if they join in with parent A and provide criticisms of parent B (new or more ammunition), they will ingratiate themselves to parent A. And the same procedure is used with parent B. It is only in joint interviews that these maneuvers may be "smoked out" and the judge's failure to employ them deprives him (her) of an important source of information about what is "the truth."

Accordingly, when interviewing a child whose mother is outside the judge's chambers, the likelihood is that the child will select to tell the judge those things that will ingratiate him (her) to the mother, because of the possibility that she might hear the proceedings or the judge might tell her what has transpired. Similarly, the child will lie in favor of the father if he happens to be at close range (even though not in earshot). Considering all these factors the judge does well to make the assumption that many of the things the child says are lies, distortions, and fabrications. And this is especially the case when one is going to touch directly on such tender issues as which parent would be preferable for the child to live with.

It is important for judges to appreciate that by the time they interview the child in chambers, there probably have been numerous earlier interrogations extending over many months and even a few years. Under such circumstances, children may no longer have an accurate recollection of many past events and may no longer know which parent they actually want to live with. So mind boggling have been the interrogations with lawyers and mental health professionals, and so great is the need of children to ingratiate themselves to adult authority, that lying may have become a *modus vivendi*. Under these circumstances, many children operate on the principle that they will say whatever is most expeditious at that particular time, that which will ingratiate them to the person with whom they are speaking at that moment. The pattern has become so deeply ingrained that the bona fide preferences and opinions have long been suppressed and repressed from conscious awareness.

Technical Considerations

The Importance of Interviewing Children Individually   On a number of occasions I have come across situations in which judges have interviewed two and even three children at the same time. This is an error. Children should be interviewed one at a time. The judge does well to recognize that in a very high percentage of cases a younger child will mimic the statements of an older one. In a joint interview, then, one is basically getting the opinions of the older child. Even when the children are seen separately, this is likely to occur. However, when seen alone the younger child especially will not have the older one to provide clues and feed answers during the course of the interview.

The Issue of Who Brings the Child to the Judge's Interview The court also should recognize that the child's comments may be colored by individuals who are outside the judge's chambers during the course of the interview. Children embroiled in custody disputes suffer with terrible loyalty conflicts. They generally say to each parent that which will ingratiate them to that parent at that time, regardless of their true beliefs and regardless of the consequences of fabrications they may provide. This principle extends itself to the *in-camera* interview wherein the child is likely to support the parent who is close by. Moreover, the parent who brings the child and/or the parent who takes the child back home is also likely to have an influence on what is said in chambers. Furthermore, children have short memories. A father who brings the child to the court on Monday morning, after a weekend of fun activities, may very well be viewed as the preferable parent. And a mother who brings the child to court on Friday afternoon, after a difficult week in which the child was forced to do homework, chores, and was disciplined for normal childhood transgressions, is likely to be viewed with disfavor. Accordingly, the court should have both parents bring the child to the courthouse and both parents bring the child home or have a neutral third party accompany the child to the courthouse. But even under such circumstances the court does well to make inquiries regarding the aforementioned considerations of recent parental involvement.

The Issue of Confidentiality Many judges will tell children, at the beginning of their interviews with them, that what the children say will be held strictly confidential and that their parents will never learn what they have revealed. Unless the court can be 100 percent certain that this promise will be fulfilled, it is a risky one to make. Generally, this reassurance is given under circumstances in which a transcriber is recording every word. The transcripts of the interview are usually sent to the attorneys, who may or may not be instructed not to reveal their contents to the parents. It is but a short step to the child's learning that the judge has divulged the "secrets." Under these circumstances the child cannot but feel betrayed – especially by someone who is held in high esteem. It is yet another betrayal added to that of a parent's leaving home. Accordingly, I generally discourage courts from making such promises. Rather, judges should proceed without such a promise and hope that the child's need to communicate important issues will override the fear that the parents may learn of his (her) disclosures. If the child does ask about whether the divulgences will be revealed, the judge does well to tell the child that his (her) comments may be available to the parents or that the judge must be given the freedom to decide which information will be revealed and which will not. It is also important for judges to appreciate that such divulgences are not necessarily detrimental. They may provide useful information for the parent whose deficiencies have played a role in the child's selection. If the child is in therapy (with or without the parents, their separated status notwithstanding), these reasons for preference can serve as points of departure for psychotherapeutic interchange.

Introductory "Basic Statistical Data" Questions The court is advised to begin the interview by asking the child simple questions which he (she) can answer with ease and freedom from anxiety, e.g., name, address, age, telephone number, etc. Each time the child gets the "right" answer, initial tensions and anxieties are reduced and it becomes easier for the child to answer the more anxiety-provoking questions that will inevitably follow. Other questions in this category would include the child's grade level, name of school, teacher(s), and names and ages of people in the family network (mother, father, stepmother, stepfather, siblings, stepsiblings, half-siblings, etc.). In the course of getting information about the names of these individuals, some useful information might be obtained. For example, the child might state, "My stepfather's name is Bob. I like to call him 'Daddy' and my real father 'Dad,' but my real father would get very angry at me if he ever knew." The response here indicates that the child's father is placing inappropriate demands upon the child.

The judge does well to appreciate that the basic information one wants to obtain in the interview with the child relates to the manifestations of *parental* capacity, especially with regard to how one parent compares to the other. This is the basic data from which the court is going to make its decision. Similarly, the child's preference is also going to derive from this data. If the court approaches this from the top (so to speak) with questions like "Which parent do you want to live with?" or "Which parent do you prefer?" meaningful answers are not likely to be forthcoming because of the child's loyalty conflicts. However, as will be described in detail below, the court can obtain information about basic parenting behavior (from which the child's preference is derived) without necessarily inducing tension or anxiety. Furthermore, the child's reasoning processes from which the conclusion may be derived may be faulty. For example, a child may say, "I want to live with my father. He's really good to me. When I see him every weekend he lets me watch television as much as I want and I don't have to do my homework. My mother is mean. She makes me go to sleep early, makes me do homework, and doesn't let me watch as much television as I want." In short, the judge should get the raw data relating to parenting capacity and use his (her) own reasoning processes.

"Blank Screen" Questions   After the initial period in which the judge simply asks "name, rank, and serial number"-type questions, the court does well to proceed in accordance with the principle that the best and most revealing responses are those that the child provides spontaneously, willingly, and without the awareness that important material is being revealed. The best way to obtain such information is to allow the child to talk about anything and hope that in the context of such conversation important material will be provided. My experience has been that information related to parental capacity is usually provided in such free discussions without the necessity to ask specific questions that the child appreciates may yield information about parental preference. Most children are deeply involved with their parents and are therefore likely to talk about them in the course of their conversations.

Along these lines, it is important for judges to appreciate the psychoanalytic principle of the "blank screen." The best way to learn about what is going on in the person's mind is to allow the individual to free associate and talk as if his (her) thoughts and feelings are being projected on a blank screen, a screen that has no contaminations that might draw out a particular thought or fantasy. This is basically what is going on in the traditional psychoanalytic couch situation. The analyst sits behind the patient, unseen, and so few if any contaminating stimuli are brought to the attention of the patient, stimuli that might contaminate the free associations. The *Thematic Apperception Test* (TAT) (Murray, 1936), an instrument that is widely used by psychologists in the course of their diagnostic evaluations, demonstrates this principle quite well. The patient is presented with a series of pictures, each of which depicts a scene in which there are vaguely depicted figures involved in some vague activity. The individuals can be distinguished from one another regarding sex and approximate age, but nothing else specific is portrayed. In fact, the pictures are specially designed to be vague in order to approximate the blank screen phenomenon. The examinee is simply asked to tell a story about what is happening in the picture. One of the cards, however, is completely blank. This card is, at the same time, the most anxiety provoking and the most revealing. Because there are no stimuli on which to project fantasies, the individual may be a little anxious regarding what story to create. However, the complete absence of specific stimuli will result in the least contaminated kind of story, i.e., a story that will be most revealing of the innermost and truest processes operative in the mind of the storyteller.

The TAT is one of many *projective tests* used in psychology. The term *projective* refers to the process by which the examinee *projects* fantasies onto what is viewed as a blank screen. A good way to think about projective questions is to view them as a way of asking a person to select responses from a *universe* of possible answers. One does well to think of the total universe and so pose a question that the child is being asked to give a particular response that is self-selected from the universe of possible responses. This is the least contaminated response.

Although the aforementioned "name, rank, and serial number"-type questions have a potential contaminant, it is generally minuscule. Any disadvantages of possible contamination from such questions are more than compensated for by the relaxation the child experiences when getting the "right" answers. Following this period of decompression of tension, the judge should attempt to elicit information with open-ended questions that facilitate the creation of the psychoanalytic blank-screen situation. A few examples: "So how are you doing?" "What would you like to talk to me about today?" "So what's on your mind?" The principles to utilize, when following through with the child's answers, are these: Extract from what the child says the information that is likely to shed light on the custody dispute. Use that material as a handle and point of departure for further inquiry. Maintain the posture of the "ignorant interrogator" (ignorant meaning not-knowing, rather than stupid) and continually ask questions.

In the course of the interview, the judge does well to ask for specifics; generalizations rarely provide useful material. It is important to obtain clarifications that provide a visual image. When a boy, for example, says that his father is "mean," this may or may not be true. It is only by obtaining specific examples of the father's alleged meanness that the judge can determine with certainty whether the statement is valid. If the concrete, visualizable examples involve making the child do homework, turning off the television in order to go to sleep, or taking his clothes off the floor, the conclusions are very different from examples involving the father's humiliating and denigrating the child. I cannot emphasize this point strongly enough. All too often interviewers, even mental health professionals, will come to conclusions on the basis of abstract statements made by patients. These may have absolutely no validity. It is only with specific examples, especially examples that one can visualize in a concrete way, that one is in a position to determine whether or not a statement is valid.

At this phase of the interview it is an error to ask the child the question: "Why are you here?" This may be anxiety provoking and may result in the child's tightening up and not providing useful information. Information given in a state of fear and anxiety is not likely to be useful. The child generally knows why he (she) is there, and to "rub the child's nose in it" may be counterproductive. Even the question, "What did your mother (father) tell you about your visit with me today?" may be anxiety provoking.

A six-year-old girl, for example, in response to one of these open-ended questions might show the judge a doll. This is the "handle." This is the point of departure from which the judge might then be able to obtain important information. Rather than shying away, running out of the room, or remaining mute, the child is engaging the judge. At this point the judge might ask what the doll's name is. It would be an error for the judge to choose a name himself (herself) because that is a contaminant. Such a name is selected from the universe of possible names. It will pull the child down the track of specific associations and is likely to divert her from material that she might have otherwise expressed—material more likely to be relevant to the issues before the court. Most dolls have a name. The judge might then ask where the name came from. The child might give a seemingly innocuous response like "I made up the name myself." However, the judge should not stop there, but should then ask, "Where did you first hear about that name?" The child might then say, "My mommy thought it would be a good name for a doll." The response tells something about the child's relationship with the mother (and possibly about the father in comparison). Following this the judge might ask, "What is the doll doing?" or "I want to see how good you are at making up a story about your doll." Another example: a seven-year-old boy comes in with a model of a boat. When asked what he would like to talk about, he proudly shows the judge the boat he built and says, "I built this boat myself, but my daddy helped me. He's a carpenter. He knows a lot about building things." The sense of pride the child has when exhibiting the boat as well as his pride in his father is important information regarding parental preference.

If children are allowed to talk about anything they wish, although their comments may initially appear irrelevant to the court's purpose, there are times when useful information regarding parental capacity may be obtained. Such discussion might be introduced with questions such as "What would you like to talk about now?" and "So tell me something else." In response to such a question, a boy might start talking about his interest in baseball. In the context of his discussion he speaks with pride about his accomplishments in Little League and how proud he is that his father is one of the coaches. He expresses regret that the rules do not permit him to be on the team that his father is coaching. Or, a 14-year-old girl, again after professing to the judge that she does not want to state her parental preference, may start talking about the fact that she goes shopping with her mother, who is quite expert at selecting perfumes, lipstick, and make-up, and with whom she can discuss such personal matters as her period and her feelings about boys. Time does not generally permit the court to indulge itself to a significant degree in this kind of inquiry, but it does well to appreciate the potential value of such seemingly innocuous lines of inquiry and recognize that its investigations are compromised without such questioning.

Other useful statements at this point might be "Tell me something about your mother" and "Tell me something about your father." Similar areas of inquiry might relate to other significant figures such as stepparents and new ongoing relationships that the parents may have. The statement is general enough to allow for a universe of possible responses within the confines of talking about a particular person. Other general statements that can provide useful specific responses are "Tell me about the best thing that ever happened to you in your whole life" and "Tell me about the worst thing that ever happened to you in your whole life." Following general inquiries about each of the parents one can get a little more specific (yet still provide the opportunity for a universe of responses) with such statements as "No one is perfect. Everyone is a mixture of things that you like and things you don't like. I want you to tell me the things about your mother that you like and the things about her that you don't like." And then one goes on to ask for similar information about the father, other parental surrogates such as stepparents, and new ongoing relationships that the parents may have. One should also ask for information about the child's relationships with extended family members such as grandparents, aunts, uncles, and cousins. Although one wants to direct one's attention primarily to the parent-child relationship, the commitment and availability of extended family members should play a role in the court's decision.

Self-created Stories In the context of a self-created story, family events are likely to be depicted. Here the child will utilize the process of projection (similar to that used when creating stories around TAT cards). It is much easier for all people (children and adults as well) to talk about third parties, fantasy figures, and others than to talk directly about themselves— especially when the depicted events are guilt evoking or anxiety producing. The self-created story serves as a disguise, as a vehicle for expressing unacceptable thoughts and feelings without the child's consciously realizing that the forbidden material is being revealed. How the children in the child's story interact with the parental figures (often symbolized) may provide the judge with useful information about the child's own interactions with parents.

"Yes-No" and "True-False" Questions The court should avoid questions that could be answered by either yes or no. Of course, this is just the opposite of what is done in cross-examination, where the yes-no question has a deep-seated heritage. Although this form of inquiry may be useful in "nailing down the facts," I do not hold it in as high regard as my legal colleagues. When one asks a question that could be answered with either yes or no, one does not really know whether the response is valid. A quick answer of yes or no may be an easy way for the responder to "get off the hook" without providing a meaningful answer. Much more valid material is obtained with questions that elicit sentences and descriptions that are self-derived by the respondent. For example, if one asks a boy whether he loves his mother, one is likely to get a yes answer — even if she has been brought up on charges of physical abuse. Or, if a child says no, one still has very little information. However, if one asks questions like, "Tell me about your mother" or "I'd like you to tell me the things about your mother you like and the things about her that you don't like," the responses are likely to be far more revealing. A similar principle holds for true-false questions. There is little if any place for them in such interviews.

"When" Questions   The court does well to avoid questions relating to *time*. To ask children about *when* a particular event took place is not likely to produce meaningful data. The younger the children, the less appreciative they are of the passage of time and the less capable they are of pinpointing the exact time that a particular event occurred. Time questions only invite fantasized answers, which only compromise the data-collection process. The court should ask questions that begin with *what, where, who, and how.* These help "nail down" the facts. The court should get specific details about each item described. One wants the child to verbalize from concrete imagery that is being visualized.

"How Did You Feel . . .?" Questions   Most mental health professionals are very enthusiastic about the "How did you feel. . .?" question. This question, borrowed by presumably sophisticated laymen from the psychiatric inquiry, is supposed to help a person express feelings and thereby feel better. In recent years radio and television reporters have been using the question with the implication that learning about the interviewee's *feelings* about a particular event enriches our understanding of what has gone on. Questions from these public media interviewers usually go like this: "How did you feel when you learned that you lost the election?" "How did you feel when you first saw your son after his release from three years in a prisoner-of-war camp?" The correct answer to these and all similar questions is identical: "How do you think I felt, you idiot? Get out of here before I hit you." Unfortunately, most people are not free enough to express this on nationwide television and so provide either the obvious answer or formulate the response that they consider will be the most acceptable to the audience.

I cannot be too critical of lay people (including judges) for using this form of inquiry. They have been taught by "experts" in the field of psychiatry and psychology that it is a most valuable question. There is hardly a trainee in psychotherapy who is not repeatedly advised by supervisors to "get out the patient's feelings" and that a good way to do this is to ask, "How did that make you feel?" With rare exceptions, the question is absurd. People who know how they feel can only consider the question naive, simplistic, extraneous, or an affront. People who are so repressed that they indeed have no conscious awareness of their emotions are not likely to get in touch with their feelings by such a question. Rather, they are likely to respond with puzzlement, denial of feelings, rationalization, or what they think the interviewer wants to hear. Eight-year-old Sarah, for example, who is afraid to express the anger she feels over Gail's having broken her doll, is asked by her mother, "How did you feel when Gail broke your doll?" Mother would deal far better with Sarah's inhibitions by saying, "Even though you're not showing it, I know that deep down you're very angry at Gail. And I don't blame you. I'd be angry as well. Now what do you think you can do about this? If you don't do anything it might happen again." This comment not only communicates to the child that anger is the expected and socially acceptable response, but it structures the situation in such a way that it is clear to the child that she must effectively express her anger if she is to avoid a repetition of the situation that provoked it. Such structuring can be far more effective than merely encouraging a child (or anyone else) to *act* in a desired fashion. Accordingly, judges do well to stay away from "How did you feel. . .?" questions. Elsewhere (Gardner, 1973, 1986b, 1988)

I discuss in detail the techniques therapists should find useful for eliciting feelings from repressed patients, techniques that do not rely on this type of question.

"Grandma's Criteria" When providing examiners with guidelines for the kinds of questions to ask children involved in custody conflicts, I generally recommend that they use what I have referred to earlier in this book as "grandma's criteria." These are the parental manifestations that grandma's ghost would consider if it were free to roam the house and then report its findings to the court. If she is like most grandmas, she does not have an M.D. or Ph.D. and has very little formal so-called psychological sophistication. She would observe the children from the time they get up in the morning until they went to sleep, and sometimes even in the middle of the night. She would determine who wakes the children in the morning and who gives them breakfast and prepares them for school. Of course, if father's work requires him to leave so early that he cannot involve himself in these activities, this cannot be considered a deficiency on his part. This is similarly the case for spending lunch time with the children and being available after school. It is during the after-work hours, when both parents traditionally are home, that grandma would get her most useful information. She would want to observe who helps the children with their homework and if this is done smoothly or whether there are typically power struggles, tears, fits, tantrums, threats, impatience, and other manifestations of a poor parent-child relationship. She would observe disciplinary measures, especially whether they are humane, consistent and benevolently administered. She would pay close attention to the bedtime scene. Are bedtime stories read? Are the children lulled into sleep in a loving manner or is it typically a time of threats and punishments? What happens during the night may also be important. Who gets up to change the diapers? To whom does the child turn for consolation after nightmares? Which parent has traditionally taken the child to the emergency room or the doctor's office when there have been evening and nighttime accidents and/or other medical emergencies? She would be particularly concerned with which parent is willing to make the most sacrifices on the child's behalf.

The judge does well to get information in these areas by discussing directly with the child the day's events, from arising in the morning to going to sleep at night. The judge should be particularly interested in which adult is involved with the child in these various activities and the exact nature of the involvement. Again, the best way to get information about this is to ask general questions. One might start with: "Tell me about your day from the time you get up in the morning to the time you go to sleep at night." One can narrow down on specifics (again with questions posed in a general way to allow a universe of possible responses), for example: "Tell me what happens at breakfast time." "What happens in your house after supper?" "What does your mother do when you're bad?" "What does your father do when you're bad?" One is especially concerned here with how humane the disciplinary and punitive measures are. One can ask about each parent's receptivity to friends visiting the home and the parental tolerance of the noise, rambunctiousness, horseplay, and minor damage that inevitably occurs when children are in the home. Do the child's friends like each of the parents? Is the parent receptive to the child visiting other homes? Although none of the aforementioned questions are in the category of "Who do you want to live with, your mother or your father?" they clearly provide useful information for the court in making its decision regarding parental preference.

Parental Involvement with School Activities Another important area of inquiry is parental attendance at school activities, both curricular and extracurricular. The court should find out who attends teacher conferences and what the parental reactions are to report cards. Is there pride and/or emotional reaction or complete indifference? Who attends various plays, concerts, recitals, and open-school activities? These are among the most valuable criteria for ascertaining parental capacity and the nature

of the parent-child relationship. The parent who is not appreciative of the importance of their involvement in these activities is
exhibiting a significant deficiency.

Inquiries into Visitation   The court may learn much by
asking the child about the details of the visitations: what was
done, who was present, where did they go, etc. When inquiring
about visitation it is useful to use open-ended statements and
questions such as "Tell me about your visits with your father." It
is not a good idea to ask questions that can be answered by yes or
no, questions such as "Did you have a good time when you
visited with your father?" Whether the child answers yes or no,
one does not really know if the child had a good time. The child
may have had a terrible time and "gets off the hook" with regard
to criticizing the father by simply saying yes. The child may
recognize, as well, that the "no" answer will be responded to with
further inquiry, and this the child may wish to avoid. When
asking a general question about visitation, a child might describe
a father who brings along every transient date, thereby fulfilling
two obligations at the same time. Some children describe a
visiting parent dropping them off at the home of third parties
(aunts, grandparents, and an assortment of other individuals)
and then pursuing their own interests. Many children describe
the visiting parent's cross-examination of them to extract information that might prove useful in litigation. Other children go on
a round of circuses, rodeos, zoos, etc. Although such overindul-
gence may serve the purpose of guilt assuagement or rivalry with
the custodial parent, in excess it is a parental deficit. In the course
of conversations about visitation one is likely to get information
about whether the visiting parent involves the child with homework and includes in the visitation time activities that are somewhat less pleasurable, but possibly more important. One should
try to ascertain whether the child spends long periods propped
up in front of a television set.
    Sometimes, in the course of a description of a visitation, the
child provides very valuable information without realizing the
importance of what is being revealed. For example, a child whose

father was litigating for a significant reduction in support payments, because of professed inability to pay, told me when discussing visitation with his father, "We had a great day last Sunday. We went out with my dad's new girlfriend Barbara. Boy is she great. And you should see the ring my dad gave her. It's the biggest diamond I ever saw in my whole life. Jane said it cost $5,000." This is the best kind of information to obtain. It is given naively and openly, without the child realizing its implications for the judge's considerations. Another response in this category, told by a child who was simply asked by his father how his week went: "I had a great week. Since Mike's moved into the house everything's been great. Because he doesn't work, he's home when I come home from school. He used to be a basketball player and he's taught me a lot of good shots." This occurred at a time when this boy's mother was asking for an increase in her support and alimony allotments.

In the course of a description of a visitation one might learn that the father is unreceptive to allowing friends in the home because of the potential damage. Committed parents recognize and tolerate these potential "dangers" of having friends in the home and appreciate that good relationships with friends are more important than intact furniture. Or, the child may not be allowed to run in the backyard because it interferes with the growth of the grass. Of course, primary custodial parents can also exhibit these manifestations of parental deficit and the examiner must be alerted to their presence in either home.

Inquiry into the Reasons for the Divorce   Sometimes questions about the reasons for the divorce may provide the court with useful information. The child's description of the nature of the marital conflict may include information about parental capacity. For example: "My mother couldn't stand my father's drinking anymore. I used to help her find the bottles that he would hide." "My mom and dad used to fight a lot about punishments. My father believes in hitting, my mother doesn't. My father said that his father used to hit him when he was a boy and that it's the best way to get children to listen." Another child stated, "My father was always angry at my mother because she was coming home very late at night. Sometimes she would stay out almost all night. She would never tell him where she was going. She put us to bed and think we were sleeping and then she'd go out. She'd lie to us and tell us that she was staying home, but we knew that she wouldn't."

Closing the Interview   Before closing the interview the court does well to ask the child a final question such as, "Is there anything else you'd like to talk to me about that you haven't mentioned." This is an open-ended question that will give the child the opportunity for final input. The court does well to make the assumption that the child wants to get across information to the judge about parental preference and needs to do it in such a way as to not feel disloyal. Such a question – just before parting ways – gives the child the opportunity for final input. The child might say, "My brother wants to live with my mother. He says he loves her very much. My brother and I are very good friends and I would never want to live in a different place." Or the child may say, "Don't make me live with someone who doesn't like to play baseball." I am not claiming that the wisdom of these final comments, or the criteria upon which parental preference is based, are necessarily the most judicious. I am only stating that the opportunity to provide a final comment before parting may provide the judge with useful information not previously mentioned.

Last, judges who, at the beginning of the interview, feel the need (sometimes by legislative mandate) to extract a promise from the child to tell the truth may end the interview by asking if the child has told the truth. Like the request for the initial oath, the request for this final vow is not useful. No matter how psychopathic the child, no matter how many lies may have been perpetrated upon the court, it is extremely unlikely that the child will confess to having provided the court with fabrications.

Interviewing Children with Parental Alienation Syndrome

Children suffering with a parental alienation syndrome may present the judge with a convincing picture. By the time such children reach the judge, they have developed a well-rehearsed litany of complaints against the presumably hated parent. This can be quite convincing, especially because the script has probably been rehearsed many times over with the allegedly preferred parent. Also, by this time, children have probably presented the scenario to a parade of attorneys and mental health professionals. This has given such children the opportunity to practice and sharpen their speeches. I have been involved in many cases in which judges have been completely taken in by parental alienation syndrome children and have not appreciated that they were being handed a "bill of goods." These children have a way of "snow balling" even experienced psychologists and psychiatrists, so I cannot be too critical of these judges.

Obviously, prior to conducting the interview, the judge should be familiar with the causes and manifestations of the parental alienation syndrome. Without such familiarity, he (she) will be seriously compromised in conducting the optimum kind of interview. I present below a series of questions that judges should find useful when interviewing these children. It is important to appreciate that the questions provided here relate to the more common situation, the one in which the father is the allegedly hated parent and the mother the professed loved one. However, when the situation is reversed (the mother the hated one and the father the loved one), obviously I reverse the questions.

Describe Your Mother to Me   Children with parental alienation syndrome typically provide only positive responses. If any negatives are provided, they will usually be minimal. If asked to elaborate upon the negatives, only inconsequential criticisms will be provided. Children who suffer with other kinds of psychiatric disturbances or are "normal" will generally be able to list both positives and negatives about each parent. The complete idealization of a parent is a clue to the presence of this disorder.

Describe Your Father to Me   The child with parental alienation syndrome will enumerate various criticisms at great length. These will be both present and past. Often the past indignities will be about experiences that other children would consider normal or would have forgotten long ago. Sometimes a complaint will be about an event the child has not actually observed but the mother has described. The child will accept as valid the mother's rendition and not give any credibility to the father's refutation. If the judge points out to the child that the mother's rendition is being given preference over the father's, the child is likely to respond, "My mother would never lie to me." An attempt to confront the child with the inequality and bias of such a response will generally prove futile. But this prejudice provides the judge with data nevertheless because it confirms the presence of a parental alienation syndrome.

When it is pointed out to the child that few if any positives about the father have been presented, the child will claim flatly that there are none. Inquiries into past good times enjoyed together by the child and father will be denied as nonexistent, or the child will claim that these events were actually painful and the child's professed enjoyment of them stemmed from the fear of punishment for not doing so. It is this complete one-sidedness of the response, the total absence of normal ambivalence, that should alert the interviewer to the fact that one is probably dealing with a child suffering with a parental alienation syndrome.

What Do You Think about Your Father's Family?   The child with a parental alienation syndrome will generally respond that all members of the father's extended family, even the child's own grandparents and previously loved aunts, uncles, and cousins, are somehow obnoxious and vile. When asked for specific reasons why there is absolutely no contact at all with any of these individuals, no compelling reasons are provided. Often inconsequential reasons are given. Attempts to impress upon the child how important it is to have relationships with these loving relatives prove futile. The child extends the view of the father as noxious to the father's extended family. The child will describe no sense of loss or loneliness over this self-imposed removal from the father's extended family. If a potential or actual stepmother is involved with the father, this hatred will extend to her and her extended family as well.

Does Your Mother Interfere with Your Visiting with Your Father? Generally the child will describe absolutely no interference on the mother's part. Often the child will proudly describe the mother's neutrality and state that the decision is completely his (her) own. The child will not generally be aware of the subtle influences that have molded the child's "own" opinion. Information about these can be obtained by asking questions about what the mother's exact statements were regarding visitation. The child may state, "She asked me whether I wanted to continue watching television or whether I wanted to go with my father, who was at the door to pick us up. She told me that she was leaving the decision to me." "She told me that she would get into trouble if I didn't go, but I still didn't go."

Why Then Don't You Want to Visit with Your Father? The child may give very vague reasons. When asked to give *specific* reasons, these children may describe horrible abuses in a very convincing way. In addition, they often provide gross exaggerations of inconsequential complaints. They make "mountains out of mole hills" and dwell on frivolous reasons for not visiting. Often they claim that they want absolutely no contact at all with the father for the rest of their lives, or at least not before they are adults. When it is pointed out to these children that the vast majority of other children would not cut their fathers off entirely, forever, for such "indignities," they insist that their total rejection is justified, and they may add that their mothers agree with them.

Does Your Mother Harass You? Healthy children generally will give some examples of "harassment," such as being made to turn off the television, do homework, or go to bed earlier than they want. Children with parental alienation syndrome describe no such "harassments." They often will describe their mother as being perfect and as never asking them to do things they don't want. This is obviously a fabrication and is a manifestation of the whitewash of the mother. I use the word *harassment* with these children because it is a common expression utilized by mothers of parental-alienation-syndrome children. The father's overtures for involvement with the child are generally referred to as harassment by the mother. If the child is unfamiliar with the word harassment, I substitute "bother you a lot."

Does Your Father Harass You?   These children are likely to describe in great detail the father's "harassments." Generally, they involve attempts on his part to gain contact with the children. Letters, telephone calls, and legal attempts to gain visitation are all clumped under the term *harassments*. Although the father's initial overtures may have been spaced reasonably, with mounting frustration over rejection and alienation, the father's overtures increase in frequency and intensity. The love and affection that is at the foundation of these overtures is denied completely by both the mother and the parental-alienation-syndrome child. Rather, they are viewed simply as onerous harassments.

Further Comments Regarding the Interview with Parental-Alienation-Syndrome Children   The above questions are general ones. The judge does well to ask more specific questions pertinent to the particular case. These might include questions regarding why the child wants to change his (her) name back to the mother's maiden name, why the father's Christmas presents were thrown in the garbage (usually in the mother's presence), why the child wants to have the father still contribute to his (her) education even though he (she) never wants to see the father again, what the siblings' reasons are for not wanting to see the father (these too often prove inconsequential), and so forth. When speaking to the parental-alienation-syndrome child it is also important to make a sharp differentiation between the child's words and the associated emotional tone and gestures. The child who describes hatred of the father may do so while smiling and may present a list of alleged indignities suffered at his hands in such a way that one gets the feeling that there was absolutely no pain involved. This is an important clue regarding whether or not one takes these complaints seriously.

Judges who interview children in chambers must appreciate that these children may be very convincing. Judges may be taken in by the litany of complaints and give such great weight to the child's statements that they may go along with the child's stated preference. Judges must be alerted to the primary manifestations of this disorder, especially the complete lack of ambivalence, the dwelling on frivolous and inconsequential "indignities," the total alienation from the extended family of the hated parent, the absolute denial of any positive input on the hated parent's part at any time in the child's life, and the definite statement that the child wishes *never* to see the hated parent again. It is hoped that judges will increasingly appreciate what is occurring when they see such children and rectify the situation in accordance with the guidelines to be presented in this book, especially in Chapter Seven.

GUARDIANS AD LITEM

I have mixed feelings about guardians *ad litem*, child advocates, and the utilization of yet another attorney in adversarial proceedings. Because of my preference for mediation, arbitration, and other methods of dispute resolution, which do not involve adversarial proceedings, I am reluctant to support a program that invites yet another attorney into the battle. Besides the extra expense, it is likely that another attorney will just add to the intensity of the conflict. However, I have found that the guardian *ad litem* can be particularly useful to the impartial examiner (and even an adversary evaluator) in the course of the evidence-gathering phase of one's evaluation. The guardian *ad litem* can generally be relied upon to assist in obtaining documents that a parent might have been hesitant to provide or to enlist the court's assistance in getting reluctant parents to cooperate in the evaluation. The guardian *ad litem*, even more than the impartial examiner, is allowed direct communication with the judge and can thereby speed the process of the evaluation and obtain information that might not be so easily acquired.

However, it is important that the judge and the attorneys (the people who are involved in choosing the guardian ad litem) be certain that the person chosen is familiar with the parental alienation syndrome. Not to do so increases significantly the risk that the disorder will be entrenched. To serve as a guardian in child custody disputes, the attorney must reorient himself (herself) regarding reflexive support of one's client's position. The guardian has to appreciate, first, that his (her) clients are children and their judgment regarding what is in their best interest may be somewhat compromised. I will elaborate further on this very important point in Chapter Seven, where I discuss the role of the guardian ad litem in the treatment of parental alienation syndrome families.

SIX
PSYCHOTHERAPY OF PARENTAL-ALIENATION-SYNDROME FAMILIES

INTRODUCTORY COMMENTS

The reader does well to note the implications of the title of this chapter. I have not entitled it "Psychotherapy of Parental-Alienation-Syndrome Children," "Psychotherapy of Children with Parental Alienation Syndrome," "Psychotherapy of Parents Who Induce a Parental Alienation Syndrome," or "Psychotherapy of Parents Who have Been the Target of Their Alienated Children." Although each of these parties may warrant a special additional psychotherapeutic approach, they all need to be seen by one therapist, the divorced status of the family notwithstanding. I have seen many cases in which the judge has ordered each of the parties to have a separate therapist. I have *never* seen this work out. The most common result of such an order is that nobody does anything, not the mother, the father, and certainly not the children. And even the judge is not likely to pursue the issue and make sure that his (her) order in this realm is being complied with. But even if the parties were to be submissive and compliant enough to follow through with this recommendation, it is not likely that the treatment will be successful. Each party would be providing the therapist with his (her) own rendition of the situation and is likely to take the therapist "down the garden path." Without the opportunity for input from the other family members, the therapist is not likely to have an accurate understanding of what is really going on.

Furthermore, the individual therapist is going to be deprived of the important information that can *only* be gained from joint interviews among the family members. Because programming parents are notoriously uncooperative regarding entering treatment in which the focus is to confront them with their pathological utilization of their children, court-ordered family therapy is crucial. Without such an order, the therapist is going to be in an impotent position regarding the implementation of recommendations necessary for the alleviation of the disorder. I know of no better example of a situation in which psychiatry and law can work together. And I can think of no better example of a situation in which the absence of one of these disciplines will leave the other impotent. The therapist is not likely to be successful without a court order requiring *all* parties to be in his (her) office and to cooperate or else suffer such consequences as fines, reduction of visitation, and even transfer of the children to the primary custody of the more cooperative parent.

Courts are not going to be successful in alleviating the problems of parental-alienation-syndrome families by simply ordering people to cease and desist from programming children or obstructing visitation. First, the programming is often subtle and even unconscious, and no court order is going to prevent the communication of these thoughts and feelings. The rage that such programming parents feel is exuding from every pore in their bodies, and even the unanimous vote of the nine members of the U.S. Supreme Court is not going to suppress completely the expression of this fury. Furthermore, the court needs someone "out there," away from the courthouse and in direct contact with all family members, in order to effect the changes necessary for the alleviation of this disorder, which is really a family disorder.

Conducting treatment with these families is not something that every therapist can do. One must be comfortable with being authoritarian and ordering people around. More of the therapy involves moving pieces on a chess board than analyzing people in order to help them gain insight into their underlying psychodynamics. This is not the kind of a therapy that should be conducted by passive types, those who are laid back, and those who are going to just sit back and listen while people spin off their fantasies. Rather, such treatment should only be done by a therapist who is comfortable with not only being active but even making threats that if a party does not comply with certain recommendations, the judge will be informed of that individual's recalcitrance with the likelihood of serious consequences. I am sure there are some readers at this point who are startled by my use of the word *threat* when it comes to working with a patient. The word *threat* is not a no-no word in my vocabulary. Life is filled with threats. If you don't pay your electric bill, the company is going to turn off your electricity. If you don't pay your phone bill, the company is going to turn off your phone. Without threats, the therapy of parental-alienation-syndrome families is likely to prove futile. Programming parents can be "tough customers," and they need a hard line if anything is going to be accomplished. Therapists working with such families, accordingly, must be hard-nosed or else the treatment will be a waste of time.

I have mentioned mothers who enter into a *folie-à-deux* relationship with a therapist (usually female) in which they join together and provide mutual support for the animosity toward the father. Actually, as mentioned, this becomes a *folie-à-trois* relationship when one includes a child. I have seen courts in which such a mother is ordered to discontinue treatment with such a therapist. The problem with such an order is that the mother is likely to find another therapist who will relate to her similarly because such therapists are not hard to find. There are many angry women around (some of whom become therapists) who lock in quickly with other angry women (some of whom become patients), and the two join forces against any man, no matter how sick and distorted the allegations against the man and no matter how detrimental such a union might be. I have also seen other situations in which the judge has refused to order a cessation of such treatment. In either case, court-ordered family therapists should be willing to operate under either circumstance, with the appreciation that the mother's involvement with such a therapist may be working against their therapeutic goals. But no therapeutic program is perfect, all have their drawbacks, and family therapy of parental alienation syndrome is no exception.

Therapists who have served previously in the litigation are extremely poor candidates for treating these families. Whether the therapist has served as an impartial examiner or as an advocate, he (she) is likely to have testified on behalf of one parent against the other. Under such circumstances, the parent against whom the therapist testified is likely to harbor significant animosity toward the therapist, and the treatment of the family is likely to be seriously compromised. Accordingly, one does well to bring in a new person, someone who has no familiarity at all with the case. This person should "start clean," without any preconceived notions about the family members. One could argue that someone who has been involved in the case to a significant degree, especially an impartial examiner, is in a good position to conduct such treatment. Certainly, knowledge of the family is a strong argument for such involvement, but the aforementioned animosity problem in most cases outweighs this advantage. A new therapist can spend a few hours reviewing reports and familiarizing himself (herself) with the details of the case. Also, the new therapist has the opportunity to conduct interviews and become more deeply entrenched. Like all rules, there are occasional exceptions. My experience has been that there is an occasional case in which the parents do not end up with an acrimonious relationship with the impartial examiner. This is especially the case if the examiner has been successful in facilitating the parents resolving their difficulties (often with the help of their attorneys) without resorting to courtroom litigation. Testimony on behalf of one parent against the other, then, does not take place. If, in addition, the evaluator's recommendations provide somewhat equal gains and losses for each side, then serving subsequently in this capacity may still be possible.

THE INITIAL EVALUATION

The therapist does well *not* to proceed until a court order is in hand, a court order specifically designating the therapist—by name—as the person who is to treat the family. Preferably, the names of all of the parties to be treated should be included in the court order. These must be spelled out in order to ensure the cooperation of all parties. In most cases, this will include the mother, father, and each of the children. In some cases, it should also include the names of stepparents and other significant parties with whom the parents may be involved, parties who are playing an active role in the perpetuation of the alienation. One is dealing here with a network of people, just the opposite of therapy with an individual patient. It is important, also, to be certain that the order is signed. Court orders are generally made up by one attorney with the approval of the other. Sometimes such approval is not obtained, and the order never gets to the judge's desk. This may occur when one attorney is very eager for the therapy to take place and recognizes that his (her) adversary will be reluctant (or will even refuse) to cooperate. The document, then, becomes worthless for the purposes of such treatment, and the examiner has absolutely no power over reluctant parties.

I generally conduct the initial evaluations along the lines described elsewhere (Gardner, 1989a) and in Chapter Four. My usual procedure is to conduct an initial two-hour interview, which I refer to as the *initial consultation.* Following this, I conduct what I refer to as the *extended evaluation.* For these families I generally set up a two-hour family interview, during which time I assess the basic problems and learn much about the interactions, the power plays, and the subsystems. In the extended evaluation, I see each of the parents two to three times alone and then follow this interview with one or two interviews with the parents together. I may interview once or twice a stepparent or adult who has a significant involvement with one of the parents, especially if that person lives in the home. I want to see each child once or twice. Furthermore, I will review pertinent court materials, especially reports submitted by impartial examiners. In my own interviews I will try to fill in any gaps that may have been present in the information previously provided me. I generally have little respect for reports submitted by "hired gun" advocates who have not seen both parties. These multiple interviews not only serve the purposes of data collection but are designed to increase the likelihood that a good therapeutic relationship with each of the parties will develop. Most important, I will try to ascertain in which category the syndrome lies—severe, moderate, or mild. Because each category requires a different psychotherapeutic approach, such determination is crucial before embarking on a therapeutic program.

At the outset I inform all parties about the modifications of the traditional rules of confidentiality that will prevail throughout the course of my treatment. Specifically, I will reserve the right, at my discretion, to reveal to any party what has been told me by any other party if it is my opinion that such revelation will enhance the efficacy of the treatment. In contrast, I will not allow myself to be constrained from such revelations if I consider such information important to divulge. Sometimes this initial statement will have been "forgotten" and a party, in the course of an individual interview, may attempt to invoke the privilege. In response I will "remind" that individual that I have no obligation to comply with the request for confidentiality, and I may or may not do so depending upon the nature of the divulgence. If a party says to me, "Doctor, I have something to tell you but I'm afraid you might reveal it to the others. I don't know what to do," I will reply, "Well, you're going to have to take your chances. I can promise you that I will use my discretion and not reveal unnecessary material. Rather, I will only reveal that which I consider necessary to divulge for the purposes of collecting the more accurate data. This is your therapy and you have to decide how much you wish to divulge. Obviously, the more information I have, the better position I will be in to be of help to you and your family." Basically, I leave the decision to the patient, and he (she) makes the final decision regarding whether or not the material will be disclosed. I consider my response here to be a good example of what I refer to as "the-ball-is-in-your-court-baby principle."

SEVERE CASES OF THE
PARENTAL ALIENATION SYNDROME

The Mother

With regard to the *therapeutic approaches* to mothers in this category, traditional therapy for the mother is most often not possible. As mentioned, some of these mothers have reached the point where they are paranoid. Some may have been paranoid previously, and others were preparanoid but become overtly so under the stresses of the custody litigation. Some are not paranoid but are so blinded by their rage that they do not alter their opinions by confrontations with reality, no matter how many times they are confronted and no matter how convincing the evidence that their ideas are false. Such mothers are totally unreceptive to treatment and will consider a therapist who does not accept their delusions as valid to be joining with their husbands in some kind of conspiracy. Or they may claim that the therapist has been "bought off" by the husband. The fact that the husband is, in all likelihood, paying for the therapy will be used as support for this accusation. Attempts to get them to recognize that the husband's paying for the therapy does not necessarily mean that he has power to control the therapist's opinions prove futile. The therapist thereby becomes incorporated into the paranoid system. The judge, as well, may be brought into the paranoid system if he (she) rules primarily in favor of the child's father. A court order that the mother enter into treatment makes a mockery of the therapeutic process. Judges are often naive with regard to their belief that one can order a person into treatment. This is an extension of their general view of the world that ordering people around is the best way to accomplish something. Most judges are aware that they cannot order an impotent husband to have an erection or a frigid wife to have an orgasm. Yet they somehow believe that one can order someone to have conviction for and commitment to therapy. Accordingly, the evaluator does well to discourage the court from such a misguided order.

The Children

Therapy for the children, as well, is most often not possible *while the children are still living in the mother's home.* No matter how many times a week they are seen, the therapeutic exposure represents only a small fraction of the total amount of time of exposure to the mother's denigrations of the father. There is a sick psychological bond here between the mother and children that is not going to be changed by therapy as long as the children remain living with the mother. While still in the mother's home, the children are going to be exposed continually to the bombardment of denigration and other influences (overt and covert) that contribute to the perpetuation of the syndrome.

Accordingly, the first step in the therapeutic process is *removal* of the children from the mother's home and placement in the home of the father, the allegedly-hated parent. This may not be accomplished easily, and the court might have to threaten sanctions and even jail if the mother does not comply. Following this transfer there must be a period of decompression and debriefing in which the mother has no opportunity at all for input to the children. The hope here is to give the children the opportunity to reestablish their relationship with the alienated father, without significant contamination of the process by the brainwashing mother. Even telephone calls must be strictly prohibited for at least a few weeks, and perhaps longer. Then, according to the therapist's judgment, slowly increasing contacts with the mother may be initiated, starting with monitored telephone calls. The danger here, however, is that these will be used as opportunities for programming the children. It is difficult, if not impossible, to protect the children completely from programming during the course of such calls. As described in detail in Chapter Three, programming parents can be extremely clever with regard to their manipulations and will often get across their alienating messages in the context of comments that may ostensibly appear innocuous and not part of a campaign of denigration. Even questions like "How are you?" can be said in a way that implies that the children are living in an atmosphere of great danger. And when the child casually says, "All right," the caller communicates a sense of relief that they are still alive.

Therefore, this period of slow and judicious renewal of contact between the children and the brainwashing parent must be monitored carefully so as to prevent a recurrence of the disorder. In some cases this may be successful, especially if the mother can see her way clear to entering into meaningful therapy (not often the case for many [if not most] mothers in this category). In some cases the children might ultimately be returned to the mother. However, if she still continues to alienate the children, it may be necessary to assign primary custody to the father and allow a frequency of visitation that will be limited enough to protect them from significant reprogramming. In extreme cases, one may have to sever the children entirely from the mother for many months or even years. In such cases the children will at least be living with one parent who is healthy. The children will then be in a position to derive the benefits of placement with the father, continuing hostile attitudes toward him notwithstanding. However, my experience has been that in such cases the animosity toward the father gradually becomes reduced. In contrast, if the court allows the children to remain living with such a disturbed mother, then it is likely that there will be lifelong alienation from the father.

Unfortunately, my experience has been that judges have not been too receptive to this proposal. Recent egalitarian criteria for ruling in custody disputes notwithstanding, most judges still hold stringently to the traditional view that mothers are generally better than fathers in the realm of raising children. Although I am generally sympathetic to this position (as evidenced by my commitment to what I refer to as the *healthy-stronger-psychological-bond presumption*), there is no question that there are many mothers who are far less capable than their husbands to raise their children. And mothers in the severe category of parental alienation syndrome are likely to be so deficient. Unfortunately, in those cases in which the court was unsympathetic to my recommendation for immediate transfer, the children became even more deeply entrenched in the *folie-à-deux* relationship they had with their mothers and continued with the pattern of refusing contact with their fathers. Although I have no formal, long-term follow-up studies, I am convinced that most of these children will probably be alienated from their father throughout the course of their lives. A psychological bond can withstand just so much attenuation before it dwindles to nothing. And I hold the courts responsible for this family tragedy, a tragedy that could have been avoided.

The Father

With regard to individual therapeutic work with fathers in this category, my comments here refer to those fathers who have been good fathers, have been significantly involved with their children, and in no way deserve the animosity being vented upon them. I mention here, once again, that the parental alienation syndrome is not an applicable diagnosis when there has been bona fide abuse. In such cases the children's animosity is warranted, and transfer to the father's home would clearly be extremely detrimental. The first step in the treatment of these fathers is to explain to them in detail what is happening to their children and help them not to take so seriously the children's professions of hatred. The fathers must be helped to appreciate that they had indeed developed a strong healthy psychological bond with their children during their formative years and that the children's allegations of hatred are generally a facade. They have to appreciate fully the ancient wisdom that the opposite of love is not hate but indifference. They have to be impressed with the fact that the children's preoccupation with them (even though an acrimonious preoccupation) is still a manifestation of involvement. Accordingly, the fathers must be helped to develop a "thick skin." This advice applies whether or not the father has the opportunity to see the children.

My further advice depends on whether or not the father has the opportunity to see the children. For those fathers who do see their children, especially those who have been successful in obtaining primary custody, some fathers become quite discouraged and think seriously about removing themselves entirely from their children, so pained are they by the rejections. Many will even have been given advice (sometimes by well-meaning therapists) to "respect" the children's desires not to see them. This is a grave mistake. Such withdrawal by the father will generally be detrimental to the children. The fathers must be encouraged to keep reaching out, to keep telling the children how much they care for them, and to divert the children's attention when they are involved in the denigration. At times, it is useful to encourage such fathers to say such things as, "You don't have to talk that way with me now. Your mother's not around" and "I don't believe a word of what you're saying. You know and I know that we love one another deeply and that we've had great times together in the past and will have more great times in the future." In some cases, with the mother out of the picture, the children will have the opportunity for having living experiences that the father is not the dangerous ogre they have been taught to believe. In such cases the fathers experience a gradual diminution in the children's campaign of denigration. As mentioned, in some cases permanent residence with the father may be the only viable option. In other cases varying degrees of visitation with the mother may be reasonable, and in some cases ultimate return to the mother (with liberal visitation to the father) may be possible.

Those fathers whose children have absolutely refused to see them and who have been unsuccessful in getting the courts to order meaningful visitation, let alone transfer of custody, are in a difficult situation indeed. Their former wives generally refuse to allow telephone calls and will destroy mail before it gets to the children. They are likely to flaunt with impunity court orders to desist from such practices. Communication through relatives may also prove futile. Sympathetic relatives hear about, and even may be direct observers of, the wrath of the children's mother and suspect (often rightfully) that if they try to intervene on the part of the father, they too will be rejected and lose out on their opportunities to see the children. This is a common situation. Most often, there is little meaningful advice I can provide such fathers. I tell them to continue with their overtures, however small the likelihood of their getting through, and hope that as the children get older they will come to appreciate what has gone on. They must resign themselves to the fact that they may never have a meaningful relationship with their children again; however, they should never lose hope completely, and it may be that the children will become reconciled with them as they get older. Again, the disorder, being an outgrowth of the burgeoning of custody litigation in recent years, is too new for us to have meaningful follow-up studies that would provide us with information regarding the ultimate prognosis of children in this category, especially children who have not had any contact at all with their fathers over many years.

MODERATE CASES OF THE PARENTAL ALIENATION SYNDROME

Introductory Comments

With regard to the *therapy* for these families, it is important that *one* therapist be utilized. This is *not* a situation in which mother should have her therapist, father his therapist, and the children their own. Such a therapeutic program, although seemingly respectful of each party's individual needs, is not likely to work for the treatment of families in which the children exhibit a parental alienation syndrome. Such fractionization reduces communication, sets up antagonistic subsystems within the family, and is thereby likely to intensify and promulgate the pathological interactions that contribute to the parental alienation syndrome. It is also important that the therapist be court ordered and have direct input to the judge. This can often be facilitated by the utilization of a guardian ad litem or a child advocate who has the opportunity for direct communication with the court. The mother must know that any obstruction on her part will be immediately reported to the judge, either by the therapist or through the guardian ad litem or child advocate. The court must be willing to impose sanctions such as fines or jail. The threat of loss of primary custody can also help such mothers "remember to cooperate."

In the last few years, the term *child advocate* has taken on a special meaning. Traditionally, the term referred to an attorney who served the children in the course of custody litigation. Some jurisdictions differentiate between the child advocate and the guardian ad litem; other jurisdictions do not. These differences sometimes relate to whether the individual is allowed to conduct cross-examinations in the courtroom. Recently, there has emerged on the scene a group of individuals, most often not attorneys, who refer to themselves as child advocates. These people may or may not have formal training in any of the traditional mental health disciplines. They generally are those who wave the banner "Believe the children" and take at face value everything and anything children say. They gravitate, especially, to sex-abuse evaluations, where they hold stringently to the position that "children never lie," especially in the realm of sex abuse. My experience has been that some of these individuals are using their seemingly benevolent advocacy of children in the service of venting rage upon men, and they are, for the most part, derived from the group of fanatic feminists who have found this field to provide a wonderful opportunity for venting rage against men. Others are poorly trained and/or simple-minded and believe that they are indeed joining a noble cause. Whatever the motivations of these individuals, examiners do well, these days, to be very careful about engaging the services of someone whose primary label is "child advocate."

It is in the moderate category that the aforementioned "hard-nosed" court-appointed therapist can be most useful, if not crucial. Before embarking on the treatment, the therapist *must* have a clear idea regarding exactly what the court's support will be. As an impartial therapist, direct communication with the judge is possible in order to clarify this issue. Such therapists must know exactly what threats they can utilize to lend support to their suggestions, instructions, and even manipulations. Empty threats are not only a waste of time but compromise the treatment. They immediately provide the therapist with a reputation of being weak and impotent and significantly compromise the likelihood that the treatment will be effective. Generally, the threats are on a hierarchy, and the therapist does well to pose them in order from the mildest to the most severe. A mild threat might simply be that the therapist will report the parent's lack of cooperation to the court. A higher-level threat might involve a court-ordered reduction in the payments the father is required to provide the mother. Of course, there are limitations to this threat in that one cannot leave the mother destitute or incur such privations that the children will not be properly cared for. Obviously, this threat will be more efficacious for the wealthy than for the poor. Sometimes a fine for each failure to produce the children will work; sometimes a more ongoing financial withholding may be necessary to help the mother cooperate. The threat of permanent transfer of the children to the primary custody of the father (with the mother then having visitation) can sometimes be invoked. The highest-level threat is jail. In recent years, fathers have certainly been jailed for failure to fulfill financial commitments, but I have no personal experience with mothers being jailed for failure to fulfill their commitment to enforce the visitation of the children with their fathers. Some well-publicized examples of this would prove therapeutic to some of these alienating parents. Again—and I cannot emphasize this point strongly enough—the therapist does well to have the judge clearly spell out exactly how far he (she) is willing to go with regard to the implementation of these threats. And all this information should be available to the attorneys and the clients at the outset, *before* the first meeting.

The Mother

As is true for mothers in the severe category, mothers in the moderate category will often find their own individual therapists with whom they develop a mutual admiration society in which the therapist (consciously or unconsciously) becomes the mother's champion in the conflict. Women in this category have a way of selecting therapists who will support their antagonism toward the father. Most often, the mother chooses a *woman* as a therapist—especially a woman who is herself antagonistic toward men. Typically, the mother's therapist has little, if any, contact with the father and so does not have the opportunity to hear his side of the story. When they do meet with him, they typically will be hostile and unsympathetic. Accordingly, the mother and the therapist often develop a *folie-à-deux* relationship. Although the court may not wish to stop the mother from seeing this therapist, it does well to prohibit the children from being "treated" by her (as mentioned, the therapist is rarely a man). Even if the court were to order the mother's therapist to stop treating her, it is likely that she would find another person who would support her position. And this is another reason why I generally do not recommend that the court order a cessation of the mother's treatment with the therapist with whom she is pathologically involved. The court should order the mother to see the court's therapist, even though her maneuvers to obstruct the therapy may be significantly supported by her own therapist.

The therapist does well to try to find some healthy "insider" on the mother's side of the family. Sometimes the mother's mother and/or father can serve in this capacity. On occasion it might be the mother's brother or sister. Here, one is looking for a person who is aware that the mother is "going too far" with regard to the animosity that she harbors toward her husband and is fostering the children's alienation from him. If a good relationship existed between the father's parents and the mother's parents prior to the separation, the therapist might prevail upon the father's parents to speak with the mother's parents. Sometimes family meetings in which all four grandparents are present—with the mother and father—can be useful in this regard. The mother's mother can be a very powerful therapeutic ally if the therapist is able to enlist her services. I cannot emphasize strongly enough the importance of the therapist's attempting to find such an ally on the mother's side of the family.

That individual can sometimes bring the mother to her senses and effectively prevail upon her to "loosen up" and appreciate how detrimental her maneuvers are to her children. Many parties who are appreciative of the mother's injudicious behavior take the position of "not wanting to get involved." In some cases, these individuals fear that if they do not support the mother's position, they too will become the targets of the same rage that is directed toward the father. The therapist does well to attempt to have access to such people and to impress upon them that their neutrality may be a terrible disservice to the children. I have no problem eliciting guilt in such individuals if it will serve the purpose of facilitating their involvement in the therapeutic process.

Most of the mothers in this category are not receptive to insight therapy in which they delve into the reasons for their exaggerated animosity. There are, however, some mothers in the moderate category who may indeed involve themselves meaningfully in the therapeutic process. At the most superficial level, one tries to get them to appreciate the importance of the father's role in the children's upbringing and that their (the mothers') manipulations, although producing grief in the father, are also contributing to the children's psychopathology. Many have been so blinded by their rage that they do not appreciate this obvious effect of their campaign of denigration and exclusionary techniques. Sometimes the rage stems from jealousy that the father has a new involvement and that the mother does not. Her jealousy is a contributing factor to her program of wreaking vengeance on her former husband by attempting to deprive him of his children, his most treasured possessions. Another factor that often contributes to the campaign of animosity is the mother's desire to maintain a relationship with her former husband. The tumultuous activity guarantees ongoing involvement, accusation and counteraccusation, attack and counterattack, and so on. Most people, when confronted with a choice between total abandonment and hostile involvement, would choose the acrimonious relationship. And these mothers demonstrate this point well. To the degree that one can help her "pick up the pieces of her life" and form new involvements and interests, one is likely to reduce the rage. The most therapeutic experience such a woman can have is meeting a new man with whom she becomes deeply involved and forms a strong relationship.

Economic factors may be contributing to the mother's anger. Generally, in our society, women of divorce suffer more financial privation than their husbands, the privations for both parties notwithstanding. If the therapist believes that the mother has been "shortchanged" in the settlement, then professional input (from accountants and knowledgeable lawyers) may be warranted. In such cases the therapist does well to inform the court (preferably by letter with copies to the parents and their attorneys) that he (she) has good reason to believe that the property and financial settlement has not been fair and that the mother's unnecessary privations are contributing to the anger that is perpetuating the psychopathology. Furthermore, it should be pointed out that, if indeed this is the case, then a more egalitarian settlement would prove therapeutic for all concerned. It is important for therapists to appreciate that they are not accountants and financial lawyers and that what may appear to the mother to be an unequal settlement may, in fact, not be. Accordingly, the therapist should not come to any conclusions on this matter, but leave this to the proper experts.

In some mothers overprotectiveness may have been a factor in producing a parental alienation syndrome in the children. Such mothers view the world as a dangerous place and may consider the father to be just another example of the children's exposure to danger. There is a wide variety of other issues that the therapist may have to deal with in the treatment of these mothers. The multiplicity of manifestations described in Chapter Three and the wide variety of psychodynamic patterns delineated in Chapter Four should give the therapist a good idea about some of the more common problems that he (she) may have to deal with. For example, if the mother is overprotective, one must treat this disorder, which, as mentioned, may contribute to her need to program her children. If she has sexual inhibition problems that result in her projecting her sexual impulses in such a way that she promulgates a false sex-abuse charge, this problem must be addressed as well. All sources of anger, both related to and unrelated to her husband, need to be looked at especially if they result in anger being channeled into the vengeance and rage being directed toward her husband.

I have been involved in many cases in which mothers in this category would suddenly decide that they wanted to move to another state. They suddenly become "homesick," after many years of comfortable adjustment in the state in which the children were raised. Some suddenly decide that they want to remove themselves (and the children, of course) from the scene of the custody conflict (including the whole state) and "start all over" and/or "find themselves" at some remote place. A few claim better job opportunities in another state. The therapist should examine the reasons for such sudden decisions to relocate. Of course, there are women who do indeed meet a new person, and involvement with that individual may only be possible if they relocate. And there are indeed women who do have better job opportunities elsewhere. However, when a parental alienation syndrome is present, the therapist does well to conduct a detailed inquiry into the request and to be very suspicious regarding the justification for the move. When it is obvious that the decision is yet another exclusionary maneuver in the context of a parental alienation syndrome, then the court should be advised to inform the mother that she is free to leave the state at any time she wishes; however, she should understand that if she does so it will *not* be with the children. And such a position can be included in the evaluator's recommendations.

The Children

The court's therapist must have a thick skin and be able to tolerate the shrieks and claims of maltreatment that these children will provide. Doing what children profess they want is not always the same as doing what is best for them. Therapists who believe that they must "respect" their child patients and accede to their wishes will be doing these children a terrible disservice. These same therapists would not "respect" a child's wish not to have a polio shot, yet they will respect the child's wish not to see a father who shows no significant evidence for abuse, maltreatment, neglect, etc. (Again, I take the opportunity here to repeat that when bona fide abuse is present, the concept of the parental alienation syndrome is not applicable.) The therapist does well to recall that prior to the separation the children were likely to have had a good, strong relationship with the father and that strong psychological ties must still be present. The therapist should view the children's professed animosity as superficial and designed to ingratiate themselves with the mother. To take the allegations of maltreatment seriously is a terrible disservice to these children. It may contribute to an entrenchment of the parental alienation syndrome and may result in years of, if not lifelong, alienation.

Similarly, when a fabricated (as opposed to bona fide) sex-abuse allegation has been introduced, if the therapist is convinced that it is false, then he (she) does well not to dwell on these allegations. Typically, over time such false allegations become elaborated and new allegations arise when the earlier ones do not work (Gardner, 1987, 1991a, 1992a). It is antitherapeutic to listen to these. Rather, it is therapeutic to say, "That didn't happen! So let's go on and talk about *real* things like your next visit with your father." The sex-abuse allegation may become an intrinsic part of the parental alienation syndrome and may become a formidable additional dimension. However, it is beyond the purposes of this book to discuss in detail the incorporation of sex-abuse allegations into the parental alienation syndrome. This important dimension, however, has been discussed elsewhere (Gardner, 1987, 1991a, 1992a).

The therapist must appreciate that the children *need* him to serve as an excuse for visiting with the father. When "forced" to visit with the father, they can say to the mother that the therapist is mean, cruel, etc., and that they really do not want to see the father, but the therapist "makes them." And the judge should appreciate that he (she) too can serve this function for the children. With a court order, they can say to their mother, "I really hate my father, but that stupid judge is making me see him." I cannot emphasize this point strongly enough. This is one of the most common errors made by therapists involved in the treatment of these children, namely, they fail to appreciate that the children actually *want* them to *force* them to visit in order that they may have an excuse to do so, but such an excuse necessarily involves complaints about the therapist's coercions and cruel manipulations.

The therapist must also appreciate that older children may promulgate the mother's programming down to younger ones. And the older children are especially likely to do this during visits with the father. The mother thereby relies on her accomplice to "work over" the younger ones when in the enemy camp (the father's house). These older children may even mastermind "inside jobs" in the father's house. Accordingly, a "divide and conquer" approach sometimes is warranted. This is best accomplished by requiring the children to visit separately—or at least separate from the older sibling programmers—until they all (including the mother) have had the actual experience that the terrible consequences of being alone with the father were not realized. For example, an older sister may be programming her two younger brothers into believing that the father is dangerous and/or noxious, when they themselves exhibit only mild manifestations of a parental alienation syndrome. When they visit with the father and relax their guard, she may quickly remind them about the indignities they are likely to suffer under such circumstances. Structuring the visitations so that the sister visits separately from her brothers (at least for a time) is the most effective way of dealing with this kind of problem. This is a good example of an important aspect of the therapy of these families, namely, that less is done via the attempt to get them to gain insight and much more is accomplished by structuring situations and providing individuals with actual experiences.

Transition periods, that is, the points when the children are transferred from mother to father, may be especially difficult for children with parental alienation syndrome. It is then (when both parents and the children are together) that the loyalty conflicts become most intense and the symptoms most severe. Accordingly, it is not a good idea to have the father pick up the children at the mother's home. In that setting—with the mother directly observing the children—they are most likely to resist going with their father and will predictably gain their mother's support (overt or covert) for their resistance. Alternative transitional arrangements must therefore be devised; arrangements that do not place the children in a situation in which they are with the mother and father at the same time.

A good transition place is the therapist's office. The mother brings the children, spends some time with them and the therapist, and then goes home, leaving the children alone with the therapist. It is important that the mother leave the therapist's office and not wait (even in the waiting room) for the father to appear. To allow her to do so sabotages the whole arrangement. The therapist then spends time with the children alone. Subsequently the father comes, spends time with the children and the therapist, and then takes them to his home. Or a truly impartial intermediary, with whom the children have a good relationship, can pick the children up at the mother's home and bring them to the father's home. A therapist, guardian ad litem, or child advocate can serve in this role.

In some families, the children warrant a gradual expansion of the relatively restricted visitation that the court may have previously ordered for the father. The court has come to recognize the limitations of such stringent visitation and has made its wishes known to all parties that an expansion is desired. Ideally, the therapist should have the freedom to make the decisions regarding just how much expansion should take place and at what rate. It is impractical (and obviously very expensive and time-consuming) to go back to court every time a modification of a visitation schedule is to be effected. With rare exception, in the course of such expansion, these mothers will complain that the therapist is going too rapidly and not giving the children enough time to adjust. When empirically monitoring such visitations, therapists must rely on their own observations of the children after visitations and recognize that the reports being given by the parties about exactly what happened may not be fully accurate. It is a serious error for the therapist to allow himself (herself) to be controlled by these mothers into slowing down and even preventing a reasonable expansion of visitation. Mention has been made previously of the mother who viewed these empirical expansions as experiments on her children and stated, "I won't subject my child to experiments." In a proper court-ordered therapeutic program, such a mother would have no choice but to allow her child to be experimented with.

The therapist does well to view one aspect of the children's treatment as a kind of "debriefing" and "deprogramming." The principles utilized are similar to those implemented with prisoners of war who were inculcated with enemy propaganda and were brainwashed into professing public hatred of the country for which they were originally fighting. An example of this is the brainwashing of American prisoners of war by their North Korean captors during the Korean War. It is also similar to the kind of debriefing utilized with youngsters who were forcibly inculcated into religious cults, cults that supported removal and alienation from their nuclear families. An example of this would be youngsters who were indoctrinated into the "Moonies" cult in the 1970s. One must try to help the children appreciate that they have been brainwashed. Obviously, older children are more likely to appreciate this than younger ones. Sometimes confrontation with absurd and ludicrous allegations may help the child gain such insights. It is also useful to say things along these lines: "I'm not asking you to take my word for it. I want you to use your own observations. I want you to think about what happened during your last visit and ask yourself whether or not the things your mother said would happen *actually* happened. During your next visit, I want you to keep your eyes open and come to your *own* conclusions regarding whether or not these dangers and practices actually exist. You say you're old enough and smart enough to come to your own conclusions. Okay, people like that come to conclusions on the basis of their *own* observations, *not* on the statements made by others—whoever they may be. Just as I asked you before to give me *proof* of what you believe on the basis of what you've seen, I want you to give me *proof* next time, after your next visit, on the basis of what *you yourself* have actually seen and experienced."

I have come across a few situations in which the children and the family were split regarding the success of the programmer's attempts at alienation. Specifically, one or more of the children were successfully programmed, and one or more were not. I have also seen cases in which a mother was successful in programming one or more children, and the father was successful in programming one or more children. This civil war resulted in two divided camps. One maneuver (I am hesitant to call it therapeutic) one might utilize in these situations is to formulate a "trade off." The children in home A will only visit home B if the children in home B visit in home A. Or, more specifically, if the mother wants to see the children who live in the father's home, then she must allow the children in her home to visit with the father. Such a requirement may be dictated by the court-ordered therapist and even by the court. One advantage of this arrangement is that it may effect visitation with an alienated parent. It can also serve to give the children "excuses" for visitation. For example, a child in such a situation might say, "I really hate my father and I really don't want to visit with him, but I do want to see my sister." As mentioned, providing such "excuses" are an important part of the therapy of these children. However, the obvious drawback of such an arrangement is that the children are truly being used as pawns in a chess game, and this cannot but be psychologically detrimental. My limited experiences with such a situation have led me to the conclusion that its advantages outweigh its disadvantages. As is true with most divorce conflicts, there is no such thing as a "good" solution or a "bad" solution. Rather, we have to decide which we consider the least detrimental of all the detrimental options available to us. I consider the swapping arrangement less detrimental than no visitation at all. As mentioned, a psychological bond, no matter how strong, can only tolerate a certain degree of attenuation beyond which it snaps and is destroyed.

When working individually with the children, they must be discouraged from "buttering up" each parent and saying to each what they think one wants to hear at the moment, regardless of the consequences. In family sessions the therapist should "smoke out" the lies. This is much more likely to be accomplished in family sessions than in individual meetings. Therapists should express incredulity over the children's vilification of the father. They should not take seriously the children's false allegations and should quickly move on to other subjects. However, following visits with the father, they should emphasize to the children that their view of their father as an ogre was not realized during the visitation. The therapist does well to appreciate that as long as the litigation goes on, direct work with the children will be difficult and complete alleviation of symptoms may not be possible. Accordingly, in communications to the judge, the therapist should be ever reminding him (her) of the fact that the longer the litigation goes on, the less the likelihood the treatment will be successful.

Once the court has made a final decision that the children shall remain living with their mother, then the children are often able to dispense with their scenarios of deprecation. This is a very important point. The children develop their campaigns of denigration because of the desire to maintain the psychological bond with the mother. The custody litigation has threatened a disruption of this bond. Once the court has ruled that the children shall remain living primarily with their mother, they can relax and allow themselves to enjoy a more benevolent relationship with their father. In short, the court's order obviates the need for the symptoms and so they can often be dispensed with.

The Fathers

The therapeutic approaches to the fathers in this category are similar to those utilized with fathers in the first category. One must explain to them what is happening and help them "thicken their skins." They must be helped not to take so seriously the children's vilifications. Many fathers recognize that the children are most difficult during the first minutes or hours following the transfer and then they "relax their guard," and enjoy the visitation. Other fathers might have to tolerate an ongoing state of animosity throughout the course of the visit. Such fathers should be encouraged, however, to continue with the visits and view the hostility as basically a mask for the mother's benefit. Some children in this category are relatively calm and happy during the first hour or two of the visit, then go through a stage of rage outbursts that last one or more hours, and then go back to their previous state of friendliness. These should be viewed as demonstrations for the benefit of the mother, and these will be reported upon on the child's return. However, at the time of such reporting, their duration and intensity will generally be expanded and described as being in response to some terrible indignity suffered at the hands of the father. Sometimes the rage outbursts represent a release of pent-up anger generated by the child's embroilment in the parental conflict.

These fathers must be helped to divert the children from their hostile provocations to healthier interchanges and not to dwell on whether a particular allegation is true or false. However, they should also be engaged as therapeutic assistants with regard to the deprogramming process. Accordingly, they should point out to the children the most egregious examples of the mother's distortions and ask them whether they themselves have had experiences that verify these allegations. This is best done at the time when an alleged indignity or persecution is supposed to have taken place. Furthermore, the fathers must be helped to provide the children with healthy living experiences—which are the most effective antidotes to the delusions regarding his noxious and/or dangerous qualities. Such fathers do well to talk about "old times" together and to engage in the playful interchanges that may have been manifestations of the bonding that took place at that time. Healthy parents and children engage in special "private" games that are unique to each relationship. These may involve singing special songs, involvement in certain playful activities, or using special terms. Engaging the children in a repetition of these activities and interchanges can be quite salutary and play an important role in reducing the symptoms of the parental alienation syndrome (at least while in the father's home) and in rebuilding an attenuated psychological bond.

Most important, the fathers have to be encouraged with the philosophy that relationships based on genuine love should ultimately prove stronger than relationships based on fear. These fathers should be helped to appreciate (if they don't know already) that the children's animosity toward them is based primarily on the fear of alienating their mothers, especially if they express any affection for their fathers. They should provide an atmosphere in which they permit the children to express *all* thoughts and feelings, both positive and negative, regarding both parents. This is a different environment from the mother's home, in which the children are not allowed to express negative thoughts and feelings toward her or positive thoughts and feelings toward their father. They live in a state of fear, lest they break these stringent rules. The hope is that, ultimately, the children will come to appreciate this difference and recognize the greater state of relaxation and pleasure they enjoy in the father's home.

Concluding Comments

Not all therapists are suited to work with such families. As mentioned, they must have "thick skins" to tolerate the children's antics as they claim that they are being exposed to terrible traumas and indignities in their fathers' homes. They must also be people who are comfortable with taking a somewhat dictatorial position. And this is especially important in their relationship with the mothers of these children. The therapist must appreciate that more of the therapy relates to manipulating and structuring situations than providing people with insight. To the degree that the therapist can provide people with living experiences, to that degree false perceptions will be altered.

Therapists with a strong orientation toward psychoanalytic inquiry are generally not qualified to conduct such treatment. I am a psychoanalyst myself and involve most of my adult patients in psychoanalytic therapy. However, when a parental alienation syndrome is present, the therapeutic approach must *first* involve a significant degree of people manipulation (usually by court order) and structure before one can sit down and talk meaningfully with the parties involved. Moreover, therapists who accept as valid the patient's wishes (whether child or adult) and consider it therapeutically contraindicated to pressure or coerce a patient are also not candidates to serve such families. I too consider myself sensitive to the needs of my patients. As mentioned, doing what the patient *wants* and doing what the patient *needs* may be two entirely different things. It is for this reason that the courts play such an important role in the treatment of families in which a parental alienation syndrome is present. Without the therapist's having the court's power to bring about the various manipulations and structural changes, the therapy is not likely to be possible.

MILD CASES OF THE PARENTAL ALIENATION SYNDROME

With regard to *therapy*, in most cases therapy is *not* necessary. What these children need is a final court order confirming that they will remain living primarily with their mother and there will be no threat of their being transferred to their father. This usually brings about a "cure" of the parental alienation syndrome. If the children need therapy it is for other problems, possibly related to the divorce animosities. In some cases the approaches outlined under the moderate category may be warranted. As mentioned, one should not view these categories as distinct; rather they should be viewed as existing on a continuum from the mildest form of the mild to the severest form of the severe. Accordingly, mild cases that approach the moderate may require the kind of treatment that is applicable to the moderate. The therapeutic approaches, then, are those that are applicable to the moderate forms of the disorder, but the therapist probably need not be as stringent.

CLINICAL EXAMPLE

In the clinical example described below, I will provide few substantive details regarding the exact signs and symptoms of the children's parental alienation syndrome. Rather, I will focus on the structure of the treatment and the various manipulations that were required. My purpose here is to give the reader examples of the kinds of maneuvers that one should utilize in the treatment of these families.

Gloria and Ned's situation provides a good example of court-ordered treatment of a family in which a parental alienation syndrome was present. In their case, I first received a telephone call from Ned's lawyer asking me if I would be willing to serve as a court-appointed therapist in a case in which the parents were having difficulty complying with a court-ordered visitation schedule. He told me that each parent's attorney was invited to submit three names and the judge would select a therapist from the six names so submitted. It was the judge's hope that there would be one or more names that appeared on both lists, so that he would be able to rule that the therapy be conducted by someone whom the parents mutually agreed upon to serve in this capacity. I told him that I was receptive to serving as a court-appointed impartial examiner but that it was crucial that, before seeing the parties, I have a court order specifically naming me as the therapist to serve in this capacity. I also told him that it is important to name specifically all individuals who would be involved in the therapy, not merely both parents and the children, but that if stepparents or significant others were involved, they too would be ordered to participate. We then discussed my fee arrangement, and he told me that this would be agreeable to his client, who recognized that he would be assuming the full obligation for paying for the treatment.

Although in the course of this telephone call there was no discussion of substantive information—other than that there was a problem complying with the court-ordered visitation schedule—some information was still obtained. First, it was Ned's lawyer who called, not Gloria's. This already told me that Ned was probably more enthusiastic than Gloria about engaging me as the therapist. Furthermore, it was Ned who was assuming the full cost of the treatment, and this too was another statement of his motivation.

About three weeks later I received a telephone call from Ned's lawyer. He told me that Gloria's attorney fought vigorously against my appointment, his main argument being that "his client didn't want me to be the court-appointed examiner." Neither he nor his client provided any specific reasons for the unreceptivity to my appointment, and this is one of the reasons why the judge decided to select me from Ned's list. He informed both attorneys that I had appeared in his courtroom before and that he believed that I would do a competent job in this case. The fact that Gloria was resisting my involvement was also a source of information. The most common reason for resisting my involvement in a case is the party's appreciation that I make every attempt to serve as an impartial examiner, even when viewed by the court as an advocate. It is known in the legal community that at times I have come to court and testified on behalf of the party who was reluctant to initially invite my participation, that is, I appeared on behalf of the inviting party's adversary. Parents who are programming a parental alienation syndrome typically resist the court's appointment of an impartial examiner (at the time of the custody litigation) and, similarly, resist the appointment of a court-appointed therapist (after the litigation is over). In both situations they want someone whom they can manipulate. I believe that I have the reputation for not being easily manipulated. I suspect that this was the reason why the mother resisted my appointment, but I could not know at that point.

About a week later, I received the court order in which, as requested, I was mentioned by name as the person to conduct the treatment. I noted that this order was drawn up by Ned's attorney rather than by Gloria's. This too is advance information. A court order is generally not drawn up by the court but rather by one of the attorneys, approved by the other, and then signed by the judge. Generally, the attorney who is more committed to the contents of the order is the one who draws it up. Accordingly, this too was advance information.

On the same day I received the order, I received a call from Ned asking me if I had received the order and requesting that we set up the first appointment. I told him that my usual procedure is to see both parents first, alone, and then proceed from there. I told him that I would get back to him as soon as I received a call from Gloria. It is important for the reader to appreciate that, in general, I am extremely reluctant to *initiate* contact with people I have not previously seen in my office, whether it be for evaluation or treatment. I consider it somewhat unethical to initiate contact with a patient, especially if one is going to charge that patient. A complaint to the ethics committee would be considered with sympathy, even though there was a court order for me to conduct the treatment. The only exception I have to this rule is when dealing with a life-or-death matter in which a previously uninvolved party's assistance may be crucial. In divorce/custody disputes, compliance with this principle may have a fringe benefit, namely, it provides the therapist with information about motivation and receptivity.

About a week later Ned called again, asking if I had heard yet from his wife. I told him I had not, and I suggested that he have his attorney call her attorney in order to encourage her to make the call. About one week later I received a message from my secretary that Gloria X had called. I returned the call and this is the conversation that ensued:

> *Gardner:* This is Dr. Richard Gardner.
> *Gloria X:* Yes, what can I do for you?
> *Gardner:* What would you *like* me to do for you?
> *Gloria X:* Get my husband to stop *harassing* me.

The reader by now should be quite familiar with this word, which is commonly heard from both parents and children when a parental alienation syndrome is present. It is one of the diagnostic signs. The conversation continued.

> *Gardner:* I want you to know that if your husband is indeed harassing you then it will be one of my jobs to do everything in my power to reduce this practice, which I am sure can be very upsetting. I suggest you bring that up in our first interview so that I may direct my attention to it and find out more about what exactly is happening.

Gloria X (angrily): What makes you assume that I'm going to be in the same room with that man?

Gardner: Why don't you want to be in the same room with him?

Gloria X: I just hate his guts. He's a despicable liar. He doesn't give a shit about those kids. They told him that they don't want to see him, and he doesn't take no for an answer. He doesn't respect their wishes or their rights. I find him despicable, and the children are disgusted with him.

We see here further confirmation for the presence of a parental alienation syndrome. The diagnosis is being made here without my having seen anyone.

Gardner: I'm sorry that you're having so much trouble in your relationship with your former husband, and I want you to know that I will do everything possible to reduce the acrimony. I don't believe that I could possibly be successful in accomplishing this goal if I were not to see you together. Joint interviews are a proviso of my involvement. If you can't see your way clear to them, then I see myself as having no choice but to withdraw from providing further services.

Gloria X: Good! (patient then hangs up)

The reader can get some idea of the rage that one deals with if one is to diagnose and treat families in which a parental alienation syndrome is present. Following that telephone call I wrote a note to the judge informing him that I would be pleased to continue providing services in this case but that joint interviews were crucial if there was to be any hope of success. As is my usual practice, copies of this letter were sent to the attorneys and parents.

About a week later I received a telephone call from Gloria's attorney. He admitted that his client could be a "difficult woman" and asked if I would reconsider my position. I told him that the only thing I would be willing to do would be to see her alone for one interview, the purpose of which would be to try to make Gloria more comfortable with the treatment and explore her reasons for not wanting to be in the room with Ned. He should know in advance, however, that the likelihood that I could conduct the treatment while seeing both parties separately was extremely small, but that I would give her the benefit of discussing this with me alone. He thanked me for my "flexibility" (not a compliment I frequently receive) and told me that his client would be getting in touch with me.

About two weeks later (passage of time not completely ignored), Gloria called for an appointment. She arrived 45 minutes late for a 90-minute appointment and informed me that her watch was broken and that she got stuck in traffic. There was absolutely nothing she said in the 45 minutes that I spent with her to suggest that she had any justifiable reasons for not being in the same room with her husband. She denied that he had ever been physically violent with her, although she claimed that she lived in fear of such and this now was her main reason for refusing to participate in joint interviews with him. By the end of the interview I told her that I was unconvinced that separate interviews were warranted and suggested that she agree to the first joint session. This she refused and angrily left the room.

Accordingly, another letter was sent to the judge (again with copies to the attorneys and clients) informing him of my conclusions regarding the joint interviews. This time the judge came down "heavily" on Gloria. He sent a letter to Gloria's attorney, with copies to Ned's attorney and me, in which he stated that if Gloria did not start cooperating in treatment, attend joint interviews, and otherwise stop obstructing the therapy, he would give serious consideration to a transfer of primary custody to Ned. From previous experiences with me, the judge was aware of this recommendation in difficult cases and had every intention of implementing it. Apparently, Gloria got the message that the judge "meant business" and called me again and agreed to a joint interview. However, she told me that she did not trust her husband and would be accompanied by someone who would "protect her." I told her that she was free to bring anyone she wished to my waiting room, but that the decision as to whether that person could be in the room was primarily Ned's decision. I myself, seeing there to be no danger, did not feel the need to have such a party present. I informed her, however, that if Ned had no objection, the party could stay in the room at this point. She informed me that she was bringing her brother who was employed as a bank security guard.

On the day of our first appointment, I entered the waiting room. On one side was Gloria and her brother, Bob, and on the other side, Ned. All three were reading magazines as if the others did not exist. I invited Gloria and Ned to come up, at which point Gloria invited her brother to join her. At that point Ned (while we were all standing in the waiting room) said that he did not want Bob to participate. Accordingly, I informed Gloria that, at that point, her brother could not come into the consultation room, but that I would be willing to discuss this as the first issue on our agenda. Accordingly, Gloria came into the office with Ned. Ned claimed that Bob was supporting her in programming the children against him and that his presence there would make my work doubly difficult. He felt that there would be two against one. With regard to the issue of Gloria's being physically assaulted by Ned, there was absolutely nothing to suggest that this would take place. Accordingly, I told Gloria that she was free to bring her brother to my waiting room at any time, but that his more active participation was not being enlisted at this time. However, I informed her that there have been occasions when I have brought into the treatment significant others and that Bob's involvement would be decided subsequently. (Needless to say, Bob somehow evaporated after about three sessions and was never heard from again.) Furthermore, his participation in the programming process was in no way as great as Ned considered it to be, and so I did not consider Bob's involvement in the treatment warranted.

During the course of the first interview, I got background information about the marriage, the marital problems, the reasons for the separation, and the course of the post-separation adjustments. They told me about their three children, Mary (age 11), Robert (age 7), and James (age 5). It was clear that I was dealing here with a parental alienation syndrome of the moderate type. It was clear, also, that Gloria had been programming the children against their father, both overtly and covertly, both actively and passively. Interestingly, although the symptoms of the parental alienation syndrome began soon after the children learned of the custody dispute, her exclusionary maneuvers dated back to the earliest years of the children's lives. She had always viewed Ned as somewhat incompetent when it came to being alone with the children and was ever predicting negligence, accidents, and other manifestations of his ineptitude. She took great pains to supervise what he was doing and would frequently take over. Ned said, "Through the years I keep wavering between feeling that all I've been is a sperm donor and the feeling that she used me as the village idiot."

As is typical of parental-alienation-syndrome families, the transition points were the most difficult. Things had gotten progressively worse and had reached the point where the children were having fits of rage every time their father came to pick them up for visitation. They would fight him off physically, spit at him, and use profanities. Gloria would stand silently by shouting at Ned, "Can't you see they hate you? . . . Why don't you respect their feelings? . . . When are you going to get the message that they just don't want to be with you? etc., etc." Accordingly, during the previous year, Ned had been unsuccessful in getting the children to leave with him about 80 percent of the time. During those 20 percent of visitations when he was successful, the children would generally give him a difficult time in the car, but once in his home they tended to quiet down, become more friendly, and even engage in meaningful activities. However, even during those periods they would frequently "catch themselves" and resume their campaign of denigration. Mary, especially, could be relied upon to remind her brothers, if they had forgotten, how despicable a person their father was.

I informed the parents that I would be setting up a series of interviews to get to know the family better. I told them that I would be seeing Ned one to three times alone, Gloria one to three times alone, and each of the three children alone for one or more sessions. After that, I wanted a family interview. Ned was eager to proceed as rapidly as possible and complained about how bitter he was over all the time that had been lost setting up the therapy. Not surprisingly, Gloria had no such complaints. It had now been about three months since the children had visited with him, and he was extremely distraught. Gloria, although professing enthusiasm for the therapeutic program, found a wide variety of frivolous excuses for stretching out this evaluation period. I told her that I considered many of her reasons flimsy excuses for procrastination and that I was making careful notes for the court regarding this point. The therapist must appreciate that we are not dealing with *patients* here so much as we are with *litigants*. We are not dealing here with insight therapy so much as we are dealing with people who need to be threatened and coerced if anything therapeutic is to happen. The therapist must provide living experiences for their patients if they are to be helped. The kind of living experiences that Gloria had to have was that if she were to continue being recalcitrant, there would be another letter sent to the judge, and this could not but weaken her position in the custody conflict. The children also needed living experiences with their father, experiences that, more than any insights, would lessen their fear of and animosity toward him.

In my individual sessions with the family members, I learned much about the psychodynamics of the parental alienation syndrome and the specific ways in which the symptoms had developed in this family. (As mentioned, my purpose with this example is not to go into psychodynamics [which have been discussed in detail elsewhere] but to focus on problems related to the structuring of the treatment process.) I then set up a family interview. This time, when I entered the waiting room, Gloria and the three children were sitting at one end and the father at the other. No one was reading magazines at this point. The three children, however, were sitting close to Gloria, huddled next to her, as if Ned would spring from his seat at any point, dash across the room, and physically assault them. When they came into the consultation room, Gloria immediately sat down in the middle of the couch. Not surprisingly, the three children scrambled for seats next to her on a couch that barely accommodated the four of them comfortably. Ned had no choice but to sit in one of the chairs opposite them. I am sure that if he had gone toward the couch, the three children would have scrambled for seats elsewhere.

In the course of our discussion, on every disputed point that was raised, the children supported Gloria's position—even for matters that they had not directly observed. When I pointed out that they did not have enough information to come to a conclusion themselves, their reflex response was, "We believe our mother. Our father is a liar." When I asked them if they could specifically describe their father's lies, the only examples they gave related to his renditions, which differed from their mother's.

Before closing the meeting, I informed all that the following arrangement was going to be implemented regarding the court-ordered visitation that was scheduled for the following Friday: Gloria was to appear at my office at 4:00 p.m. with all three children. I would spend a half-hour with the four of them and then Gloria would leave. It would be understood that she would get into her car and drive away from my office and not linger there for any reason whatsoever. She expressed great reluctance to do this, but could not identify the specific fear she had other than that something terrible would happen if the children were alone with their father. I informed her that I had conducted a series of interviews and had no reason to believe that anything dangerous or detrimental would happen to them and nothing I had read in previous reports provided substantiation for her allegations. She insisted that she would wait in the waiting room. I told her that I had no reasonably good way of controlling where she was and that I was not going to call the police, although I could in that it was my private waiting room. Rather, I told her that if she did not cooperate, a letter would be faxed to the judge's office that very afternoon. She then told me that she planned to wait in the parking lot. I told her that I was not going out into the parking lot to check her out. However, if I did learn that she was there, a letter would be faxed to the judge. I told her that it was her decision, but she should know in advance just what the consequences would be. Although I found this interchange demeaning, I considered myself to have no alternative. To have let her sit in the waiting room, or even the parking lot, would have compromised the treatment significantly. It would also have given her the message that I was going to permit her to control the conduct of the treatment and this, obviously, could not but be antitherapeutic. Therapists who agree to treat such families must be willing at times to engage themselves in such unpleasant interchanges.

I informed the family that after the first half-hour meeting with the mother and the three children, I would see the three children alone from 4:30 to 5:00 p.m. Then Ned was to arrive at 5:00 p.m., at which time I would spend a half-hour with him and the three children. Then, Ned would leave with the three children for their visitation with him that weekend. Needless to say, the children joined with their mother in expressing reluctance for this program. Interestingly, their professions of reluctance did not have the same force as Gloria's. Last, I informed them that I would see them all on the following Tuesday in order to discuss what happened during the previous weekend.

On the appointed day Gloria, not surprisingly, was late by 15 minutes. I decided to stick to the schedule and told her that she must leave promptly at 4:30. Again, she expressed reluctance, and again I reminded her of what actions I would take. At 4:30 p.m. I asked her to leave. And as she walked out of my office she turned to me and screamed, "You're a stupid idiot! You're ruining my children!" She then slammed the door. During the first five to ten minutes the children were somewhat tense, yet still complained bitterly about their forthcoming visit with their father. At one point, James peeked out the door to see whether his mother was in the waiting room and informed me that he did not see her. Interestingly, following this disclosure the children relaxed significantly. I was not surprised by this, because I had every reason to believe that they were strongly bonded with their father and were afraid of expressing this emotion in front of their mother. Ned arrived at 4:55 p.m. and spoke to me through the intercom. The children exhibited some tension at that point, and Robert asked me if I knew whether his mother had come back into the waiting room. I told him that I did not know and that we would see when it came time for his father to join us. At 5:00 p.m., when I went to the door to invite his father in, the two boys came with me and peeked out to see whether their mother was there. Their father then joined us. As he entered the office, he reached out for the children and they were all somewhat stiff. They asked him if their mother was in the parking lot, and he responded that he did not see her. Subsequently, the two boys loosened up in the course of the half-hour meeting, but Mary maintained her aloofness from her father.

The following Tuesday I learned that Gloria had made no less than 25 telephone calls during the visitation, which ended on Sunday evening. She continually asked the children, "Is everything all right? . . . Don't worry. If there's any trouble you call me and I'll get right over there and take you home. . . . I don't think Dr. Gardner knows what he's doing. . . . I have a lawyer to protect you children." I also learned that Mary was continually reminding the children to "be careful" and to "watch out for him." Gloria never got specific about what the children should be careful about or what they should watch out for, but her calls caused them to be fearful and compromised their capacity to enjoy the weekend. As a result of this, I informed Gloria that during the next visit (two weeks later), there would be *one* ten-minute call on Saturday and *one* ten-minute on Sunday and that each call was to last not one minute longer. I informed her, as well, that if she went beyond this, I could count on Ned to inform me of this and that a letter would be faxed to the judge describing her failure to cooperate in the "treatment." Not surprisingly, Gloria had a fit when she heard this, but recognized that I meant every word of what I said and that she was not going to convince me to retract my threat. I have absolutely no hesitation using the word *threat*; in fact, it is one of my favorite words. And in the treatment of these families, if there are no threats, there is no treatment.

I also decided to make a different arrangement with regard to the three children being with their father together. It was clear that Mary was serving as the mother surrogate, programming the boys and thereby effecting "inside jobs" at Ned's house. The logistics here were more difficult. Of the various possible arrangements, I decided on their church serving as the transition point in mid-weekend, when there would be a switch and Mary would go to their father and the two boys back to their mother. Mary had learned—by living experience—that her programming the boys would result in her not being permitted to visit along with them, something she really wanted to do. The mother was to come at 4:00 p.m. Friday with all three children. At 4:30 p.m. she would leave with Mary, and I would spend another half-hour with Robert and James. Then, at 5:00 p.m., Ned would come, spend a half-hour with me and the boys, and then take the two boys. On Sunday, both parents would go to church, mother accompanied by Mary and father by the two boys. Then, the children would "switch." Ned would then leave church with Mary and Gloria would go home with the two boys. In individual sessions I told all three children that when Mary stopped turning the boys against their father and they stopped listening to her when she did, then all three could spend more time with their father. I was appealing here to those deep forces within all three of them that really wanted to have a good relationship with their father.

Fortunately, the church proved to be a good transition site. Mary was not that disturbed that she would make a scene in church, and she knew that I had established a reputation for myself of being quite stringent. She knew, also, that if there was any trouble with the transition in church, the judge would learn of it.

After two weeks of the "split visitation" arrangement, I once again tried the children visiting together and it proved successful. Gloria, too, controlled herself with the telephone calls. This family's treatment lasted about six months. It would not have been successful had I not had the power of the court behind me. Without it, none of the maneuvers would have been successful, and the children probably would have become completely alienated from their father. I cannot say that Gloria gained any insight into her difficulties. Nor can I say that the children were not left with residual animosity and fear of their father. However, both of these feelings were reduced significantly, and they had living experiences that provided proof that their mother's fears would not be realized in actuality.

There are some readers, I am sure, who, when reading this clinical example, must have thought that there are better ways to make a living, either within or out of the field of psychiatry. And I am in full agreement. I myself find such an approach distasteful (and at times demeaning) and certainly would leave the field if this was how I had to spend my whole day, every day, throughout the course of my career. However, it is the only treatment plan I know of for such cases. Every professional has his (her) share of dirty work, and this is an example of the dirty work of psychiatry. My hope is that the reader who is willing to utilize such an approach will be willing to tolerate its discomforts because of the knowledge that such toleration may bring about the salvaging of young human lives and the prevention of complete alienation from a parent, a child's most treasured possession.

CONCLUDING COMMENTS

The parental alienation syndrome rarely exists in pure form. Children who have been subjected to the psychological traumas attendant to their parents' divorce are likely to suffer with a wide variety of other symptoms, often unrelated to the parental alienation syndrome. Accordingly, if the therapist is successful in treating the disorder, he (she) does well to assess for the presence of other difficulties as well. These have been described elsewhere (Gardner, 1976, 1986a), and it is beyond the scope of this book to discuss such treatment in detail. Also, as I am sure the reader appreciates, every patient and every family is different and each treatment program must be tailored to the needs of that particular family. I have described here the general principles of the psychotherapeutic approach, principles that can only serve as guidelines for the particular families in treatment.

On many occasions I have been consulted by distraught parents (more often fathers than mothers) whose spouses have been successful in effecting a complete alienation over a long period. These fathers have been completely depleted of all their financial resources, and the courts have basically been unreceptive to their situation, especially because judges have been reluctant to implement the recommendations described in this chapter. Not only have the judges been reluctant to order a transfer of custody to the father, but they have even refused to impose the sanctions described in detail here. The wives have scorned the court's directives with the recognition that absolutely nothing will happen to them for such defiance. These fathers have come to me for advice regarding what to do at this point about their children. Some of them were advised by well-meaning therapists that ultimately the children would come to see what was going on. I believe that this advice, although benevolently motivated, was injudicious and indicates that the adviser was not familiar with the parental alienation syndrome and the way it can insidiously bring about an attenuation (and even complete destruction) of a parent-child psychological bond.

My general advice to such fathers is that they continue to make every reasonable attempt to communicate with their children and work on the assumption that, the children's ongoing animosity notwithstanding, there is still residua of the early bonding operative. I try to help them find the balance between making nuisances of themselves and making no overtures at all. I advise them to recognize birthdays, graduations, confirmations, bar mitzvahs, etc., by mail and by grapevine communications. I generally discourage their sending significant amounts of money or expensive presents, because doing so could easily result in their being exploited. Even though their letters might be destroyed (before or after being read), and even though the children may hang up on them, I advise them to "keep plugging." Again, I emphasize that the frequency of such overtures not be so great that they will be making nuisances of themselves. I recommend that they remember the bonding of the earlier years and hope that love will ultimately win out over fear. Because we have no long-term follow-ups of these children at this point, I do not know the frequency with which this advice ultimately proves useful. I suspect that it is useful only in a small percentage of cases, but this should not discourage therapists from making these recommendations.

This chapter should not end on this note of pessimism. I am basically optimistic about the psychotherapeutic treatment of children with parental alienation syndrome if the evaluator can convince the court of what is going on and then use its powers to support a treatment program of the kind outlined here.

Comment on Addendum II for the Second Printing—1995

Since the publication of the first printing of this book in 1992 I have come upon a solution to the problem of dealing with mothers and children in the severe category of parental alienation syndrome. My experience has been that the severe category represents about 10 percent of PAS families. Whereas the children of mothers in the mild and moderate categories usually do better remaining with their mothers, many—but not all—the children in the severe category would probably do better living primarily with their fathers. The problem of transfer has been a formidable one. This problem, I believe, has been solved by the proposal included in the back of this book as Addendum II. It describes a series of transitional sites of varying degrees of restriction and supervision that can be very useful, both for deciding where the children shall ultimately live and facilitating their easement into the father's home, if that proves to be the final optimum disposition.

 **SEVEN**

THE ROLE OF LAWYERS AND JUDGES IN DEALING WITH PARENTAL-ALIENATION-SYNDROME FAMILIES

INTRODUCTION

I know of no better example of the value of psychiatry and the law joining forces than when one is dealing with parental-alienation-syndrome families. When the law and psychiatry work together, there is a good likelihood of success when dealing with these families. In contrast, an approach to this disorder in which either discipline works independently is almost doomed to failure because the therapist does not have the power of the court, and the court does not have the expertise of the mental health professional nor the opportunity to work in depth on an ongoing basis with these families. The judge in the courthouse is not available to reach out and deal with the details that are crucial to attend to if one is to be helpful to these families. And lawyers, although they are certainly more available to their clients than judges, are still not as accessible to deal with the whole family. And, as mentioned, judges and lawyers do not have the training to provide these families with the psychiatric services they require.

Mental health professionals are basically impotent when it comes to requiring their patients to do anything. They can analyze, help people gain insight, suggest and recommend, but they have little if any power over their patients. They basically cannot order anybody to do anything. When the power of the courts is *judiciously* placed in the hands of the mental health professional, the combination can be quite useful. I emphasize the word *judiciously* because at no point do I envision a mental health professional to have anywhere near the power of the judge. Rather, it is *through the judge*—specifically by recommendations to the judge—that he (she) wields power, and it is through the threat cf reporting to the judge those who are not cooperating in treatment that the power is wielded.

LAWYERS

As was true in my discussion of the lawyer's role in gathering evidence when working with parental-alienation-syndrome families, I will have little to say about the individual lawyer's role in the therapy of these families. The most therapeutic thing a lawyer can do is to do everything possible to obtain an appropriate ruling as quickly as possible. The longer the children are exposed to the programming, the longer they are subjected to the loyalty conflict, the more deep-seated become their symptoms, and the more difficult it will be to alleviate them. Unfortunately, there are many lawyers who operate under the principle that the more protracted the litigation, the more money they will make. Of course, this is not frequently professed openly, but there is no question that this factor operates for many of the lawyers whom I have personally encountered. Law is an overcrowded profession, there are many "hungry" lawyers, and under these circumstances it is not surprising that this factor frequently overrides ethical and therapeutic considerations. Lawyers in this category do their clients a terrible disservice indeed. And there are lawyers who are not in this category, who are not prolonging the litigation for personal monetary gain, but who are doing so because they recognize that time is on the side of their client, especially when the client is the one who is programming the children. Their need to zealously support their client's position overrides their willingness to recognize that such procrastination is psychologically detrimental to their client's children.

The attorney who supports the programming parent, especially the parent who is filled with vengeful rage, is doing the whole family (including the client) a terrible disservice. Even worse, the attorney who is swept up in the paranoid parent's delusion will do even more damage. Operating under the principle that it is the lawyer's role to support the client, people may be driven to psychotic decompensation, homicide, and suicide (and I have personally been witness to all of these outcomes of protracted custody litigation [Gardner, 1986a, 1989a]). The knowledgeable and ethical lawyer will recognize the client's psychopathology under these circumstances and will not be party to a program that supports such destructive maneuvers. Rather, the ethical lawyer will support the utilization of the guidelines for custody assignment presented below—in my discussion of the judge's role in dealing with these families. The ethical lawyer, also, will support the kind of treatment program described in Chapter Six.

JUDGES

Guidelines for Judges for Making Custody Decisions

Courts do well to make custody decisions on the basis of what I refer to as the *stronger-healthy-psychological-bond presumption.* Implementation of this presumption is a three-step process:

> 1. Preference (but not automatic assignment) should be given to that parent (regardless of sex) with whom the child has established *over time* the stronger *healthy* psychological bond.
> 2. That parent (regardless of sex) who was the primary caretaker during the earliest years of the child's life is the one with whom the child is more likely to have established the stronger bond. Residua of that early bonding are likely to influence strongly subsequent bonding experiences with the parents.
> 3. The longer the gap between the early bonding and the time of the dispute, the greater the likelihood other experiences will

affect the strength of the bond. Whether or not these have resulted in the formation of an even stronger bond with the parent who was not the primary caretaker during the earliest years has to be assessed in the course of the evaluative process.

I believe courts have not been paying enough attention to the formidable early-life influences on the child's subsequent psychological status. Early-life influences play an important role in the formation of the child's psychological bond to the parent who was the primary caretaker during the earliest years. Courts have been giving too much weight to recent and present-day involvement, ignoring the residual contributions of early bonding to present experiences. Mothers have been much more often the primary custodial parents during the early child-rearing process. This produces a bond between the two that results in strong attachment cravings when there is a rupture of the relationship. Accordingly, when there is a threatened disruption of this relationship by a sex-blind judge or joint-custodial mandate, mother and child fight it vigorously. Commonly, the mother brainwashes the child and uses him (her) as a weapon to sabotage the father's attempts to gain primary custody. The children develop their own scenarios, as well, in an attempt to preserve this bond. I believe that residua of the early influences are playing an important role in the attempts on the part of both parties to maintain the attachment bond.

It is to be noted that these guidelines strictly avoid a specific age cut-off point. Rather, I use the more vague time frame of "the earliest years of the child's life." Although I generally try to avoid being vague (and I hope that the reader will agree with me on this point), there are times when vagueness is crucial, and this is one of them. To indicate a specific age cut-off point would be both dangerous and grandiose. It would be dangerous because I would run the risk that a judge might use it as a line of demarcation for deciding whether or not a parent satisfied this requirement. It would also be grandiose because it would imply that I know with certainty that there is such a cut-off point (there is not). Rather, one does better to view this principle on a continuum. The longer a particular parent has been the primary caretaker during the child's formative years, the greater the likelihood the bonding is likely to take place.

It is also important to note that the parent-child bonding referred to here is *healthy* bonding. I am not referring to sick bonding. A child who was brought up by a paranoid mother, for example, may very well become more strongly bonded to her than with the father. Obviously, one would not give preference to this mother in a custody dispute, her stronger bonding notwithstanding. In many cases, the father's bonding with the child is healthy but, because of the inevitable differences in time that children spend with each of their parents in the average household, the bonding with the father will be weaker.

It is important also for courts to appreciate that the psychological bond can withstand just so much attenuation before it begins to weaken and even become entirely destroyed. For example, a mother may have had the stronger bond prior to the onset of the custody dispute. And it may even have been a healthy one. At the same time, the father's bonding with the children, although somewhat weaker than the mother's, was still quite strong, and if anything were to have happened to the mother, most would agree that the father would serve better than anyone else as the primary caretaker of the children. However, if in the course of a child custody dispute, the mother becomes so enraged that she successfully indoctrinates the children against the father, then a certain amount of weakening of their bond with him is likely to take place. If this goes on uninterrupted over many months and possibly extending over a few years, there will be a progressive deterioration of that bonding—sometimes to the point where it may be obliterated almost entirely. After many such years of alienation, the father may become a stranger to them. And this is one of the reasons why the courts must act quickly.

Furthermore, there are situations in which the mother was the primary caretaker and the father has been successful in indoctrinating the children against the mother. Although initially they may have resisted such indoctrination—especially because of their stronger bonding with their mother—the bonding may still be corruptible; over time, especially if he is successful in utilizing exclusionary maneuvers—he may tip the balance in his direction. In such cases the children may actually develop a parental alienation syndrome against their mother, in spite of the fact that she was the primary caretaker and it was she with whom they had the stronger bond prior to the onset of the litigation. A rapid transfer back to the mother as the primary custodial parent is the best treatment in this situation.

The implementation of the presumption that children do best when placed with the parent who is most involved in child rearing, especially during the formative years, would reduce significantly the custody litigation that we are currently witnessing. It would result in many mothers being automatically awarded custody. It would not preclude, however, fathers obtaining custody because there would be some fathers who would easily satisfy this important criterion for primary custodial assignment. The implementation of this presumption would still allow those parents (whether male or female) who were only secondarily involved in the child's rearing to have the opportunity to seek and gain custody. They would, however, have to provide compelling evidence that the primary custodial parent's child-rearing input was significantly compromised and their own contributions so formidable that they should more justifiably be designated primary custodial parents.

I believe that the implementation of these guidelines will reduce significantly the likelihood that mothers will brainwash their children and that parental alienation syndromes will develop. Furthermore, it will reduce the likelihood of injudicious decisions regarding custodial placement and prevent, thereby, the wide variety of psychopathological processes that can develop therefrom.

Last, I recommend that we replace the best-interests-of-the-child presumption with the *best-interests-of-the-family presumption.* The best-interests-of-the-child presumption is somewhat narrow. It does not take into consideration the psychological effects on the parents of the child's placement and the effects of the resultant feedback on the child's welfare. As mentioned, the strong bond that forms in early life between the child and the primary caretaker produces immensely strong cravings for one another when there is threatened disruption of the relationship. Just as the child suffers psychologically from removal from the adult, so is the adult traumatized by removal from the child. The psychological trauma to the adult caused by such disruption can be immense, so much so that parenting capacity may be compromised. This negative feedback, of course, is not in the best interests of the child. But we are not dealing here simply with the question of placing the child with a parent in order to protect that parent from feeling upset about the child's being placed with another parent. Rather, we are considering the ultimate negative impact on the child of the disruption of the bond with the primary caretaker.

Accordingly, I am recommending that courts assign primary custody in accordance with the presumption that the *family's* best interests will be served by the child being placed with that parent who was the primary caretaker during the formative years. Furthermore, the longer that parent continued to be primary caretaker, the greater likelihood the *family's* interests will be served by placement with that parent. The implementation of this presumption will, I believe, also serve as a form of preventive psychiatry in that it will not only reduce custody litigation significantly but will also serve to obviate the terrible psychological problems attendant to such litigation.

The Role of the Judiciary in Dealing Optimally with Parental-Alienation-Syndrome Children and Their Parents

I believe that the courts can play a crucial role in helping families in which a child manifests a parental alienation syndrome. The courts have the power to make custodial assignments that can be quite therapeutic—a power that therapists do not have. Without the court's utilization of its powers , it would be extremely unlikely, if not impossible, to treat certain children in this category.

In previous chapters I have discussed in detail the categories of mothers who contribute to their children's parental alienation syndrome. In Chapter Six I described for mental health professionals the therapeutic approaches to each of these three categories. The recommendations I made for mental health professionals there are applicable to the judiciary. Whereas the mental health professional can only make recommendations, the courts have the power to effect the kinds of transfers (parent and/or child) that are warranted. I will, however, review here (for judges) certain aspects of my recommendations previously made for mental health professionals.

It is important for judges to ascertain in which category the parental alienation syndrome lies: severe, moderate, or mild. This differentiation is crucial if the court is to make proper rulings. Without the court's providing proper placement of the children, the therapist may be left impotent. I present here the approaches courts do well to utilize for each of the three types of parental alienation syndrome.

When appointing therapists and guardians ad litem to implement the recommendations below, it is *crucial* that the judge appoint individuals who are thoroughly familiar with the parental alienation syndrome. Without such knowledge, the likelihood of such therapists helping these families is almost at a zero level. They must choose therapists who will not "respect" the child's wishes to do sick things. They should appoint therapists who operate on the principle that serving the best interests of children is not necessarily doing what they ask, but doing what is good for them. They must appoint therapists who do not accept at face value what children say, but recognize that often what they say and what they need are two very different things. Furthermore, they must choose guardians who will not reflexively support their child clients' requests and who recognize that child clients with parental alienation syndrome often need strong adults to do just the opposite of what they claim they want.

They do well to indicate in the court order the exact name of the therapist who is to be appointed (rather than a vague term like *a psychologist* or *a psychiatrist*) and the names of the parties who are being ordered to cooperate in the treatment. This should not only include the mother, the father, and all children but any other parties who might be part of the network that supports the parental alienation syndrome. This should include stepparents as well as live-in parties who are significantly involved with each of the biological parents. If these additional parties are not subject to the court's authority, then their active participation should strongly be supported by the court, and their failure to involve themselves should be viewed unfavorably by the court.

Furthermore, and this is quite important, the court does well to be quite clear, at this point, regarding the exact sanctions that will be imposed for parties who do not cooperate with the impartial examiner. If these are not spelled out clearly, the therapist's work will be compromised. As discussed in Chapter Six, these fall into the category of fines, reduction in support/alimony payments, loss of primary custody, and jail. The judge who is not willing to impose such sanctions is not fulfilling his (her) role and is undermining at the outset the treatment being ordered.

As mentioned previously in this book, the parental denigration by children who are suffering with a parental alienation syndrome is in no way warranted. The hated parent does not warrant such a campaign of denigration. In contrast, when bona fide abuse has taken place, the alienation may very well be warranted, and the parental-alienation-syndrome concept is not applicable.

Severe Cases of the Parental Alienation Syndrome The mothers of children in this category are often fanatic. In many cases they are paranoid. Court-ordered treatment is likely to prove futile, so meager is their insight into their psychopathology. Rage and vengeance against the husband for having abandoned them are often present, but less important than the paranoid mechanism. Some were paranoid before the litigation; most were preparanoid and exhibited paranoid deterioration as a result of the litigation (Gardner, 1986a). The children join the mother in a *folie-à-deux* relationship and may harbor the same delusions about the father that their mother exhibits. I wish to emphasize again that the fathers I am discussing here are those who have had reasonably good relationships with their children prior to the onset of the child custody dispute and, although they may certainly have some problems, are far healthier than the mothers.

It is crucial that the court make an early decision regarding primary custody (especially in support of fathers in the severe category and mothers in the moderate and mild categories). This in itself is probably the most therapeutic thing the court can do. As mentioned, the symptoms in both mothers and children arise, in part, from the threat of disruption of the mother-child bond. For children in the moderate and mild categories, a court order that the children will live permanently with their mothers will remove one of the most important factors operative in bringing about the symptoms and, in many cases, is the most important factor in the alleviation of the disorder. Courts are traditionally slow and thereby prolong the family's grief and the entrenchment of the parental alienation syndrome. I recognize that judges are often overwhelmed by heavy court calendars, and lawyers are not famous for their speed in moving along such cases. And this is especially the case for the attorney who supports a client for whom time is on her (his) side. These impediments to the court's quick action notwithstanding, everything should still be done to bring about the earliest possible decision regarding primary custodial designation.

The court must take care to enlist the services of a therapist who is thoroughly familiar with the parental alienation syndrome and who is comfortable utilizing the more coercive maneuvers necessary to the treatment of these families. Therapists who do not satisfy both of these requirements are not likely to be effective in helping such families. Ideally, the therapist should be someone whom both parents respect. Unfortunately, mothers of parental-alienation-syndrome children, especially in the severe and moderate categories, do not generally respect any therapist who takes a neutral position or who is going to utilize coercive techniques in the service of bringing about rapprochement between the children and their father. Accordingly, if the court is going to withhold such an order until a mutually agreed-upon therapist is found, it will have a long time to wait. Rather, the court does well to maintain a roster of therapists who are familiar with the techniques necessary to utilize in these cases, are comfortable using them, and allow the parents (with the help of their attorneys) to select one from a list of two or three such qualified people.

Therapy with these children is often not possible while they are still living in the mother's home. There is a sick psychological bond between the children and the mother that is not going to be changed by therapy as long as they remain in her home. While still there they are going to be exposed continually to the bombardment of denigration of the father that contributes to the perpetuation of the parental alienation syndrome. The only hope for these children, therefore, is court-ordered removal to the home of the father, the allegedly hated parent. Often, this is not accomplished easily, and the court might have to threaten sanctions and even jail if the mother does not comply. Following the transfer there must be a period of decompression in which the mother has no opportunity at all for input to the children. This is the only possible way they can reestablish their former relationship with the father and protect themselves from the reindoctrinations of the mother. Even telephone calls must be strictly prohibited for at least a few weeks, and perhaps longer. Although this may sound like an extremely stringent requirement, my experience has been that programming can easily take place in the course of such conversations, even when monitored by the father. Many of the programming communications are subtle, and even a statement like "Thank God you're all right" communicates that the children have survived terrible risks and dangers. Then, according to the therapist's judgment, slowly increasing contacts with the mother may be initiated, starting with monitored telephone calls.

It is important that the therapist be court ordered and that *one* therapist serve the whole family, separated or divorced status notwithstanding. In many of the cases in which I have been involved, the courts have ordered that each of the parties be in therapy with a separate therapist. Although seemingly egalitarian, it is basically an injudicious recommendation. First, the family would have to be quite wealthy to implement this recommendation. Second, I have never seen a family in which the order has been followed in a meaningful way. Furthermore, ordering separate therapists will only fractionate the family more (beyond that which related to the separation) and contribute to the perpetuation of the parental alienation syndrome. Not only is communication reduced, but family subsystems are set up that only add to the animosity of the family members. Although, as mentioned, the mothers in this category are not usually candidates for meaningful insight therapy, they can still be required to comply with the court- appointed therapist's instructions in the course of the child's treatment. The therapist must be given certain powers through the court. Obviously, the judge cannot delegate his (her) authority directly to the therapist. However, the therapist can have an open line to the court, either directly or through a child advocate or guardian ad litem.

If the father had established a good and reasonably healthy psychological bond with the children prior to the litigation (the more common situation), then these children are likely to exhibit such manifestations of affection once separated from the programming mother. Although initially the children may be quite resistant to visiting with the father, and may fight the transfer vehemently, they ultimately settle down. At that point *carefully monitored* visits with the mother may be possible. The determinant of how much contact they will have with the mother should be made by the therapist. The main criterion for deciding how much time the children will spend with the mother should be determined by the extent of the mother's programming and the degree of complying scenarios manifested by the children. For most cases in this category, permanent transfer to the father is the best course of action for the court to take. The mother's psychological bond with the children is often quite sick, whereas that with the father is more likely to be a healthier one. Transfer back to the home of the mother may result in lifelong alienation from the father. The degree of contact with the mother, during visitation, depends upon the mother's degree of programming. And, as mentioned, this is determined by the therapist with monitoring and input by the court.

One of the fringe benefits of the court-ordered transfer is that it provides the child with a face-saving alibi for the mother. Specifically, the child, when with the mother, can profess unswerving loyalty to her and need not admit that there is any affection for the father, even after the child has lived (sometimes even peacefully) with the father for a number of months following court transfer. The child can complain to the mother about all the indignities suffered at the father's home and the stupidity of the judge for having ordered the transfer. The child often professes innocence of any wish to live with the father: "The stupid judge makes me live with him. I hate every minute of it. Most judges don't know what they're doing. And that Dr. Gardner is a bigger idiot, because he told the judge that he thought it would be a good idea for me to live with my father. He's just a stupid ignoramus psychiatrist."

Moderate Cases of the Parental Alienation Syndrome   The mothers of children in this category are not as fanatic as those in the severe category and are less likely to be paranoid. Most often they have established a healthy psychological bond with the children prior to the custody litigation. They are, however, programming their children against the father, but to a lesser degree than mothers in Category One. Such programming often relates to vengeance maneuvers and the desire to maintain the healthy psychological bond. These mothers may be in therapy, but often with a therapist (more often a woman than a man) who supports the mother's antagonism toward the father. The court's ordering a discontinuation of such therapy often proves futile in that the mother is likely to find another therapist who will support her in her animosity toward the father. Accordingly, here again, the mother should be ordered to attend sessions with a court-ordered therapist who sees the whole family, the parents' separated or divorced status notwithstanding.

Here the children can continue living with the mother, but

the therapist needs the court's power to require the mother to cooperate in the visitation and not to obstruct it. This may involve the utilization of neutral parties at transfer points, or transfers taking place in the therapist's office. The details of the kinds of maneuvers and manipulations required by the therapist in such treatment have been presented in Chapter Six. Whereas the therapist dealing with the severe category of mothers needs the court's support for monitoring visitation from the father's house to the mother's, here the court's power is necessary to enforce implementation of visitation from the mother's house to the father's. The court may also have to threaten monetary sanctions, removal of custody, and even jail in order to get such mothers to cooperate in facilitating visitation.

Mild Cases of the Parental Alienation Syndrome The mothers in this category also have established a healthy psychological bond with their children prior to the onset of the custody litigation. They are less enraged than mothers in the moderate category, but there is some anger, especially regarding the misguided egalitarianism of recent legislation—which does not give proper respect to the importance of the parent with whom the child has developed the stronger psychological bond (most often the mother). The children's scenarios of denigration of the father are created in an attempt to maintain the stronger bond with the mother. The symptoms, in both mother and children, are likely to disappear (most often dramatically) as soon as the court makes a final decision that the children shall remain permanently with the mother. From that point on the symptoms serve no purpose and can be allowed to evaporate. Here again, the judge can do much more than even the most skilled therapist. To attempt therapy while the parents are still litigating for custody—when there is still the threat that the children might be ordered to reside permanently with the father—is not likely to be effective.

Concluding Comments

My experiences with judges have been mixed with regard to the implementation of the aforementioned guidelines and recommendations. Some have been quite receptive to my ideas and have implemented them fully. At the other end of the spectrum are those who have been completely unreceptive to what I have to say, much, I believe, to the detriment of the families involved. A complaint I have about many of the judges in whose courts I have testified is the slowness of the process. In many cases this has nothing to do with the judge in that the courts are overcrowded. In some cases it relates to attorney delay, because it is well known that time is on the side of the parent who lives with the children, regardless of whether or not that particular home would be best for them. However, I have seen far too many cases in which the stalling maneuvers are clearly the judge's. There are many who have difficulty making a decision. They are constantly finding excuses for continually pushing ahead a final ruling. Some will threaten sanctions against an uncooperative mother, but never follow through on them. These mothers are notorious for flaunting judicial rulings and judges must be aware of this. These mothers believe, sometimes to a fanatical degree, that any contact with the father would be detrimental, and they are willing to face jail sentences if necessary. However, in extreme cases, that may be the only thing that will get them to cooperate. However, my experience has been that monetary privation or the threat of permanent transfer of custody to the father will work.

Another complaint I have against judges is their quickness to order people into therapy. First, I suspect that many of them recognize that one really cannot order anyone into treatment. The same judge may recognize that he (she) could not order into medical treatment an adult whose religious beliefs are antithetical to such medical care. Yet, they do not seem to hesitate to order into treatment parents who are litigating over their children. Furthermore, such a judge would not order a frigid woman to have an orgasm or an impotent man to have an erection, yet he (she) has no hesitation ordering a person to involve himself (herself) in a meaningful therapeutic process. Such orders are an extension of their general view of the world that ordering people around is the best way to accomplish something. Often, the therapy tack becomes incorporated into the stalling maneuver and unnecessarily prolongs the litigation. In such cases the therapy has been ordered in order to get the parent to stop programming the children. Such a parent knows that as long as they remain "sick," the children will remain with them. With such a boon benefit for not getting "better," the parent will remain "sick" for years. Such judges do not seem to appreciate that the "therapy" lies more in their hands than in that of the mental health professional. A quick decision regarding primary custodial status is far more therapeutic than anything even the most skilled and experienced therapist can accomplish. In short, we need more decisive judges who will act firmly and swiftly, and we need more judges who will support and stand behind the kind of impartial therapist described in this book.

GUARDIANS AD LITEM

Once again, a guardian ad litem who is not familiar with the parental alienation syndrome may cause serious psychological damage to children suffering with this disorder. A guardian ad litem who is not familiar with the causes, manifestations, and proper treatment of children with parental alienation syndrome may prove a definite impediment in the course of their treatment. The guardian who takes pride in supporting what children profess they want is likely to perpetuate the psychopathology of children suffering with parental alienation syndrome. The guardian must recognize that parental-alienation-syndrome children need to be forced into doing things that they profess they do not want to do. In order to do this, the guardian must "switch gears" and unlearn certain principles learned in law school regarding being a zealous supporter of one's client's requests and demands. He (she) must be ever aware that the client is a child, not an adult. Furthermore, he (she) must be ever aware that the client is just not any child, but a child with a parental alienation syndrome. If these considerations are taken into account, then the guardian will be comfortable doing just the opposite of what the client requests. Such a guardian must be comfortable with the children's criticisms and must be willing to be used as the excuse for the children going to the allegedly hated parent: "I really hate that lawyer. He says I *must* visit my father. I really hate my father. You know, Mommy, I love you and I don't want to go there but he makes me go there." In this way, the guardian is used as a vehicle for assuaging the child's guilt over disloyalty to the mother implied by any willingness to visit the father.

Guardians who do their work properly will impress upon the adversary attorneys and the court the importance of ordering the kind of therapeutic program described in Chapter Six. They will help educate judges and attorneys who are not familiar with the parental alienation syndrome. If lawyers are still on the scene at the time of the aforementioned therapeutic program, then the guardian should serve to help implement the treatment. Sometimes the guardian can serve as an intermediary between the court-appointed neutral therapist and the court. I am not recommending here that the guardian serve merely as a messenger boy (girl). Rather, the guardian would clarify for uncooperating parents the legal consequences of their recalcitrance and add clout to the therapist's warnings and threats.

# EIGHT
RECOMMENDATIONS FOR THE FUTURE

INTRODUCTION

In this last chapter I will focus on changes that, if implemented, should reduce the frequency of development of the parental alienation syndrome. Because I believe that the parental alienation syndrome is primarily a derivative of seemingly benevolent and egalitarian, but misguided criteria that have been utilized for determining primary custodial status, I think that a reconsideration of these criteria is in order. Furthermore, believing that an important contributory factor to the parental alienation syndrome is the adversary system as the primary method for resolving child custody disputes, I think that a reconsideration of that method of adjudication is also warranted. These changes, however, cannot be made without changes in the educational systems of the lawyers and mental health professionals who are directly involved in such disputes and their resolution. Recommendations for changes in the training of people in both of these realms is therefore desirable. I believe that the implementation of the recommendations described herein provide us with an excellent opportunity for practicing preventive psychiatry. The parental alienation syndrome focused on in this book is only one of a wide

279

variety of psychiatric disturbances caused by the embroilment of parents and children in child custody disputes. (Elsewhere [Gardner, 1986a] I have described these other disorders in detail.) The implementation of the recommendations provided in this chapter would, I believe, also reduce the incidence of these disorders as well.

THE EDUCATION OF LAWYERS

If the recommendations made in this book are to be brought about, it is crucial that significant changes be made in the education of attorneys. If law schools continue to churn out graduates who are as committed to the adversary system as those of past years, then it is unlikely that many of the proposed reforms will be realized. At this time there is good evidence that many law schools are beginning to make such changes. Some schools have introduced courses in mediation and other alternative methods of dispute resolution. However, the schools still have a long way to go. In this section I focus on what is starting to be done and what still needs to be done.

Law School Admissions Procedures

Most of the major law schools with which I am familiar do not interview students who are being screened for admission. Rather, the criteria upon which the decision is made are mainly class standing, grade point average, the academic prestige of the institution(s) from which the student has graduated, letters of recommendation, and last (but certainly not least) the applicant's score on the Law School Aptitude Test (LSAT). This information is fed into a computer and a decision is often made without human intervention. A school will often grant an interview if an applicant requests it, but this aspect of the admissions procedure is not well publicized or encouraged. The faculty generally prefers to use the above criteria to determine suitability for admission rather than devote significant time to interviewing the sea of applicants who apply to the best law schools. Some of these applicants have been discouraged from applying to medical school because of the glut of physicians in densely populated areas and because of the AIDS epidemic. Others have been discouraged by the paralysis that many physicians experience in association with the glut of paperwork required to practice medicine in recent years. Bureaucratic snags and failure of health insurance providers to fulfill their obligations have made medicine an onerous occupation for many physicians, some of whom have actually left medicine because of their frustration over these developments.

I believe that the failure to interview applicants is an unfortunate practice. Medical schools also receive floods of applicants (recent drops notwithstanding) and yet routinely interview those among the highly qualified group under serious consideration for admission. Medical school admissions committees consider themselves to have an obligation to both the school and society to learn something about the morals, ethics, values, and psychological stability of potential candidates. Although the law schools claim that such information will be found in the undergraduate school's letter of recommendation, there is no question that colleges try to portray candidates to graduate school in the best possible terms. The more prestigious the schools their graduates enter, the more prestige the undergraduate school will enjoy. Under these circumstances, hyperbole characterizes the letters of recommendation because even a hint of impairment is likely to doom the candidate—*especially* at the more prestigious law schools.

Such an admission policy contributes to the development and continuation of some of the problems described in this book. Specifically, those lawyers who perpetrate the evils described herein must have certain personality defects in order to operate in the way they do. They must have significant impairments in their sensitivity to the feelings of others and be capable of blinding themselves to the psychological damage they are inflicting on clients—both their own clients and those of their adversaries. They must be people with little sense of guilt concerning their actions. In extreme cases such individuals are called *psychopaths*.

Psychopaths, by definition, are people who have little guilt or remorse over the pains and suffering they cause others. They have little capacity to place themselves in the positions of those whom they are exploiting or traumatizing. The primary deterrent to their exploitative behavior is the immediate threat of punishment or retribution from external sources. They have little, if any, internal mechanisms to deter them from their heinous activities. Psychopathic types can be very convincing and ingratiating; they are often master manipulators. They may do quite well for themselves at the undergraduate level, demonstrating their brilliance to professors and convincing school administrators and faculty that they are major contributors to their academic institutions. Such individuals often receive the most laudatory letters of recommendation to law schools and other graduate institutions. It is important for the reader to appreciate that I am not by any means claiming that all lawyers who engage in protracted custody litigation are psychopaths or psychopathic types. I am only claiming that law school admissions procedures are not well designed to screen such people, and the legal educational process intensifies such tendencies when they exist.

It is important for the reader to appreciate that the terms *psychopath* and *psychopathic type* do not refer to clearly defined categories. There is a continuum from the normal to the psychopathic type to the extreme psychopath—with varying gradations of impairment. When I use the term *psychopath* I am referring to the people at the upper end of the continuum. Psychopathic types are found lower down on the continuum, but they still exhibit occasional psychopathic traits. Individuals in both of these categories may very well gain acceptance into law school, especially if no interview is required. I am not claiming that interviewers would routinely detect such individuals, only that astute interviewers should be alerted to their existence. Interviewers who screen applicants for medical schools are generally concerned with such types. Although medical school interviewers may certainly be fooled by psychopaths, they are less likely to be duped than computers.

It is also important for the reader to appreciate that this

negative comparison between medical school and law school admissions procedures is not a statement on my part that we do not have psychopathic types in medicine. Rather, I believe that we have too many and that admissions screening procedures are not stringent enough and interviewers not astute enough always to detect such individuals at that point. I do believe, however, that there are fewer psychopaths in medicine than in law, partly due to admissions interviews. Moreover, I fully appreciate that we in medicine have our own brands of psychopathology and personality disorder, as does every field. I am not whitewashing medicine here; I am only pointing out certain differences in admissions procedures relevant to the issues in this chapter.

Another category of psychopathology likely to be found among members of the legal profession is *paranoia*. A paranoid individual is generally defined as someone who has delusions of persecution. Specifically, paranoids believe that others are persecuting, plotting against, exploiting, and engaging in a variety of other harmful acts against them when there is no evidence for such. These individuals may be always on the defensive and may seize upon every opportunity to "fight back." *Paranoid types* are individuals who have paranoid tendencies, but are not grossly paranoid. They are at a point along the continuum between normal and paranoid, but closer to the paranoid end. Paranoid tendencies and the practice of law go well together. These individuals may view legal education as a vehicle for providing themselves with ammunition for protection against their persecutors. Again, we certainly have our share of paranoids in medical school; however, because our admission procedures lessen the likelihood that paranoids will gain admission, I believe that there is a higher percentage in the legal profession. Paranoids are very likely to encourage litigation, whether it be custody litigation or any other type. And they thereby contribute to the grief of parents involved in custody/visitation conflicts.

Of particular pertinence to this book is the paranoid type or paranoid lawyer who does not appreciate that a mother in the severe category of parental-alienation-syndrome parents may be basically paranoid. Such an attorney is more likely to support her delusions, much to the grief and detriment of all concerned. And if the judge as well has such tendencies (not a remote possibility considering judges are generally drawn from the pool of lawyers), then the mother's paranoia may be even more harmful. In short, when a paranoid mother is supported by a paranoid lawyer and presents her case before a paranoid judge, the likelihood of family devastation approaches the 100 percent level.

Then, there is the plethora of lawyers graduating from law schools. At this time the best estimates are that there is approximately one lawyer for every 320 people in the United States. The ratio in Japan is one to 10,000. Although we live in the most litigious society in the world, even we cannot use so many lawyers. In such a situation, there are many "hungry" lawyers willing to take on any clients who are simpleminded or sick enough to engage their services. The lawyer and client work together as a team. Both must commit themselves to the "cause." The client who is foolish and gullible enough to believe that adversary litigation is the best first step toward resolving a custody/visitation dispute then teams up with an attorney who is hungry enough to exploit such a client and we have a "team."

The cure for this problem, obviously, is to reduce the number of people entering law school. This is not going to be easily accomplished. Many schools (including law schools) are money-making propositions. There is no medical school in the United States that earns money on each medical student, regardless of how high the tuition. Hospitals, laboratories, faculties in more than twenty specialities, and extremely expensive equipment make the cost of medical education extremely high. By comparison, legal education is relatively inexpensive. There are no laboratories and expensive equipment as is necessary in departments of chemistry, psychology, physics, biology, engineering, and other scientific disciplines. Of course, a law library is necessary; otherwise all that is required are classroom facilities. Legal training, then, may be a "money-making proposition" and may help to offset the costs of the more expensive departments within a university (such as medical schools). So there is little likelihood that universities are going to curb law school admissions.

Imposing restrictions on the number of people entering the legal profession would generally be viewed as undemocratic. In this "land of opportunity" we believe that everybody should have the chance to pursue any reasonable goal. But every single discipline and trade has restrictions on membership. Certainly the maintenance of standards of competence is a factor. Also, many disciplines restrict the number of trainees because they want to maintain high earning power for those who have gained admission. Unions do this routinely; in fact, nepotism is the rule among many trade unions. Although considered undemocratic, the practice is widespread. As long as there is a sea of lawyers, many of whom are hungry, there will be many attorneys available to perpetuate the kinds of family psychopathology described in this book.

Teaching Law Students about the
Deficiencies of the Adversary System

Prevention is best accomplished if one's attention is directed to the earliest manifestations of the processes that bring about a disorder. With regard to the prevention of the parental alienation syndrome and other disorders that arise from protracted adversarial proceedings, one does well to start at the law-school level, where lawyers first learn the system. Although all law schools teach that the adversary system is not perfect, most professors teach their students that it is the best we have for ascertaining the truth when such determination is crucial to resolve a dispute. Law students are taught that the system has evolved over centuries and that it is the best method yet devised for determining whether or not a defendant has indeed committed an alleged crime. It is based on the assumption that the best way of finding out who is telling the truth in such conflicts is for the accused and the accuser each to present to an impartial body (a judge or jury) his (her) argument, in accordance with certain rules and guidelines of presentation. More specifically, each side is permitted to present any information that supports its position and to withhold (within certain guidelines) information that would weaken its arguments. Out of this conflict of opposing positions, the impartial body is presumably in the best position to ascertain the truth.

Many in the legal profession have never given serious consideration to the system's weaknesses and hence blindly adhere to its tenets. Essential to the system is the principle that the impartial body attempts to rule on and/or resolve the dispute through the application of some general rule of law. Although this certainly serves to protect individuals from misguided justice, it produces in many legal professionals what I consider to be an exaggerated deference to "the law." This may result in a blind adherence to legal precedents, statutes, and laws—often with little consideration to whether they are just, honorable, or fair. I would like to focus in this section on what I consider to be some of the grievous weaknesses of the adversary system, weaknesses that directly contribute to the kinds of family psychopathology already described.

Lies of Omission and Lies of Commission Lies can be divided into two categories: lies of omission and lies of commission. A merchant who sells a piece of glass while claiming it is a diamond is lying by commission (a lie has been committed). A pregnant woman who does not tell her husband that he is not the father of the child she is carrying is lying by omission (she has omitted telling him the truth). In both cases someone is being deceived. The adversary system basically encourages lies of omission. It encourages withholding information that might compromise a client's position. This is lying. The same attorneys who routinely justify such omissions in their own work would not hesitate suing a physician for malpractice for the omission of information that could be detrimental to a patient. Many lawyers get defensive when one tries to point out that lies of omission are still lies, and that teaching law students to utilize them is to teach deceit. The argument that this is how the adversary system works is not a justifiable one. It is a rationalization. Psychiatrists, and physicians in general, work on the principle that all pertinent information must be brought to their attention if they are to make the most judicious decisions regarding treatment. The same principle holds with regard to the solution of other problems in life. The more information one has, the better is one's capacity to deal with a problem. The adversary system encourages the withholding and covering up of information. The argument that the other side is very likely to bring out what is withheld by the first is not a valid one. The other side may not be aware that such information exists. Furthermore, the procedure encourages nit-picking and other time-wasting maneuvers, delays, and interrogatory procedures that usually impede rather than foster the divulgence of information. These time-wasting elements in the procedure often so becloud an issue that important facts get lost or are not given proper attention. Furthermore, only the wealthiest can afford a trial that attempts to ensure that all the pertinent information will ultimately be brought forth.

It is unreasonable to expect that one can teach law students how to lie in one area and not to do so in others. These practices tend to become generalized. Attorneys have been known to say to clients, "Don't tell me. It's better that I don't know." The next step, after a client has unwittingly provided the compromising information, is for the attorney to say, "Forget you told me that" or "Never tell anyone you said that to me." And the next step is for the attorney to say, "You know it and I know it, but that is very different from their *proving* it." This "deal" is, by legal definition, collusion: an agreement between the lawyer and the client that they will work together to deceive the other side. Like chess, it is a game whose object is to trick and entrap the opponent.

Professors at many law schools may respond that such criticism does not give proper credit to or demonstrate respect for the "higher" principles taught at their institutions. They claim that their students are imbued with the highest ethical and moral values known to humankind. Although they may actually believe what they are saying, my experience has been that the graduates of these same institutions are still prone to involve themselves in the aforementioned deceitful maneuvers with their clients. Moreover, even these institutions teach the adversary system. When one begins with a system that is intrinsically deceitful, one cannot expect those who implement it to use it in an honest manner. To use it is to deceive and to risk an expansion of deceit into other areas. If one teaches a child to steal pennies and only pennies, one should not be surprised when the child starts stealing nickels. To say I only taught the youngster how to steal pennies is no defense. If one teaches a child to lie to the butcher but not to the baker, one should not be surprised when the child lies to the baker as well. After years of involvement with adversarial deceit in the professional realm, many attorneys no longer appreciate how deep-seated their tendency to fabricate has become. Cover-ups and lies of omission become incorporated into their personality and lifestyle. Many reach the point where they no longer appreciate that they have been corrupted by the system within which they earn their livelihood.

The Failure to Allow Direct Confrontation between the Accused and the Accuser   It amazes me that after centuries of utilization, adherents of the adversary system do not appreciate that they are depriving themselves of one of the most valuable and predictable ways of learning the truth. I am referring here to the placing of the accused and the accuser together in the same room in direct confrontation. Proponents of the system will immediately take issue with me on this point. They will claim that one of the reasons for the development of the adversary system was the appreciation that the system's predecessor, the inquisitorial system, left accused parties feeling helpless, especially with regard to this issue. During the early use of the inquisitorial system, accused individuals were not permitted direct confrontation with their accusers, and frequently did not even know who they were. This insistence upon the right of accused individuals to face their accusers is considered to be one of the strongest arguments for perpetuating the adversary system.

Unfortunately, many of the system's proponents fail to

appreciate that the confrontations insisted upon are not as free and open as they would like to believe. When referring to this practice, the general assumption is that the confrontation will take place in an open courtroom. This too is considered an advance over inquisitorial procedures, in which the proceedings were often held in secret. On the one hand, this is an advance because there are many witnesses to the confrontation: a judge, a jury, and often observers in the audience. On the other hand, the confrontation is extremely constrained by rites of courtroom procedure, and both parties are required to work under very confining circumstances. They are rarely allowed direct communication with one another; rather, communication is usually through their attorneys. These elements significantly compromise the benefits that are presumably obtained from the confrontation. In short, the principle of direct confrontation between accused and accuser is certainly a noble one, but its implementation in the adversary system has reduced its efficacy enormously.

The central problem with the adversarial courtroom confrontation is that the two individuals are not permitted to speak directly to one another. The argument that in more volatile situations they might cause one another physical harm is no justification for such formidable constraints. Litigants for whom such a risk exists could, if necessary, be provided with some kind of physical barrier such as a perforated steel screen (through which they could still converse). The argument that the accused and the accuser are still better off having representatives is, I believe, a residuum of the medieval practice of trial by champion. No matter how brilliant the lawyer and the judge, no matter how obsessive they are with regard to getting the details of the alleged incident, no matter how devoted they are to the collection of their data, the fact is that *they were not present as observers of the alleged incident*. The accused and the accuser know better than anyone else whether or not the events actually occurred. Similarly, they often know each other better than any of the other parties involved in the litigation. If the system were to allow the two to talk directly to each other, and confront each other with their opinions of one another's statements, much more "truth" would be obtained. Of course, less money would be made by the "middle men." In some cases their "services" could be dispensed with entirely. In other cases attorneys would still be necessary because of their knowledge of the law and other genuine services that they could provide their clients. It would be an error for the reader to conclude that I am suggesting that we dispense entirely with traditional courtroom procedures and that lawyers never be used. I am only suggesting that there be some place in the legal system for truly direct confrontation between the accused and the accuser.

These factors are especially valid for custody litigation. The litigants know one another "inside out." Each knows better than anyone else when the other party is fabricating. Each knows the signs and symptoms of the other's lying: stuttering, the hesitations, the embarrassed facial expressions, and the wide variety of other manifestations of duplicity. The adversary system does not give individuals the opportunity for an "eyeball-to-eyeball" confrontation. I am convinced that this is one of the best ways of finding out who is telling the truth, and I am astounded that after all these years, the system still deprives itself of using this valuable source of information.

It is for this reason that I make joint sessions mandatory in my custody evaluations (Gardner, 1982, 1986a, 1989a). In such meetings the parents can immediately "smoke out" one another's lies in a way far superior to the procedures used in the courtroom. Furthermore, in joint interviews the examiner has the opportunity to telephone other individuals immediately who might be able to provide important information regarding which parent is telling the truth. The judge cannot do this; an impartial evaluator can do so readily. It might take weeks or months to bring in a third party to provide testimony, and even then one might not be successful because of the reluctance on the part of the person to "get involved." However, a telephone call made by one of the spouses is much more likely to elicit the third party's comments during a brief conversation over the telephone. Such participation is very different from appearing on a witness stand in a courtroom. And the spouse who lies and risks being exposed by such a call is not likely to resist strongly because of the knowledge that such resistance implies guilt, shame, or some kind of cover-up that will compromise the resistor's position in the custody evaluation. There is no lawyer involved to "protect" the client's rights and to justify thereby cover-ups and the perpetuation of the fabrication. There is no time lag to allow the individual to "prepare a response" and thereby selectively withhold information or even introduce fabrications.

I recall one situation in which the mother claimed that the father had a problem with petty thievery and described how he prided himself on how much food he could steal from supermarkets as well as other items from a wide variety of stores. I asked the mother how many times, to the best of her knowledge, her husband had involved himself in such thievery. (The reader will note here the importance of trying to get numbers and frequency in association with custody visitation/allegations.) The mother replied, "I really don't know how many times, but I'm sure it's been in the hundreds." The father flatly denied any such behavior. The mother then stated that he would often do this with a certain friend, George. Again, the father denied that this was the case. I then asked them if they would have any hesitation over my calling George. Both agreed that I could do so immediately; however, the father did so with a slight but definite tone of hesitation. I asked them who they preferred to make the call and the father agreed that he would let the mother do it. I suspected again that this related to some reluctance on his part to put through the call, but I was pleased to have the mother make it in that there would be less chance of her communicating any messages (even subtly) to George regarding cover-up of the father's activities.

I instructed the mother to call George and merely tell him that she was in my office and that a custody evaluation was being conducted. I asked her to ask George to speak with me, without giving him any further information. Once on the phone, I told George who I was and informed him that I was conducting the evaluation under court order and that he should understand that any information he provided could be transmitted to any of the involved parties and used in any way whatsoever in the course of the litigation. He agreed to speak with me. I then simply asked him if he had any information about any possible stealing habits on the part of either of the parents. George immediately described the exact same pattern of stealing related by the mother. I asked George if he would be willing to come to a court of law and describe under oath what he had just told me. He stated that he would, although he was most reluctant to get involved. The father suddenly "remembered" that perhaps on one or two occasions he had stolen items, but denied that the problem was as serious as George and his wife had described. When I asked George how many times he himself had actually observed the father engaged in thievery, he said, "I'm ashamed to admit it, but I myself must have gone with him 20 or 30 times. He told me that he had done it hundreds of times, but I never saw him do it other than the times I was with him. But he was proud of what he was doing and I believed him when he said he had done it hundreds of times." I am sure the reader will agree with me that I succeeded here in accomplishing in a few minutes what might never have been accomplished in the courtroom or, if it had been, it would have taken a much longer period and would only have been accomplished at far greater expense.

Accordingly, when I conduct custody evaluations under the aegis of the court, I do so with the proviso that I be free to bring the involved parties together in the same room at the same time. And I implement this pattern in custody evaluations conducted in the context of mediation. Obviously, this pertains to the parents who are mediating, but also I obtain their agreement to invite other parties to participate as warranted. Any reluctance is viewed as an obstruction to the mediation process and results in my considering whether the parties are indeed candidates for mediation. And the same considerations hold when I am asked to conduct other kinds of evaluations, such as sex-abuse evaluations (Gardner, 1987, 1992a). Here, again, I am surprised that the tradition is for the courts to send a child to examiners such as myself and ask us to evaluate the child alone to find out whether or not there has been sex abuse. Or, I may be asked to evaluate a

RECOMMENDATIONS FOR THE FUTURE 293

man with regard to the question of whether he sexually abused a particular child, but I am not permitted to interview the child. In fact, it is extremely rare in criminal proceedings for the same evaluator to interview both the accused and the alleged victim, even in situations when both would be willing to participate in an evaluation by the same party. But even in civil cases, where there are absolutely no legal reasons to justify such a separation of evaluations, I have found it extremely difficult to accomplish this goal. When I have asked for the opportunity to bring the alleged abuser and the child into the same room at the same time (at my discretion), I was often met with an incredulous response. This too amazes me. Admittedly, there are extra complicating factors in such situations, such as the child's fear of the confrontation and the repercussions of the disclosures. However, these drawbacks notwithstanding (there is no situation in which there are no drawbacks), not including such joint interviews seriously compromises the evaluation.

The Issue of Conviction for the Client's Position Most lawyers believe that they can be as successful helping a client whose cause they may not be particularly in sympathy with as they can with one whose position they strongly support. From their early days in law school, they are imbued with the idea that their obligations as lawyers are to serve the client and work as zealously as possible in support of his (her) position. They are taught that they must do this even though they may not be in sympathy with the client's position and even though they might prefer to be on the opponent's side. This is another weakness of the adversary system. It assumes that attorneys can argue just as effectively when they have no commitment to the client's position as when they do.

In most law schools students are required to involve themselves in "moot court" experiences in which they are assigned a position in a case. The assignment is generally made on a random basis and is independent of the student's own conviction on the particular issue. In fact, it is often considered preferable that the assignment be made in such a way that students must argue in support of the position for which they have less conviction. On other occasions, the student may be asked to present arguments for both sides. Obviously, such experiences can be educationally beneficial. We can all learn from and become more flexible by being required to view a situation from the opposite vantage point. However, I believe that attorneys are naive who hold that one can argue just as effectively without conviction as one can if one has conviction. Noncommitted attorneys are going to serve less effectively in most cases. Accordingly, before they enter the courtroom, their clients are in a weakened position. Most (but not all) attorneys are not likely to turn away a client whose position they secretly do not support. (One doesn't turn away a paying customer so quickly.) Accordingly, it would be very difficult for a client to find a lawyer who is going to admit openly to a lack of conviction for the client's position.

I recall a situation in which I had good reason to believe that an attorney was basically not supporting his client, the father in a custody case, and that his lack of conviction contributed to his poor performance in the courtroom. In this particular case I served as an impartial examiner and concluded that the mother's position warranted my support. However, once in the courtroom, I was treated as an advocate of the mother (the usual situation). Early in the trial, the guardian ad litem suggested that I, as the impartial examiner, be invited into the courtroom to observe the testimony of a psychiatrist who had been brought in as an advocate for the father's side. The father's attorney agreed to this, which surprised me because I did not see what he had to gain by my having direct opportunity to observe (and potentially criticize) his client's expert. I thought that there would be more to lose than gain for this attorney because his own expert's testimony would be likely to provide me with more "ammunition" for the mother.

While the advocate expert testified, I took notes and, as was expected, the father's attorney provided him ample time to elaborate on his various points. When I took the stand, I was first questioned by the mother's attorney, the attorney whose position I supported. He gave me great flexibility with regard to my opportunities for answering his questions. Then the father's attorney began to question me. To my amazement, he allowed me to elaborate on points on which I disagreed with him. At no point did he confine me to the traditional yes-no answers that are designed to weaken and distort testimony. He persistently gave me the opportunity for elaboration, and naturally, I took advantage of it.

During a break in the proceedings, when the judge and attorneys were conferring at the bench, I heard the judge ask him, "Why are you letting Gardner talk so much?" I suspect this was an inappropriate statement for the judge to make, but it confirms how atypical and seemingly inexplicable was the attorney's cross-examination of me. The lawyer shrugged his shoulders, said nothing, and on my return to the stand continued to allow me great flexibility in my answers. I had every reason to believe that he was a bright man and "knew better." I had no doubt that he did not routinely proceed in this way. To me, this attorney's apparently inexplicable behavior was most likely motivated by the desire (either conscious or unconscious) that his own client lose custody because of his recognition that the mother was the preferable parent. He "went through the motions" of supporting his client, but did so in such a way that he basically helped the other side win the case.

Therapists, in contrast, generally work in accordance with the principle that if they have no conviction for what they are doing with their patients, the chances of success in the treatment are likely to be reduced significantly—even to the point of there being no chance of success at all. If, for example, the therapist's feelings for the patient are not strong, if there is no basic sympathy for the patient's situation, if the relationship is not a good one, or if the therapist is not convinced that the patient's goals in therapy are valid, the likelihood of the patient's being helped is small. Without such conviction the therapy becomes boring and sterile—with little chance of any constructive results.

Watson (1969), an attorney, encourages lawyers to refuse to support a client's attempts to gain custody when the attorney does not consider the client to be the preferable parent. He considers such support to be basically unethical because one is likely to be less successful with a client for whose position one does not have conviction. This is a noble attitude on this attorney's part. Unfortunately, far too few lawyers subscribe to this advice, and most succumb to the more practical consideration that if they do not support their client's position, they will lose that client and the attendant fee.

The Issue of Emotions and Objectivity Attorneys are taught in law school that emotions compromise objectivity. They use the word *objectivity* to refer to the ability to "stay cool," think clearly, and thereby handle a situation in the most judicious and "clear-headed" way. Emotions are viewed as contaminants to such clear thinking, i.e., they are *subjective*. Objectivity is equated with the ability to deal with a situation in the most judicious way. And this is the concept of the word that I will utilize here. Accordingly, they are taught that if one gets emotional in a legal situation, one's clients may suffer. This polarization between emotions and objectivity is an oversimplification and compromises many attorneys' capacity to represent optimally their clients. I believe there is a continuum between objectivity and emotions. To set up a dichotomy is not consistent with the realities of the world. An emotion in fact *exists*. That one cannot measure it or weigh it does not negate its existence. To say that a thought is objective and a feeling is not is to make an artificial distinction between two types of mental processes. Emotions have many more concomitant physiological responses outside the brain than do thoughts, but this does not mean that emotions are thereby "not real" (the implication of the word *subjective*). At one end of the continuum are thoughts with little if any emotional concomitants. At the other end are emotions with little if any associated thoughts. As one moves from the cognitive (thoughts) end toward the affective (emotional) end, the percentage of thoughts decreases and the percentage of emotions increases. At some point along this continuum, closer to the affective end, are *mild* emotions. As I will discuss in detail below, I believe that extremely strong emotions generally will compromise objectivity, but mild ones are likely to *increase* objectivity – if used judiciously.

Again, I use the word *objectivity* here to refer to the capacity to handle a situation in the most effective way.

Attorneys generally do not differentiate between strong and mild emotions; they simply view all emotions as potentially contaminating attempts to learn the truth. *Both mild and strong emotions are sources of information.* When a psychotherapist, while working with a patient, exhibits emotions, he (she) does well to determine whether or not they are in the mild or severe category. The therapist has to differentiate between emotions that will compromise objectivity and those that will enhance it. If a therapist experiences mild emotions—which are engendered by the patient's behavior and are similar to emotions that the vast majority of individuals are likely to have in that situation—then the expression of such emotions to the patient can prove therapeutic. For example, if a therapist becomes irritated because the patient is not fulfilling financial obligations, the therapist does well not only to confront the patient with the default but also to express the frustration and irritation thereby engendered. After all, if a psychotherapist is not going to be open and honest with the patient about his (her) *own* emotional reactions, how can the therapist expect the patient to do so. Also, one of the services for which the patient is paying is the therapist's honest responses. Such expression of feelings by the therapist is a good example of the proper use of a mild emotion in the therapeutic process. It enhances the efficacy of the treatment. I am therefore in sharp disagreement with those who consider the presence of such emotions in the therapist to be necessarily inappropriate, injudicious, psychopathological, or a manifestation of a lack of objectivity.

Now to the issue of very strong emotions. These may be useful or not useful, therapeutic or antitherapeutic, in the treatment process. Because the therapeutic process is another "slice of life" in which the same general principles of living are applicable, my comments on the roles of emotions in treatment apply to their role in handling situations elsewhere. First, an example of a severe emotion in the therapeutic process: If a patient threatens to kill a psychotherapist, the therapist is likely to be frightened and/or extremely angry. And such feelings may be very powerful. If these feelings are used judiciously, the therapist may save his (her) life and may even protect the lives of others. We see here how a strong emotion may be useful and not necessarily becloud objectivity. If the therapist, however, fears for his (her) life when there is no actual threat, then he (she) is likely to be delusional and is clearly compromised in his (her) capacity to help the patient. Here inappropriate, strong emotions are operative in reducing the therapist's objectivity.

Now to a more common situation. If a therapist overreacts because of neurotic reactions to what the patient is saying, he (she) becomes compromised as a therapist, e.g., getting angry at a patient for leaving treatment or having sex with a patient. Such overreaction results in injudicious, antitherapeutic, or unethical handling of the matter—again reducing the therapist's objectivity. In short, emotions per se do not compromise objectivity; they may or they may not. When mild they are less likely to; when severe they are more likely to. Even severe emotions, used judiciously, can enhance one's efficacy (and thereby objectivity) in dealing with a situation.

Accordingly, lawyers have to appreciate that the traditional advice that they should be unemotional is injudicious. They should try to be sensitive to their emotions and make the kinds of discriminations I have just described. They should recognize that emotional reactions are not necessarily a hindrance to their work, nor do they interfere with objectivity. They should view their own emotions as a potentially valuable source of information about what may be going on with their clients. Lawyers should use their emotions to help their clients; they should not deny their emotions and conclude that their expression will be a disservice to their clients. It is better for them to recognize that mild emotional reactions can often enhance their efficacy. We fight harder when we are angry to a reasonable degree. We lose our efficiency in fighting when our anger deranges us and we enter into states of rage and fury. We flee harder when we are frightened. However, if the fear becomes overwhelming, we may become paralyzed with our fear.

The failure of attorneys to appreciate these principles relating to emotions and objectivity has caused me difficulty on a number of occasions in the course of adversary litigation. By the time of my courtroom appearance I generally feel a deep conviction for a particular client's position. This was often an outgrowth of my having committed myself strongly to the custody evaluation, worked assiduously at the task, and come to the point where I could firmly support one parent's position over the other. In the course of the litigation I had expressed feelings—sympathy, irritation, frustration, and a variety of other emotions. Some lawyers have seized upon my admission of such feelings as a justification for discrediting me as being compromised in my objectivity. My attempts to explain that these emotions were engendered by the reality of the situation, and that I was reacting like any other human being, often proved futile. My efforts to impress upon the attorneys that such emotions have an objectivity of their own and could enhance my understanding of the case were met with incredulity and distrust. And even presiding judges usually agreed with the attorneys that it was inappropriate of me to have these emotions. Because of this prevailing notion among members of the legal profession, I came to consider it injudicious to express my emotions and I was much more cautious about revealing them—so as not to compromise the position of the parent whose position I was supporting.

This is an unfortunate situation. On the one hand, I would have preferred to state, with a reasonable degree of emotion, the position I held and then explain that these attendant emotions did not necessarily compromise my objectivity. I would have preferred to describe how they are not only an important source of information for me, but enhance my efficiency. On the other hand, to have done so would have just invited refutation. It would give an adversary attorney "ammunition," even if unjustifiable. Accordingly, I generally follow the judicious course of not revealing the emotional factors that have played a role in the decision-making process. My hope is that attorneys will become more sophisticated regarding this issue so that evaluators might ultimately be able to provide more complete and honest testimony. My hope also is that the comments I have made here will play a role (admittedly small) in bringing about some elucidation in the legal profession on this point.

Other Changes in Law School Education That Would Benefit Attorneys and Their Clients

Medical schools require certain courses be taken at the premedical level, courses that serve as foundations for medical education. It is generally recognized that certain science courses at the undergraduate level, especially chemistry, biology, and physics, are so useful in medical school that a candidate who has not proven significant efficiency in them would not be considered for admission. Law schools generally do not have any prescribed prelaw curriculum. Most require only three or four years of college. It matters not whether one studied engineering, political science, anthropology, biology, psychology, or any other subject. This is unfortunate. I believe more serious attention should be given to this issue. Obviously, if one is going into patent law, one does well to acquire some training in the sciences and engineering. If one is going to use the law as a route to politics, then one should have some background in political science, sociology, and psychology. If one is going to go into family law and involve oneself in divorce litigation, then one should certainly have some background in normal and abnormal psychology as well as child development. And students who are not sure which aspect of the law they wish to enter should be required to take such courses subsequently.

It is unfortunate (to say the least) that attorneys have been so slow to recognize the importance of postgraduate specialization. Most lawyers are viewed by the public as "jacks of all trades" and even "masters of all trades" within the law. People go to "a lawyer," whether the problem be divorce, preparation of a will, or getting a mortgage on a house. The assumption is that good lawyers are trained in all of these areas. Actually, they are trained in very few of them. Most attorneys learn from their experiences over the years. These same individuals will, however, go to an orthopedist, gynecologist, surgeon, or other specialist. Most people recognize that the general medical practitioner is a "jack of all trades, but a master of *none.*" The arguments given by attorneys for not setting up rigorous programs of specialization are not, in my opinion, valid. They will argue that it is very difficult to decide what the criteria should be for certifying someone in a particular legal specialty and they question who should be doing the examining. Medicine seems to have worked out these problems. No one is claiming that the specialization system is perfect, but most physicians agree that it is better than having no system at all for specialty training and certification.

Accordingly, some of the damage done to clients in the course of custody litigation would be reduced if people planning to go into family law were required to include courses in clinical psychology (normal and abnormal) in their undergraduate training. Furthermore, there should be a postgraduate discipline, involving one or two years of further study, in which there would be specific preparation and experience in family law. During such training many of the issues raised here would be taught—issues such as the drawbacks of the adversary system in general, the disadvantages of the adversary system as it applies to custody litigation, and psychopathological disorders that result from protracted custody litigation. Moreover, I would include such topics as ethics and values in the law, sensitivity to the feelings of clients, psychopathy and paranoia among lawyers, and how these conditions harm clients. Again, I recognize fully that we in medicine are not free from our share of psychopaths and paranoids, nor incompetents, but we in medicine do much more to screen such individuals at every level of training.

Concluding Comments

Riskin, a law professor who is very critical of the adversary system and the educational system that emphasizes it inordinately, states (1982):

> Nearly all courses at most law schools are presented from the

viewpoint of the practicing attorney who is working in an adversary system. . . . There is, to be sure, scattered attention to the lawyer as planner, policy maker, and public servant, but 90 percent of what goes on in law school is based on a model of the lawyer working in or against a background of litigation of disputes that can be resolved by the application of a rule by a third party. The teachers were trained with this model in mind. The students get a rough image with them; it gets sharpened quickly. This model defines and limits the likely career possibilities envisioned by most law students.

In further criticism of the narrowness of the adversary system he states:

> When one party wins, in this vision, usually the other party loses, and, most often, the victory is reduced to a money judgment. This "reduction" of nonmaterial values—such as honor, respect, dignity, security, and love—to amount of money, can have one of two effects. In some cases, these values are excluded from the decision makers' considerations, and thus the consciousness of the lawyers, as irrelevant. In others, they are present by transmutation into something else—a justification for money damages.

These "irrelevant" issues—"honor, respect, dignity, security, and love"—are certainly professed by attorneys involved in custody litigation, especially when they wave the banner of the best-interests-of-the-child philosophy. In reality the children are often merely the objects that are "won." Often there may be a trade-off of the children for monetary awards. Children become chattel, objects, or booty—with only lip service paid to the emotional consequences of the litigation. Due to the adversary system and the legal education that promulgates the method, attorneys are programmed in their earliest phases of development to ignore these crucial elements in their work.

THE EDUCATION AND TRAINING OF NONLEGAL PROFESSIONALS

On a few occasions I have been asked, when presenting my credentials to testify in court, what my formal training has been in custody litigation. My answer simply has been, "none." The questioning attorney has generally been quite aware that I had no formal training in this area because there was no such training in the late 1950s when I was in my residency. The attempt here was to compromise my credibility by attempting to demonstrate to the court that I was not qualified to testify on child custody matters. Asking me that question is the same as asking an internist, who like myself attended medical school in the mid-1950s, to state what education he had at that time on the subject of AIDS. (Obviously, this question was not asked by the attorney whose position I supported.) Unfortunately, there are young people today who are asked the same question and must also provide the same answer. Considering the widespread epidemic of custody litigation that now prevails, the failure to provide training in this area at the present time represents a significant deficiency in the education and training of professionals doing such evaluations. Most people, like myself, have "learned from experience." Some have learned well and some have not. Accordingly, I would consider it mandatory that all child therapy programs in psychology, psychiatry, social work, and related disciplines require training and experience in custody litigation.

I would emphasize in such programs the point that having professionals automatically serving as advocates ("hired guns") in child custody litigation is a reprehensible practice and a terrible disservice to the family, the legal profession, and the mental health professions as well. The attempt here would be to bring about a situation in which attorneys looking for hired guns would not be able to find any mental health professional who would allow themselves to be so utilized. Although I believe that this is an ideal that will never be reached, we would still do well to have the principle promulgated at the earliest levels of education and training. It is my hope that this principle would be incorporated into the ethical standards of the various professional societies. A strong statement that such advocacy is unethical would certainly help protect and discourage mental health professionals from this type of prostitution of their talents and skills. Such refusal could be considered to be a kind of preventive psychiatry in that it would remove us from contributing to legal maneuvers that play a role in bringing about the parental alienation syndrome and other disorders that result from protracted divorce/custody litigation.

Such training would also involve impressing upon the trainees the importance of their doing everything possible to discourage their patients from involving themselves in such litigation and to point out the variety of psychopathological reactions that can result. Elsewhere (Gardner, 1986a), I have described many of these in detail. In addition, trainees should be advised to encourage their patients to involve themselves in mediation as a first step toward resolving divorce/custody disputes. They should be helped to appreciate that adversary litigation should be the parents' very last resort, after all civilized attempts at resolution have failed.

At the present time mediation is very much a "growth industry." Lawyers and mental health specialists are the primary professionals attracted to the field (Coogler, 1978; Fisher and Ury, 1981; Haynes, 1981; Folberg and Taylor, 1984). However, there are many others with little if any training or experience who have gravitated to the field. Currently, there are no standards with regard to training requirements. These will inevitably have to be set up, and I believe that they should be set up soon. At the time of this writing, mediation has been popular for about ten years. This might be considered too short a period to give us enough information to decide what the standards should be. Still, I think sufficient time has elapsed to enable us to propose guidelines for a training program. My own view is that it should take place at the graduate level. I would consider two years of course work and a year of practical work under the supervision of experienced mediators to be optimum. During the first two years the program should provide courses in both law and psychology. There should be courses in basic law as well as marriage and divorce law. Courses in finance should cover the kinds of financial problems that divorcing people are likely to encounter. In the mental health area there should be basic courses in child development, child psychopathology, family psychodynamics, and interviewing techniques. Furthermore, there should be courses in mediation techniques and conflict resolution. This academic material would serve as a foundation for the clinical work in the third year.

At this time universities in the United States do not appear to be particularly enthusiastic about setting up such programs. My hope is that they will become more appreciative of the need for these in the near future. In addition, I believe that graduate programs in psychology, social work, and residency training programs would also do well to incorporate mediation training as part of their general curricula. However, training at these levels cannot provide the same kind of in-depth experience that one gets from a full two- or three-year program of the aforementioned type.

DO "SEX-BLIND" CUSTODY DECISIONS NECESSARILY SERVE THE BEST INTERESTS OF CHILDREN?

During the last few years, in association with my increasing involvement in child custody litigation, I have often had the thought that perhaps we should not have dispensed with the tender-years presumption. If we are to consider the greatest good for the greatest number, I believe we probably would have done better to retain it. The new egalitarianism has caused much suffering, among both parents and children. Of course, there would have been some children who would then have remained with the less preferable parent; however, many more children would have been spared the psychological traumas attendant to the implementation of the best-interests-of-the-child doctrine (especially the gender egalitarianism principle of determining parental preference) and the widespread enthusiasm for the joint custodial concept. There is no question that custody litigation has increased dramatically since the mid-1970s, and there is no question, as well, that this increase has been the direct result of these two recent developments.

What should we do then? Go back to the old system? I think

not. I believe that there is a middle path that should prove useful. To elaborate: First, the displacement of the tender-years presumption with the best-interests-of-the-child philosophy was initiated primarily by men who claimed that the tender-years presumption was intrinsically "sexist" because women are not necessarily preferable parents by virtue of the fact that they are female. State legislatures and the courts agreed. As a result, the best-interests-of-the-child doctrine has been uniformly equated with the notion that custody determinations should be "sex blind." Considerable difficulty has been caused, I believe, by fusing these two concepts. *It is extremely important that they be considered separately.* Everyone claims to be in support of doing what is in the best interests of the children. Everyone waves that banner: each parent, each attorney, the mental health professionals who testify, and certainly the judge. No one claims to be against children's best interests. The situation is analogous to the position politicians take with regard to their support for widows, orphans, the handicapped, and the poor. All politicians wave that banner. Even the suggestion that a politician might not be in strong support of these unfortunates would be met with denial, professions of incredulity, and righteous indignation.

With regard to all those who claim that the best interests of the child is their paramount consideration, one could argue that a wide variety of possible custodial arrangements could serve children's best interests. One could argue that automatic placement with the father serves their best interests, and this was certainly the case up until the early 20th century. Or one could claim that automatic preference for the mother serves the children best, and this was the case from the mid-1920s to the mid-1970s. One could argue that placing them with grandparents, uncles, aunts, in foster homes, adoption agencies, or residential cottages might serve children's best interests. At this time, the prevailing notion is that sex-blind custody evaluations automatically serve children's best interests. Although it may be an unpopular thing to say in the early 1990s, I do not believe that sex-blind custody decisions necessarily serve the best interests of children. Somehow, the acceptance that fathers can be as paternal as mothers can be maternal was immediately linked with the concept that such egalitarianism serves the best interests of children. I do not accept this assumption of gender equality in child-rearing capacity and would go further and state that the younger the child, the less the likelihood that this assumption is valid. It follows then that I do not believe that sex-blind custody evaluations and decisions serve the best interests of children. I recognize that this is an unpopular position to take at this time, that it might appear to be very undemocratic and even sexist (here with the prejudice being against men), but it is the opinion that I have. My hope is that the reader will read on with some degree of receptivity and will come to the same conclusion.

To elaborate: No one can deny that men and women are different biologically. No one can deny, either, that it is the woman who bears the child and has within her own body the power to feed it (although she may choose not to do so). I believe that this biological difference cannot be disassociated from certain psychological factors that result in mothers' being more likely to be superior to fathers in their capacity to involve themselves with the newborn at the time of its birth. After all, it is the mother who carries the baby in her body for nine months. It is she who is continually aware of its presence. It is she who feels its kicks and its movements. It is she who is ever reminded of the pregnancy by formidable changes in her body and by the various symptomatic reminders of the pregnancy: nausea, vomiting, fatigue, discomfort during sleep, and so on. Even the most dedicated fathers cannot have these experiences and the attendant strong psychological ties that they engender. The mother, as well, must suffer the pains of the infant's delivery. Even though the father may be present at the time of birth and be an active participant in the process, the experience is still very much the mother's. And, as mentioned, it is the mother who may very well have the breast-feeding experience, something the father is not capable of enjoying. All these factors create a much higher likelihood that the mother—at the time of birth—will have a stronger psychological tie with the infant than will the father. This "up-front" programming places her in a superior position with regard to psychological bonding with the newborn at the time of birth. I believe that most individuals would agree that, if parents decided to separate at the time of birth and both were reasonably equal with regard to parenting capacity, the mother would be the preferable parent.

Some might argue that even if the aforementioned speculations are valid, the superiority stops at the time of birth and men are thereafter equal to women with regard to parenting capacity. Even here I am dubious. It is reasonable to assume that during the course of evolution there was a selective survival on a genetic basis of women who were highly motivated child rearers. Such women were more likely to seek men for the purposes of impregnation and more likely to be sought by men who desired children. Similarly, there was selective propagation of men who were skilled providers of food, clothing, shelter, and protection of women and children. Such men were more likely to be sought by women with high child-rearing drives. This assumption, of course, is based on the theory that there are genetic factors involved in such behavior. Women with weaker child-rearing drives were less likely to procreate, and men with less family-provider and protective capacities were also at a disadvantage with regard to transmitting their genes to their progeny. They were less attractive to females as mates because they were less likely to fulfill these functions so vital to species survival. As weaker protectors, they were less likely to survive in warfare and in fighting to protect their families from enemies.

Accordingly, although it may be the unpopular thing to say at the time of this writing (1991), I believe that the average woman today is more likely to be genetically programmed for child-rearing functions than the average man. It would be an error for the reader to conclude from this that I believe that women should be forced to go back into the home and function primarily in the kitchen and nursery. To believe that women are genetically superior to men as child rearers, especially during infancy, does not necessarily mean that they should be imprisoned in the home with their children. I still hold that they should be given the same extradomestic privileges as men, but we should be aware of the implications of this difference. (The ideal solution to this problem is that both men and women be given the opportunity to spend time both in the home and in the extradomestic realms during a child's infancy.) Even if my theory regarding the genetic basis for the female's child-rearing superiority is true, one could argue that we are less beholden to our instincts than lower animals and that environmental influences enable us to modify these more primitive drives. I do not deny this, but agree only up to a point. There are limitations to how much environment can modify heredity, especially in the short period of approximately 10-15 years since the tender-years presumption was generally considered to be sexist. Environment modifies heredity primarily by the slow process of selective survival of those variants that are particularly capable of adapting to a specific environment. Accordingly, these genetic factors are still strong enough in today's parents to be given serious consideration when making custody decisions.

THE STRONGER-HEALTHY-PSYCHOLOGICAL-BOND PRESUMPTION

It would appear from the aforementioned comments that I am on the verge of recommending that we go back to the tender-years presumption. This is not completely the case. *What I am recommending is that we give preference in custody disputes to the parent (regardless of sex) who has provided the greatest degree of healthy child-rearing input during the children's formative years.* Because mothers today are still more often the primary child-rearing parent, more mothers would be given parental preference in custody disputes adjudicated under this principle. If, however, in spite of the mother's superiority at the time of birth, it was the father who was the primary caretaker—especially during the early years of life—such a father might very well better serve as the preferable primary custodial parent. This presumption, too, is essentially sex blind (satisfying thereby present-day demands for gender egalitarianism) because it allows for the possibility that a father's input may outweigh the mother's in the formative years, even though he starts at a disadvantage. It utilizes primarily the *psychological bond* with the child as the primary consideration in custody evaluations. I would add, however, the important consideration that the longer the time span between infancy and the time of the custody evaluation and decision, the greater the likelihood that environmental factors will modify (strengthen or weaken) the psychological bonds that the child had with each parent during his (her) earliest years.

I refer to this as the stronger-*healthy*-psychological-bond presumption, which, I believe, is the one that would serve the best interests of the child. It is important for the reader to appreciate that the parent who had the greater involvement with the child during infancy is the one more likely to have the stronger psychological bond. However, if the early parenting was not "good," then the bond that develops might be pathological. Accordingly, I am not referring here to any kind of psychological bond, but a *healthy* psychological bond. It is not a situation in which *any* psychological bond will do. A paranoid mother, who has so programmed her son that he too has developed paranoid feelings about his father, may have a strong psychological bond with her son, stronger than that which he has with his father. But this *folie à deux* is certainly not healthy, and its presence is a strong argument for recommending the father as the primary custodial parent. It is for this reason that I refer to the presumption as the stronger-healthy-psychological-bond presumption. To clarify my position on these principles, I will first present a vignette that will serve as a basis for my subsequent comments.

Let us envision a situation in which a couple has one child, a boy. During the first four years of the child's life, the mother remains at home as the primary child rearer and the father is out of the house during the day as the breadwinner. When the child is four, the mother takes a full-time job. During the day the child attends a nursery school and afterward stays with a woman in the neighborhood who cares for the children of working parents. At the end of the workday and over weekends both parents are involved equally in caring for the child. The same situation prevails when the child enters elementary school. When the child is seven, the parents decide to separate. Each parent wants primary custody. The father claims that during the three years prior to the separation, he was as involved as the mother in the child's upbringing. And the mother does not deny this. The father's position is that the court should make its decision solely on the basis of parenting capacity—especially as demonstrated in the most recent three years of the child's life—and claims that any custody decision taking his gender into consideration is "sexist" and is an abrogation of his civil rights.

In the course of the litigation the child develops typical symptoms of the parental alienation syndrome. He becomes obsessed with hatred of his father, denies any benevolent involvement with him at any point in his life, and creates absurd scenarios to justify his animosity. In contrast, his mother becomes viewed by the boy as faultless and all-loving. I believe that in this situation the child's psychological bond is stronger with the mother, and the symptoms of alienation are created by him in an attempt to maintain that bond. Because the child's earliest involvement was stronger with the mother, residua of that tie are expressing themselves at the age of seven. If the father had been the primary caretaker during the first four years of the boy's life, and, if subsequently (ages four to seven), both mother and father shared equally in child-rearing involvement, I would predict that the child would develop symptoms of alienation from the mother, the parent with whom the psychological tie is weaker. Under such circumstances, I would recommend the father be designated the primary custodial parent.

In summary, the stronger-healthy-psychological-bond presumption is best stated as a three-step process:

> 1. Preference should be given to that parent (regardless of sex) with whom the child has developed the stronger-healthy-psychological bond.
> 2. That parent (regardless of sex) who was the primary caretaker during the earliest years of the child's life is more likely to have developed the stronger-healthy-psychological bond.
> 3. The longer the time lag between the earliest years and the time of the custody evaluation or decision, the greater the likeli-

hood other factors will operate that may tip the balance in either direction regarding parental capacity.

This presumption is sympathetic to the present-day emphasis on sexual egalitarianism but it gives priority to the more important consideration, namely, the strength of the psychological bond that the child has with each of the parents. In accordance with the third principle, a parent who might have been considered preferable for primary custodial designation during the infancy period might not be viewed as such in the adolescent period. During the many years that have intervened, other factors may have been introduced that tipped the balance away from the parent with whom the stronger-healthy-psychological bond originally existed. The reader should note, as well, the use of the word *healthy* in these principles. It is not a situation in which *any* psychological bond will serve. Clearly, if a parent has a sick psychological bond with a child, that is a serious compromise, and evaluators must give consideration to transfer of custody to the parent with whom the child has the healthier psychological bond, even though that parent may not have been the primary caretaker during the earliest years of the child's life.

I believe that legislators would do well to give serious consideration to these principles with an eye toward substituting them for the present best-interests-of-the-child philosophy. I believe that this would reduce significantly the incidence of the parental alienation syndrome as well as the false allegations of sex abuse that so often arise in the context of this disorder.

AN ALTERNATIVE SYSTEM FOR RESOLVING CHILD CUSTODY DISPUTES

Introduction

I present here a three-phase system for resolving child custody disputes that would, I believe, reduce significantly the psychopathology and other forms of grief caused by embroilment in custody disputes. This system would be the *only one available* to parents involved in such conflicts. It is completely legal and does not in any way deprive parents of their constitutional rights. However, it would prevent them from involving themselves in adversarial proceedings at any level. It may be of interest to the reader that I have reviewed this proposal with attorneys who are knowledgeable in this area, and they agree that all U.S. Constitutional safeguards are preserved in this proposal, its uniqueness and atypicality notwithstanding. This method of child custody dispute resolution would, I believe, provide a judicious way to determine which parent should be designated the primary custodial parent.

Mediation

In the first stage, *mediation* toward resolution of a child custody dispute would be required. This is very much the situation in the state of California, where the Conciliation Courts routinely attempt to mediate all custody disputes at the outset (McIsaac, 1983). In recent years many other states, as well, have introduced mandatory mediation before parents are permitted to embark on adversarial litigation. Moreover, in many countries (Japan, Norway, and Sweden, for example) mediation is the routine method for resolving divorce and custody disputes, and only a very small fraction of all divorcing parents resort to litigation, which is generally viewed as uncivilized and results in social stigma.

In the system I propose, parents could choose to mediate their dispute within or outside the court system. They could avail themselves of the services of psychiatrists, psychologists, social workers, lawyers, mediators, arbitrators, pastoral counselors, clergymen, and others qualified to conduct such evaluations— either privately or in clinics. Obviously, training programs and standards would have to be set up in order to ensure that only qualified mediators could be utilized at this stage. Crucial to the success of such mediation would be the reassurance that the content of the deliberations would, under no circumstances, be made available to outside individuals, such as lawyers and judges. No written reports would be formulated and no verbal conversations between the mediator and lawyers would be permitted. And these provisos might be stipulated in a contract. Parents involved in a custody dispute would also be free to avail themselves of such services provided under the aegis of the court or court-designated mental health clinics. These would provide mediation services at a fee commensurate with the parents' financial situation. Again, there would be absolutely no transmission of the mediator's findings and recommendations to others — even to the legal system under whose authority the mediation might have operated. My hope is that such mediation would serve to resolve the vast majority of custody disputes.

The mediated parenting plan would be verbally communicated to the attorney preparing the separation agreement. Because divorce is still a legal matter (and probably will be for the foreseeable future), the services of an attorney would still be necessary. However, my hope is that other possible disputes related to the divorce would also be resolved by mediation. Whether or not the parents are successful in accomplishing this, the custody dispute (the focus of my three-step proposal) could not be dealt with — at any of the three levels — by proceedings within the adversary system.

Arbitration Panel

But mediation, like everything else in the world, is not without its drawbacks. All of us are fallible, all of us make mistakes, and the most skilled mediator is no exception. Mediation may break down for a variety of reasons, one of the most common of which is the refusal by one or both parties to provide full disclosure of finances. Or, each spouse may be so convinced of the other's ineptitude as a parent that the compromises necessitated by mediation may not be possible. Psychiatric problems may interfere with a parent's ability to make the necessary compromises. When mediation breaks down, most people today have no choice but to involve themselves in adversarial custody litigation. In the system I propose, the parents would then be required to submit their dispute to an *arbitration panel,* working within the court structure. I believe that the best panel to deal with such a dispute would be one consisting of two mental health professionals and one attorney. The panel members would be selected by the parents from a roster of properly qualified individuals provided by the court. (The training and experience requirements for such certification have yet to be determined.)

The mental health professionals on the panel would be expected to conduct the kind of custody evaluation described elsewhere (Gardner, 1989a). The lawyer would be involved in the legal aspects of the dispute and would draw up the panel's final decision in proper legal form. Like a judge, the panel (especially the lawyer) would have the power to subpoena medical records, request financial documents, and so on. This power would be especially important when there is reluctance or refusal by one or both parties to disclose pertinent information. The panel would meet either in a courthouse or in a place directly under the jurisdiction of a court of law. In this way the proceedings would be very much under the control of our legal system. Most important, the parents would meet directly with the panel members. Although the discussion would be free and open, the panel would still have the authority to prevent the proceedings from degenerating into a free-for-all. By having three panelists there would be no chance of a tie vote. The majority decision would prevail. Obviously, a panel of three is less likely to be biased than an individual mediator or judge. Equally (if not more) important is the panel's data-collection process. Whereas the judge is confined to the constraints of the adversary method of data collection (gathering of evidence), the panel would be free to avail itself of the more flexible and far more preferable procedures used by mental health professionals serving as impartial examiners. Especially pertinent here would be the utilization of joint interviews, a procedure rarely used by judges and attorneys.

The panel would be free to bring in any parties who might provide useful information, and such parties could include attorneys who would provide independent representation. However, such attorneys, as all other participants, would be required to involve themselves in free and open discussion. They would not be permitted to impose upon the proceedings courtroom procedures of inquiry, which constrain open discussion and could serve to hide information from the panel. For example, an attorney might ask someone a question that could be answered by "yes" or "no." However, the respondent would be completely free to add the word "but" and then provide whatever qualifications and additions warranted to provide clarification. This would be a crucial difference between the panel's method of inquiry and that of the courtroom. Such independent representation might be especially useful, for example, for a passive wife who might not be able to hold her own against an overbearing husband. The panel, as well, would serve to protect such a person from being squelched and possibly exploited.

Appeals Panel

The crucial question remains as to whether the findings and recommendations of the arbitration panel should be binding. On the one hand, one could argue that even three people could make a mistake (the nine-member United States Supreme Court often has made what it subsequently came to realize were mistakes), and the parents should be free to enter into adversarial proceedings in order to appeal to a higher authority. Such an option, however, would undermine completely the whole purpose of this proposal, which is to prevent entirely the possibility of parents involving themselves in adversarial litigation and subjecting themselves to the psychological traumas attendant to such embroilment. On the other hand, one could argue that the process has to end somewhere and that such a panel, as the next step after mediation, is a good enough place to make final decisions in matters such as custody disputes.

At this point, I am in favor of a plan (again removed from adversarial proceedings) in which there would be the possibility of appeal to another panel of three individuals (again an attorney and two mental health professionals) who would have had significant experience in child custody mediation and arbitration. This panel would have the power to make a final decision. These panel members, as well, would be selected by the clients from a roster provided by the court. Many would be people who had served previously on arbitration panels. This *appeals panel*, as well, would operate either in a court of law or under its jurisdiction. The Constitution guarantees individuals the right to settle their disputes in a court of law, and this proposal is not blind to this requirement. The arbitration and appeals panel levels are entirely under the jurisdiction of the court. The lawyers on these panels are serving as judges; however, they are judges who do not operate under the constraints of the adversary system, which, as mentioned, is nowhere required by the Constitution. And even the mediation level may very well be conducted under the aegis of the court. Those who choose to use mediators voluntarily, outside of the court's jurisdiction, are free to do so. The Constitution does not require individuals to settle their disputes in a court of law; it only provides them with the opportunity to do so if they choose.

The appeals panel would involve itself in a two-step process of review. The first step would be similar to that of traditional courts of appeal, wherein the members review the documents at the trial court level. The judges on this appeals panel, however, would review the documentation of the arbitration panel's proceedings. At this stage they would have the power to refuse to consider the case further (like the power given to the United States Supreme Court), and then the findings of the arbitration panel would be final. The appeals panel might direct the arbitration panel to collect further data or reconsider its decision because of certain considerations. Or, after reviewing the arbitration panel's documents, the appeals panel might consider another hearing warranted and could then hear the parties directly and conduct whatever evaluations were necessary. This could involve interviews as well as other forms of data collection similar to those conducted by the original arbitration panel. The appeals panel might even meet with the arbitration panel and the parents all together. The appeals panel, as well, might choose to hear parties brought in by the parents, and such parties might include attorneys serving as advocates. However, once again, traditional courtroom procedures of examination would be replaced by open and free discussion (again moderated by the panel, to prevent deterioration of the proceedings). Whereas traditional courts of appeal allow lawyers only to provide testimony, the appeals panel would have the power to interview directly any and all parties it considered useful to hear. The conclusion of this appeals panel would be final.

In order to discourage frivolous use of the appeals panel, it would have to establish for itself the reputation of being quite stringent with regard to the possibility of changing the recommendations of the lower arbitration panel. In addition, litigious individuals would come to appreciate that they not only might not gain from such appeal, but that they could lose, in that the panel might take away more than they give. Another deterrent to the reflex appeal often seen in litigious people would be the panel's practice of reviewing the arbitration panel's records for the presence of perjury, slander, and libel. In all the years that I have been involved in divorce and custody litigation, there was hardly a case in which I did not see blatant examples of all of these practices. Yet, not once had anyone ever been prosecuted for these crimes. Not once had such behavior even been brought to the attention of the litigants by the court. If the appeals panel were to establish for itself the reputation of reviewing the arbitration panel's records for such behavior, this too could serve as a deterrent for reflex appeal by disgruntled parties.

It should be noted that the three-step procedure I have outlined above (mediation, arbitration panel, and appeals panel) does not involve adversarial proceedings at any level. The system would protect parents from the polarization and spiraling of animosity that frequently accompanies the utilization of adversarial procedures and contributes to the development and perpetuation of psychopathology. It replaces the cumbersome and inefficient method of evidence gathering used by the courts with the more flexible and efficient data-collection process used by mental health professionals. The parents would be given the opportunity to choose their own panel, protecting them thereby from the sense of impotence suffered when they are "stuck" with a judge who all recognize to be ill equipped to deal judiciously with custody conflicts. In short, they choose their own judges. By requiring decisions to be made by the majority of a three-member panel, the likelihood of bias is reduced. Last, and most important, it is a system that precludes any possibility of involvement in adversarial proceedings by people involved in a custody dispute. There would be no such forum for such individuals, and the law would thereby protect them from involvement in a system that was never designed to deal with the question of who would serve as a better parent for children of divorce.

I recognize fully that my proposal would be expensive and possibly available only to those who were affluent. However, I believe that it is still far less expensive than protracted custody litigation which has in many situations made rich people poor. At the present time, middle-income people generally receive watered-down representation (until depleted of funds). I am not claiming that the same situation would not prevail under the system proposed here. Currently, poor people receive even more watered-down services and are most likely to suffer with injudicious decisions. The claim of social services that they provide adequate evaluations and representation is rarely valid. Unfortunately, under my proposal the same situation would probably prevail. I am not presenting this proposal as a perfect solution. The rich have always been better off in this world than the poor, and there is good reason to believe that this will always be the case. This proposal fits in with the reality of today's (and I believe tomorrow's) world and, this drawback notwithstanding, it is still far superior to what we have at this point.

Due Process and Constitutional Rights

The system does not deprive the parents of any of their rights of due process guaranteed by the Constitution of the United States. They have the right to representation by counsel at both the arbitration and appeals levels. Nowhere in the Constitution is anyone (including lawyers) given the right to subject another individual to the frustrations and indignities of yes-no questions. (I have sometimes wondered whether yes-no questions deprive witnesses of their right to freedom of speech guaranteed under the Bill of Rights.) The constitutional right of the accused to confront his (her) accuser is being protected. Even better, in this system the accuser is given the opportunity for direct confrontation with the accused without the utilization of intermediaries (adversary lawyers) and the restrictions of court-room procedures. Although individuals now have the opportunity for such direct confrontations in the courtroom if they represent themselves (*pro se*), this is not commonly done. In the system I propose, the parents are essentially operating *pro se*. But even when they choose to bring in attorneys to represent them, the discussion will still be far freer than that found in the courtroom.

The Constitution guarantees an accused person the right to confront his (her) accuser in a court of law. As mentioned, both the arbitration and appeals panels are conducted under the direct jurisdiction of the court, whether or not they are actually in a courthouse. The members of the panel (essentially judges) are selected from a roster of individuals who have been approved by the court for providing such services. The lawyer on the panel would have the right to subpoena and impose legal sanctions (fines and even jail) for noncompliance. Although the mediation might very well be done privately (there is nothing unconstitutional about this), it might also be done under the aegis of the court and even in a facility within the courthouse.

The constitutional right of a hearing before an impartial judge is being protected. Here, the parents not only have one judge but three (serving in a sense as a tribunal). And protection against bias is enhanced by the requirement that the majority vote will prevail. The requirement that two of the "judges" be mental health professionals is not only desirable for the purposes of the custody evaluation, but is in no way unconstitutional. Nowhere in the Constitution is anything said about the educational or professional requirements that need to be satisfied to serve as a judge. Last, the Constitution presumably guarantees a speedy trial. It requires a morbid expansion of the meaning of the word *speedy* to believe that this constitutional requirement of due process is being protected for the vast majority of litigants in custody disputes. This proposal is more likely to provide such speed, primarily because of the advantages of its method of data collection over that of traditional adversarial courtroom proceedings.

It is important for the reader to appreciate that this proposal is just that, a proposal. It outlines what I consider a reasonable approach to the resolution of custody disputes. I am not claiming that it is perfect, and I suspect that, if implemented, it would probably warrant modification. Although the three-step procedure may appear cumbersome, there is no question that it would prove to be far more efficient and less expensive than adversarial proceedings. Although the plan is designed to protect disputing parents from injudicious decisions, I suspect that the professionals involved in making the custody decisions, being human, will certainly make their share of mistakes. However, I believe that the number of people so harmed will be far less than the number inevitably traumatized by traditional adversary litigation. Although the three-step procedure is most relevant to custody disputes, I believe that the model, with proper modifications, lends itself well to being applied to other kinds of disputes.

Final Comments on the Three-Phase Proposal for Resolving Child Custody Disputes

The system can be instituted in the structure of the present legal system. Although it does not require any changes in the U.S. Constitution, I recognize that it may not be a viable plan in certain states where state constitutional requirements may preclude the implementation of one or more aspects of this proposal. I recognize, therefore, that changes in certain state constitutions might be necessary before the plan could be utilized. It is my hope that legislators would come to appreciate that changing state constitutions and modifying state statutes would be worth the trouble because of the enormous advantages of this proposal.

We are also faced with the problem of training individuals to serve at the various levels of my proposal. We need mental health professionals and lawyers who have received more training in mediation, because such training is crucial at all three levels. We need more mental health professionals who are trained to conduct the kind of intensive custody evaluation described elsewhere (Gardner, 1989a). Traditional mediation training does not generally involve experience with such exhaustive investigations. Rather, mediators traditionally work at a more superficial level and attempt to resolve the dispute by negotiation and compromise. However, this is all many couples require. It is for the more complex problems that the more intensive kind of custody evaluations are often necessary.

At this point there are certainly many people who have enough experience to serve at the mediation level. However, we have to set up standards of certification so that parents will be protected from involving themselves with mediators who are not competent to handle a custody dispute. Furthermore, standards have to be set up for individuals functioning at the arbitration panel and appeals panel levels. The primary consideration for such appointments should be knowledge and experience. People who have served for prescribed periods of time at the mediation level would qualify for consideration to serve at the higher levels. At this time a "grandfather clause" would probably have to be utilized in order to allow people to serve at these levels who are currently experienced enough. In the future, very specific requirements need to be set up in order to decide which individuals would qualify for service at the higher levels.

The three-phase proposal has been designed to deal with custody disputes. However, at this time, false allegations of sex abuse often have to be dealt with in the context of custody disputes because of the ubiquity of such allegations in these conflicts. This is especially the case when a parental alienation syndrome is present. Because sex abuse is a crime, it cannot be dealt with simply in a civil proceeding such as the above three-phase proposal. Currently, individuals who are accused of sex abuse in the context of a custody dispute often involve themselves in two parallel legal procedures: the civil and the criminal. This often involves a double trial and even two attorneys. The information from one trial, however, may become available to the court conducting the other. I believe that my proposal would still be applicable in sex-abuse cases if one dispensed with the mediation level. If such cases went directly to the arbitration level, they would be dealt with directly under the aegis of the court. State legislatures, of course, would have to decide whether the panel here would be operating as a civil, criminal, or combined civil/criminal court. The same panel would make the recommendations regarding custody. The accused would still have the right to appeal to the appeals panel, who could deal with the problem in the very flexible manner described here. Once again, state legislatures would have to decide whether the appeals panel was operating on the civil, criminal, or civil/criminal tracks.

CONCLUDING COMMENTS

At this point, I am attempting to promulgate, through lectures and writing, the aforementioned *stronger-healthy-psychological-bond presumption* to serve as a guideline for courts and mental health professionals when dealing with custody disputes. Furthermore, I am also attempting to call attention to the aforementioned three-phase system that I have proposed for dealing with custody disputes within the legal system, but without the utilization of traditional adversarial proceedings. It is my hope that this book will also play a role in implementing the changes that I believe are crucial if we are to protect people from the psychological ravages of custody litigation.

I appreciate that my efforts will probably prove futile and that the chances of these changes being brought about are extremely small. As described earlier in this book, the United States is probably the most litigious society that has ever existed in the history of the human race. Lieberman (1983) describes in detail the reasons for this phenomenon. It may be that a total reorientation of society is necessary before my proposals could be implemented. We are a country obsessed with litigation. People sue one another for the most frivolous reasons. Protracted adversarial proceedings are an immense source of income for many members of the legal profession who basically do not welcome shorter and less expensive methods of dispute resolution, their public professions of receptivity notwithstanding. And the legislators, to whom I am appealing with my proposals, are most often members of the legal profession. Accordingly, it is unrealistic to expect them to enact legislation that will result in lost income for themselves and/or their legal associates. Furthermore, there are many mental health professionals out there who are also eager to serve as hired guns for attorneys involved in custody litigation. There are psychiatrists, psychologists, social workers, pastoral counselors, family counselors, and a variety of other types of therapists who want to enjoy the benefits to be derived from involvement in custody litigation. Therefore, I do not consider it likely that many of my colleagues in the mental health professions will take the course that I have taken by removing themselves from such adversarial involvement.

On the positive side, judges appear to be sympathetic to my proposals because implementation might very well lessen their burden and reduce their overloaded schedules. Unfortunately, my experiences with judges do not provide me with significant hope. Some judges, indeed, are making attempts to enact changes along the lines described in this book, but these represent a small minority. Most seem to flow with the adversary system and accept it as the best method for resolving child custody disputes (and most other disputes, for that matter). Considering what they observe in their own courtrooms, I sometimes find this hard to accept. Yet, this is exactly what the situation appears to be. Human beings are very distrustful of new ideas, no matter how compelling the arguments for their implementation. I believe that I have provided in this book some very compelling arguments for change.

CONCLUDING COMMENTS

My investigations into the etiology, pathogenesis, manifestations, and treatment of the parental alienation syndrome have
indeed been a labor of love. I genuinely believe that I have broken
new ground here and that the implementation of my guidelines
for treatment has been extremely beneficial for many families and
has prevented the development of significant psychopathology.
An understanding of the parental alienation syndrome places us
in a position to practice preventive psychiatry in its highest form.

Unfortunately, there are many children (I believe there are
tens of thousands of them) who suffer with the disorder and are
not being dealt with properly by either mental health or legal
professionals. As a result, we are breeding a group of children
who will continue to suffer with a disorder that, in many cases,
could have been prevented. I believe that parents who deliber-
ately program their children against a hated spouse are indeed
exhibiting a form of emotional abuse of their children and, when
this is extreme (that is, when they fall into the severe category of
parental alienation syndrome), custody should be transferred to
the allegedly hated parent. Not to do so is to allow for further
attenuation of the psychological bond between the children and a

parent who could otherwise have provided healthy input into their growth and development.

It is still too early to know exactly what happens to children who have been subjected to years of such alienation. As mentioned, the psychological bond can withstand just so much attenuation before it snaps completely and irrevocably. It is too early for follow-up studies. My suspicion is, as is true with most disorders, that there will be a range from those who suffer few if any untoward effects of the syndrome to those who not only exhibit lifelong alienation but who also manifest the psychological problems that derive from such deprivation. Yet all this is preventable in most cases, not only the development of the disorder, but its perpetuation when it does arise. It is my hope that this book will play a role in bringing this rectifiable situation to the attention of those professionals, both in the legal and mental health realms, who are in a position to bring about the prevention and eradication of this widespread disturbance.

ADDENDUM I

PROVISIONS FOR ACCEPTING AN INVITATION TO SERVE AS AN IMPARTIAL EXAMINER IN CUSTODY/VISITATION LITIGATION

Whenever possible, I make every reasonable attempt to serve as a court-appointed impartial examiner, rather than as an advocate, in custody/visitation litigation. In order to serve optimally in this capacity I must be free to avail myself of any and all information, from any source, that I consider pertinent and reasonable to have. In this way, I believe I can serve best the interests of children and parents involved in such conflicts. Accordingly, before agreeing to serve in this capacity, the following conditions must be agreed upon by both parents and both attorneys:

1) The presiding judge will agree to appoint me impartial examiner to conduct an evaluation of the concerned parties.

2) I will have available to interview all members of the immediate family—that is, the mother, father, and children—for as many interviews (individual and in any combination) as I consider warranted. In addition, I will have the freedom to invite any and all other parties whom I would consider possible sources

of useful information. Generally, these will include such persons as present or prospective parental surrogates with whom either parent may be involved and the housekeeper.

Usually, I do not interview a series of friends and relatives each of whom, from the outset, is particularly partial to one of the parents (but I reserve the right to invite such parties if I consider it warranted). The decision to interview such additional parties will be based solely on the potential value of their contributions to the data-collection process and not on whether one parent is represented by more such people than the other.

3) Information will be gathered primarily from the aforementioned clinical interviews. Although I do not routinely use formal psychological tests, in some evaluations I have found certain psychological tests to be useful. Accordingly, the parents shall agree to take any and all psychological tests that I consider helpful. In addition, they will agree to have one or more of the children take such tests if I consider them warranted. Some of these tests will be administered by me, but others by a psychologist of my choosing if I do not consider myself qualified to administer a particular psychological test.

4) In order to allow me the freedom of inquiry necessary for serving optimally families involved in custody/visitation litigation, the parents shall agree to a modification of the traditional rules of confidentiality. Specifically, I must be given the freedom to reveal to one party what has been told to me by the other (at my discretion) so that I will have full opportunity to explore all pertinent points with both parties. This does not mean that I will not respect certain privacies or that I will automatically reveal all information provided me—only that I reserve the right to make such revelations if I consider them warranted for the purpose of collecting the most meaningful data.

5) The parties shall agree to sign any and all releases necessary for me to obtain reports from others, e.g., psychiatrists, psychologists, social workers, teachers, school officials, pediatricians, hospitals (general and psychiatric), etc. This includes past records as well as reports from professionals who may be involved with any of the parties at the time of the litigation.

Although I may choose not to request a particular report, I must have the freedom to request any and all such reports, if I consider them useful sources of information.

6) My fee for conducting a custody evaluation is $200 per hour of my time. Time spent in interviewing as well as time expended in report preparation, dictation, telephone conversations, responses to letters (regardless of which side submits them), court preparation, and any other time invested in association with the evaluation will also be billed at the $200 per hour rate. My fee for court and deposition appearances is $350 per hour while in court and $150 per hour travel time to and from my office. During the data-collection phase of the evaluation, payments shall be made at the time services are rendered. Payments for the final conference at which my findings and recommendations are presented (item #9 below), the court report, and my court appearance shall be made in advance—in accordance with estimates provided prior to the rendering of these services.

Prior to the initial interview (with both parents together) the payer(s) will deposit with me a check (in my name) for $2,500. This shall be deposited in the Northern Valley-Englewood Savings and Loan Association branch in Cresskill, New Jersey, in my name, in a day-to-day interest bearing account. This money, with accrued interest (taxable to the payer), shall be returned *after* a final decision has been made regarding custody/visitation and after I have received a letter from *both* of the attorneys that my services are no longer being enlisted.

This payment is a security deposit. It will not serve as an advance retainer, in that the aforementioned fees will not be drawn against it, unless there has been a failure to pay my fees. It also serves to reassure a nonpayer that my objectivity will not be compromised by the fear that if I do not support the paying party, my fee will not be paid.

The average total cost for an evaluation is generally in the $3,000-$6,000 range. Although this figure may initially appear high, it is generally far less costly than protracted litigation. If as a result of the evaluation the litigation is shortened (often the case) or the parties decide not to litigate further over custody/visitation (also a common occurrence), then the net savings may be significant. It is very difficult, if not impossible, to predict the cost of a particular evaluation, because I cannot know beforehand how many interviews will be warranted and whether or not I will be asked to testify in court.

On occasion, I am invited to conduct evaluations in cities at varying distances from Cresskill, New Jersey. This generally entails situations in which there is a choice between my traveling to the family's location and all interviewees traveling to New Jersey and acquiring temporary accommodations in the area of my office. Although I prefer that the evaluation take place in my office, I have on occasion agreed to conduct the evaluation elsewhere. However, my fees for such evaluations are higher than for those conducted in my office and are determined by the distance I have to travel and the time I am being asked to be away from my office. My fee schedule for such distant evaluations is available on request.

7) Both attorneys are invited to send to me any material that they consider useful to me.

8) After receiving 1) the court order signed by the presiding judge, 2) the signed statements (page 8) from both parties signifying agreement to these provisions for my conducting the evaluation, and 3) the $2,500 deposit, I will notify both parties that I am available to proceed with the evaluation as rapidly as is feasible. I generally cannot promise to meet a specific deadline because I cannot know in advance how many interviews will be required, nor can I predict how flexible the parties will be regarding availability for appointments I offer.

9) Upon completion of my evaluation—and *prior to* the preparation of my final report—I generally meet with both parents together and present to them my findings and recommendations. This gives them the opportunity to correct any distortions they believe I may have and/or alter my opinion before it becomes finalized in my report. In addition, it saves the parents from the unnecessary and prolonged tension associated with wondering what my findings are.

Both attorneys are invited to attend this conference. However, this invitation should be considered withdrawn if only one attorney wishes to attend because the presence of only one attorney would obviously place the nonrepresented parent in a compromised position. When a guardian ad litem has been appointed by the court, he or she will also be invited to attend this conference. Before accepting this invitation, attorneys should appreciate that the discussion will be completely free and open. Accordingly, during this conference it would be improper for an attorney in any way whatsoever to restrict or discourage the client from answering questions or participating in the discussion. On occasion, the litigants have used this conference as a forum for resolving their custody/visitation dispute and thereby avoiding the formidable expense and psychological trauma of courtroom litigation. After this conference the final report is prepared and sent simultaneously to the court, attorneys, and parents.

10) After this conference I strictly refrain from any further communication with either parent or any other party involved in the evaluation. However, I am willing to discuss any aspect of the case with *both* attorneys at the same time, either personally or by conference telephone call. Such communication may occur at any time from the end of the aforementioned conference to the end of the trial. This practice enables me to continue to provide input to the attorneys regarding what I consider to be in the children's best interests. And this may be especially important during the trial. At that time, in order to preserve my status as impartial, any discussions I may have with an attorney and/or parent is only conducted under circumstances in which the adversary attorney and/or parent is invited to participate.

11) When there has been a significant passage of time between the submission of my report and the trial date, I will generally invite the primary participating parties for an interview update prior to my court appearance. This conference enables me to acquaint myself with developments that succeeded my report and ensures that my presentation in court will include the most recent information. All significant adult participants will be

invited to this meeting and on occasion one or more of the children (especially teenagers). This conference will be held as long as at least one party wishes to attend.

My experience has been that conducting the evaluation in the manner described above provides me with the optimum conditions for providing the court with a thorough and objective recommendation.

SERVING AS AN ADVOCATE

12) Often one party will invite my services as an impartial examiner and the other will refuse to participate voluntarily. On occasion, the inviting party has then requested that the court appoint me impartial examiner and order the reluctant side to participate. Generally, there are three ways in which courts respond to this request:

A. The court responds affirmatively and appoints me its impartial examiner. In such cases I then proceed in accordance with the above provisions (#1-#11).

B. The court is not willing to formally designate me its appointed impartial examiner, but rather orders the reluctant side to cooperate in interviews with me as if I were the advocate of the initiator. (This usually occurs when the presiding judge orders both parents to be evaluated by each one's selected adversary examiner.) In such cases, I still do not view myself to be serving automatically as the advocate of the initiating party. Rather, I make it understood to all concerned that I will proceed as closely as possible with the type of evaluation I conduct when serving as impartial examiner—*even to the point of testifying in court as an advocate of the initially reluctant party*. In that eventuality, if the initially reluctant party requests a court appearance, that party will be responsible for my fees (item 6) beyond the point at which my final report has been sent to the court, attorneys, and the clients. The party who initially invited me, however, will still have the obligation to pay for my report, whether or not it supports that party's position. I believe that this plan ensures my input to the court regarding what I consider to be in the children's best interests and precludes my serving merely as a hired advocate.

C. The court refuses to order my participation but recognizes the right of the inviting party to enlist my involvement as an advocate. In such cases I proceed in accordance with provision 13.

13) A. On occasion, I am willing to *consider* serving as an advocate in custody/visitation litigation. However, such participation will only be considered after evidence has been submitted to me that: 1) the inviting party's adversary has been invited to participate and has refused and 2) the court has refused to order such involvement. If I do then suspect that the inviting party's position merits my consideration, I would be willing to interview that party with no promise beforehand that I will support his (her) position. On occasion I have seen fit to support the participating party's position, because it was obvious to me that the children's needs would be served best by my advocacy and/or not to do so would have deprived them of sorely needed assistance. On other occasions I have concluded that I could not serve with conviction as an advocate of the requesting party and so have refused further services to the client.

B. If I do decide to serve as an advocate, I ask for the standard $2,500 security deposit, which is dealt with as described in item #6. Furthermore, if in the course of my evaluation in which I am serving as an advocate, the non-participating party decides belatedly to participate I will, at that point, no longer consider myself automatically committed to serve as an advocate for the original party. Rather, I will conduct the evaluation, as far as possible, in accordance with the provisions for my serving as an impartial examiner—even to the point of testifying in court in support of the belated participant. Before interviewing the belated participant, however, all parties will have to agree upon any possible modifications of the fee-paying arrangement that may be warranted.

Richard A. Gardner, M.D.

I have read the above, discussed the provisions with my attorney, and agree to participate in the evaluation procedures delineated above. I agree to pay _____% of the $2,500 advance security deposit and _____% of the fees in accordance with the aforementioned payment schedules. I recognize the possibility that Dr. Gardner may *not* ultimately support my position in the litigation. Nevertheless, I will still fulfill my obligation to pay _____% of his fees. I appreciate that this may entail the payment of fees associated with his preparing reports that do not support my position and even testifying in court in support of my adversary (with the exception of the situation in which items 12B and 13B are operative).

Date: _____   _____

                                         Parent's Signature

Revision No. 38

ADDENDUM II

As mentioned in this book, the parental alienation syndrome (PAS) is a developing concept, and I am ever updating my understanding of the disorder with regard to its etiology, manifestations, pathogenesis, and treatment. An addendum is now warranted because I have been provided with a suggestion for dealing with one of the knottiest problems I have encountered regarding the treatment of families in which the children are suffering with the severe type of PAS. Specifically, my recommendation that the court remove such children from the home of a parent who is suffering with a *severe* type of PAS (especially when paranoia is present) has not been met with great receptivity by judges and some mental health professionals.

One source of this unreceptivity relates to the deep-seated notion that children should not be removed from their mother, no matter how disturbed she may be. (As mentioned throughout this book, for simplicity of presentation, I will refer to the programming parent as the mother because she, much more often than the father, is the programmer. However, the same principles apply when the father is the primary promulgator of the PAS.) Courts have generally been much more receptive to my recommendations for the *mild* and *moderate* categories of mothers, because these do not include removal of the children from the mother's home. Another source of unreceptivity relates to the fact that the children in the severe category are often so frightened of their father, and have been so imbued with the notion that being in his home is dangerous and might even be lethal, that transfer is considered impossible. My frustration, resulting from the unreceptivity of courts to implement this recommendation, was made especially poignant by the recognition that the children's remaining in the mother's home dooms their relationship with their father and predictably results in their developing longstanding psychopathology, even paranoia.

At a recent conference, Dr. Dale Fruman, a child psychiatrist, suggested hospitalization as an intermediate disposition. I was struck immediately by the potential of this recommendation. I recognized that the concept of an intermediary disposition, an arrangement that did not involve *immediate* transfer from the home of the mother to the home of the father, might solve many of the problems attendant to a direct transfer and might also reduce unreceptivity to this proposal.

Before describing the details of the program, it is important to reemphasize a point mentioned in many places throughout this book, namely, that the transition points are particularly difficult for PAS children. In such circumstances, with both parents present, their loyalty conflict is most acute. In the case of children suffering with the severe type of PAS, transition under such circumstances is practically impossible. The father is generally unable to get the children out of the mother's home and, even if they are transferred to his home by force, they are likely to run away and do everything possible to return to their mother's home. Temporary placement in a transitional site appears to be an excellent solution to this problem. In such a transitional site, the aforementioned confrontation is obviated in that the children are not placed in a position in which they are with both parents together.

It is also important to reiterate that mothers in the severe category are not going to comply readily with court orders to cease and desist from their brainwashing. In fact, their ignoring of court orders is one of the reasons why they warrant placement in the severe category. The main purpose of the program outlined here is to enforce the mother's separation from the children—for varying periods depending upon the case—in order to protect the children from the mother's ongoing campaign of manipulation and programming. Accordingly, during this early phase it is crucial that there be *no contact at all* between the children and their mother, either directly or indirectly, e.g., via telephone or mail. All these contacts will be utilized by the mother to continue her brainwashing and will thereby lessen significantly the likelihood that this transitional program will be successful.

THE THREE LEVELS OF TRANSITIONAL SITES

After giving further thought to Dr. Fruman's proposal, I have formulated a plan that is based on the concept of a *transitional site*, but I would not automatically involve hospitalization as the transitional place. Specifically, less restrictive environments would be tried first, hospitalization used only as a last resort if the less restrictive facilities did not prove adequate for the purposes of the transfer.

Level 1. In this category of transitional site, I include the home of a friend or relative with whom the children have a reasonably good relationship. Although this might be the home of one of the father's relatives, it would not be a suitable place for transition if the mother has been successful in programming the children to believe that these individuals are part of the father's extended network of people who will also cause them significant harm. While living with these people, arrangements have to be made for the children's attending a local school. In order to serve effectively, these caretakers have to appreciate the depth of the mother's pathology and have to be strong enough to prohibit mail and telephone calls (during a prescribed period—see below) and report to the proper authorities (e.g., a guardian ad litem or a court-appointed therapist) the failure of the mother to obey the court order restraining her from visiting the children or even coming into their neighborhood or school. The caretakers at this site would also have to be able to exert control over the children's antics during the periods of their father's visits with them (see below).

Another type of transition site in this category would be a foster home. Here, again, the foster parents would have to satisfy the aforementioned criteria of vigilance and stringency.

If the situation is so bad that a level-1 transitional site is not feasible, then a more restricted environment must be considered. This would be necessary if the mother continued to ignore court orders not to call or visit the children (either in the transitional home or in the school environment). It would also be necessary if the children continued to run away from a level-1 transitional site in order to return to their mother. Under such circumstances, a level-2 transitional site would have to be considered.

Level 2. A possible site in this category would be a community shelter—the kind of setting where are placed delinquents, abandoned children, abused children, and others warranting removal from their homes. It is preferable that the school be incorporated into this facility (sometimes the case). Here there would be much more stringent surveillance and control of the children's behavior, especially when the father visits (see below), as well as the mother's potential to visit and/or communicate with the children.

This facility might not prove feasible if the children's antics became unmanageable, if the mother continues to visit the premises (in spite of a court order), and/or if the children's behavior becomes uncontrollable at the time of the father's visits. Under those circumstances, a level-3 transitional site would have to be considered.

Level 3. Hospitalization. Obviously, this is the most restrictive environment, one in which there is the greatest degree of control over the situation. This should only be tried after transitional sites 1 and 2 have been considered and, preferably, tried. Obviously, here the children would have the least opportunity to go back to their mother's home, and there would be the greatest degree of control over mail, telephone calls, and visits by the mother. Here, too, there would be the greatest degree of control over the children's behavior at the time of the father's visits. It is crucial that the treating personnel have knowledge of the, PAS *and* the opportunity for input to the court, either directly or indirectly. Because most hospitals have affiliated schools, the children could attend school while hospitalized.

THE TRANSITIONAL PROGRAM

At this point I will address myself to the details of the transitional program. As mentioned, although the program may be under the auspices of a therapist, what is done here is far less therapy than "movement of bodies." The main goal is to provide the children with *living experiences* that their father is not the terribly dangerous person he has been portrayed to be by the mother. The ultimate aim is to get the children into the father's home as soon as possible, but it is important to recognize that the amount of time spent in the transitional site will vary from case to case, and this must be monitored carefully by the people involved in administering the transitional program. I propose a program that follows this sequence:

Phase 1. Placement in the transitional site. Here, the children are removed from the mother's incessant campaign of programming, yet they are not with their father, with whom they believe terrible things will happen to them. During this period at the transitional site, *all* contact with the mother should be cut off, including mail and telephone calls. Then, after a few days of accommodation to the new site, the father should visit the children *at the site*. There, they will start to have the living experience that no harm will come to them. Over the next few days or weeks (depending upon their tolerance), visits with the father (again at the site) should increase in both frequency and duration.

Phase 2. At some point (hopefully in a short period), the children should begin visiting their father for short periods *in his home*, after which they return directly to the transitional site. Gradually, the visits to the father's home should be lengthened, until the point where they can start living there on an ongoing basis. During this period there should be *no* contact with the mother, even via mail and telephone calls.

Phase 3. The children are discharged from the transitional site and live with their father on an ongoing basis. In the early part of this phase, once again, no mail or telephone calls from the mother should be allowed. If she is seen in the area of the father's home, this is to be reported immediately (through proper channels) to the court, after which serious sanctions, such as a fine, a reduction in alimony payments, and even incarceration (or hospitalization [in selected cases]) should be seriously considered. The children *require* the living experience that the terrible consequences that they have anticipated will not be realized. Any interruption of this process by the mother is likely to cause them to regress.

Phase 4. Carefully monitored contact with the mother can be permitted—on a trial basis. The first step should be limited and monitored telephone conversations. It is not likely that the mother will reduce her programming, but at least limitations can be placed on it. If it appears that she has enough self-control and/or that her obsession with brainwashing the children is somewhat under control, longer telephone conversations can be permitted. During this phase, similarly monitored mail communications may be allowed.

Phase 5. Monitored visits with the mother *in the father's home* may be tried, the frequency and duration determined by how much she can reduce her inculcation of animosity toward the father.

Phase 6. In some cases, carefully monitored and judiciously restricted visits *to the mother's home* might be tried. Obviously, this would only be possible in those situations in which the mother's animosity has become reduced to the degree that there is only limited risk of programming (which runs the risk of undoing all the benefits derived from the implementation of the previous phases in this program). There are some cases in which this phase would never be reached because the mother might kidnap the children, refuse to return them, or otherwise subject them to unrelentless programming against the father. It is to be hoped, however, that this does not prove to be necessary and that some contacts with the mother might be possible.

FURTHER COMMENTS

This program might be conducted under the auspices of a psychologist, psychiatrist, or guardian ad litem, who is court appointed and who has the freedom to report back to the court any problems that may arise. In recent years, courts have become increasingly appreciative of the importance of strong sanctions (fines, garnisheeing of wages, attachment of property, and even incarceration) for fathers who have failed to fulfill their financial obligations to their former wives. Courts, however, have not been equally receptive to recommendations that PAS mothers be warned that they cannot ignore the court's orders with impunity. The threat of fine and incarceration can help most such women "cooperate." Another relevant issue is the power of the court to hospitalize the children. Courts certainly hospitalize insane people and/or individuals who are a danger to themselves and others. Many people are committed for short periods, such as thirty days, pending a final decision of the court regarding their permanent disposition. A similar procedure could be utilized to hospitalize PAS children, and a thirty-day limit would, I suspect, be adequate to achieve the aforementioned goals.

Community shelters and psychiatric hospitals are not famous for their plushness. In fact, many are referred to as "zoos," and this reputation is sometimes warranted. However unfortunate this situation may be in other circumstances, it may serve to speed up the transfer program for PAS children. Recognizing that they cannot return to their mother and appreciating that their antics may prolong their stay in the transitional site, may enhance their motivation to move rapidly into the home of their father. And even the level-1 transitional site may serve this purpose if it is inhospitable enough for the children. I am not recommending that one go out of one's way to select the most inhospitable sites for these children; but I am not recommending that one search for the most plush arrangements either.

To date, I have had no actual experience with this proposal, but I believe that it is sensible and is worthy of being tried. I recognize that this proposal, like many of the other proposals in this book, are more likely to be put into effect if there are financial resources to support it. In this regard, this proposal is no different from any of the other recommendations proposed in this book. And it is no different from any other recommendation made in psychiatry, or in medicine in general. The facts are that the more money available for any program (medical or otherwise), the greater the likelihood it will be implemented and the greater the likelihood its success. To the degree that community and/or personal resources are available to implement this program, to that degree is it likely to prove successful.

Last, it is crucial to reiterate that the only hope these children have for bonding with their father and being protected from the induction of their mother's severe psychopathology is permanent transfer to the home of the father and his designation as the primary custodial parent. Without such transfer, the bonding with the father is inevitably going to be destroyed, and the children will predictably develop the mother's psychopathology. I believe that Dr. Fruman has made an important contribution to my thinking here, and I have every reason to believe that, if implemented, this plan will prove valuable for PAS families in the *severe* category. Finally, this plan is not designed for PAS families in the mild and/or moderate categories. Mothers in these categories generally have healthier bonding with their children, have most often been the primary caretakers, and (their antics notwithstanding) still warrant being designated the primary custodial parent. Accordingly, no such transfers are indicated for mothers in the mild and moderate categories.

COMMENTS FOR THIRD PRINTING
SEPTEMBER 1996

Unfortunately, my experiences with the transition-site proposal have been disappointing and frustrating. Courts have been predictably unreceptive to implementing recommendations that provide repercussions for mothers who are inducing a PAS in their children. In recent years, courts have taken strong action against fathers who have reneged on their support and alimony payments. Such fathers have been placed on weekend house arrest, have spent weekends in jail, and even have received longer sentences. The wives and children of such fathers are being psychologically abused. Similarly, inducing a PAS in a child is a form of psychological abuse. Yet the same judges who would have no hesitation incarcerating a defaulting father will allow PAS-inducing mothers to continue their manipulations with impunity. Some judges may threaten such mothers with sanctions, but my experience has been follow-through is rare.

The PAS is a preventable disorder were courts to use the healthy-psychological-bond presumption when deciding primary custodial status. The PAS can also be interrupted with meaningful court sanctions. Yet, courts are not imposing such sanctions.

With regard to placement of PAS children in transitional sites, as is often warranted in the severe cases, I have not personally seen courts implement the proposals described here. I have received some feedback from colleagues who have reported successful utilization of the transitional-site program, but such feedback is rare. Most professionals involved in PAS cases decry the fact that the courts do nothing to effectively dissuade PAS mothers. I believe that one of the many reasons for such unreceptivity is political. In recent years, it has been politically injudicious for judges to come down too heavily on women. Whatever other factors may be involved, there is no question that this factor is operative. As long as any political consideration is the overriding factor, then courts will continue to fall short of their goal of serving the best interests of children.

REFERENCES

Alexander, G.J. (l984), Trial by champion. *Santa Clara Law Review,* 34(3):545-564.

American Bar Association (1991), Membership Report, July 1991. Chicago: American Bar Association.

Bazelon, D.L. (l974), The perils of wizardry. *The American Journal of Psychiatry,* 131:1317-1322.

Berger, S.J. (1985), Personal communication.

Campbell, R.J. (1989), *Psychiatric Dictionary, Sixth Edition.* Oxford: Oxford University Press.

Coogler, O.J. (1978), *Structured Mediation in Divorce Settlement.* Lexington, Massachusetts: Lexington Books (D.C. Heath and Company).

Derdeyn, A.P. (1976), Child custody contests in the historical perspective. *American Journal of Psychiatry,* 133:1369-1376.

_____ (1978), Child custody: a reflection of cultural change. *Journal of Clinical Child Psychology,* 7(3):169-173.

Encyclopedia Britannica, Macropedia, (1982), Law of Evidence, 7:1-6.

Encyclopedia Britannica, Macropedia, (1982), Legal Profession, 10:779-784.

Epstein, M.A., Markowitz, R.L., Gallo, D.M., Holmes, J.W., and Gryboski, J.D. (1987), Munchausen syndrome by proxy: considerations in diagnosis and confirmation by video surveillance. *Pediatrics,* 80(2):220-224.

Finlay v. Finlay, 240 N.Y. 429, Court of Appeals of New York, 1925, Cardozo.

Fisher, R. and Ury, W. (1981), *Getting to Yes.* Boston: Houghton Mifflin Co.

Folberg, J. and Taylor, A. (1984), *Mediation: A Comprehensive Guide to*

Resolving Conflicts Without Litigation. San Francisco: Jossey- Bass Publishers.

Forer, L.G. (1975), *The Death of the Law.* New York: David McKay Co., Inc.

Freud, S. (1905), Three contributions to the theory of sex: II-infantile sexuality. In *The Basic Writings of Sigmund Freud,* ed. A.A. Brill, pp. 592-593. New York: Random House, Inc. (The Modern Library), 1938.

Gardner, R.A. (1973), *Understanding Children: A Parents Guide to Child Rearing.* Cresskill, New Jersey: Creative Therapeutics.

_____ (1976), *Psychotherapy with Children of Divorce.* Northvale, New Jersey: Jason Aronson, Inc.

_____ (1977), *The Parents Book About Divorce* (paperback). New York: Bantam Books, Inc.

_____ (1979), Death of a parent. In *Basic Handbook of Child Psychiatry,* ed. J.D. Noshpitz, vol. 4, pp. 270-283. New York: Basic Books, Inc.

_____ (1982), *Family Evaluation in Child Custody Litigation.* Cresskill, New Jersey: Creative Therapeutics.

_____ (1985a), Recent trends in divorce and custody litigation. *Academy Forum (A Publication of the American Academy of Psychoanalysis),* 29(2):3-7.

_____ (1985b), *Separation Anxiety Disorder: Psychodynamics and Psychotherapy.* Cresskill, New Jersey: Creative Therapeutics.

_____ (1986a), *Child Custody Litigation: A Guide for Parents and Mental Health Professionals.* Cresskill, New Jersey: Creative Therapeutics.

_____ (1986b), *The Psychotherapeutic Techniques of Richard A. Gardner.* Cresskill, New Jersey: Creative Therapeutics.

_____ (1987), *The Parental Alienation Syndrome and the Differentiation Between Fabricated and Genuine Child Sex Abuse.* Cresskill, New Jersey: Creative Therapeutics.

_____ (1988), *Psychotherapy with Adolescents.* Cresskill, New Jersey: Creative Therapeutics.

_____ (1989a), *Family Evaluation in Child Custody Mediation, Arbitration, and Litigation.* Cresskill, New Jersey: Creative Therapeutics.

_____ (1989b), A psychiatrist's opinion of the adversary system, especially as utilized in custody disputes. *The New Jersey Family Lawyer,* 8(8):158-163.

_____ (1991a), *Sex Abuse Hysteria: Salem Witch Trials Revisited.* Cresskill, New Jersey: Creative Therapeutics.

_____ (1991b), *Parents Book About Divorce, Second Edition* (hardcover). Cresskill, New Jersey: Creative Therapeutics.

_____ (1991c), *Parents Book About Divorce, Second Edition* (paperback). New York: Bantam Books, Inc.

_____ (1992a), *True and False Accusations of Child Sex Abuse.* Cresskill, New Jersey: Creative Therapeutics.

_____ (1992b), *Psychogenic Learning Disabilities: Diagnosis and Treatment.* Cresskill, New Jersey: Creative Therapeutics. (in press)

Gettelman, S. and Markowitz, J. (1974), *The Courage to Divorce.* New York: Simon and Schuster.

Glieberman, H.A. (1975), *Confessions of a Divorce Lawyer.* Chicago: Henry Regnery Co.

Goleman, D. (1988), Lies can point to mental disorders or signal normal growth. *The New York Times,* May 17, 1988, pp. Cl, C6.

Haynes, J.M. (1981), *Divorce Mediation: A Practical Guide for Therapists.* New York: Springer Publishing Co.

Kolb, L.C. and Brodie, H.K.H. (1982), *Modern Clinical Psychiatry.* Philadelphia: W.B. Sanders Co.

Kopetski, L.M. (1988), Personal Communication.

Landsman, S. (1983), A brief survey of the adversary system. *Ohio State Law Journal,* 44(3):713-739.

Libow, J.A. and Scherier, H.A. (1986), Three forms of factitious illness in children: when is it M.S.P.? *American Journal of Orthopsychiatry,* 54(4):602-611.

Lieberman, J.K. (1981), *The Litigious Society.* New York: Basic Books, Inc.

Lindsley, B.C. (1976), Custody proceedings: battlefield or peace conference. *Bulletin of the American Academy of Psychiatry and the Law,* 4(2):127-131.

_____ (1980), Foreword to *Custody Cases and Expert Witnesses: A Manual for Attorneys.* M.G. Goldzband. New York: Harcourt Brace Jovanovich.

McIsaac, H. (1983), Court connected mediation. *Conciliation Courts Review,* 21(2):49-56.

Money, J. (1986), Munchausen's syndrome by proxy: update. *Journal of Pediatric Psychology,* 11(4):583-584.

Money, J. and Werlwas, J. (1976), Folie à deux in the parents of psychosocial dwarfs: two Cases. *Bulletin of the American Academy of Psychiatry and the Law,* 4:351-362.

_____ (1980), Folie-à-deux in the parents of psychosocial dwarfs: two cases. In *Traumatic Abuse and Neglect of Children at Home,* ed. G.J. Williams and J. Money, pp. 160-174. Baltimore: Johns Hopkins University Press.

Murray, H. (1936), *The Thematic Apperception Test.* New York: The Psychological Corp.

Neef, M. and Nagel, S. (1974), The adversary nature of the American legal system from a historical perspective. *New York Law Forum,* 20:123-164.

Nizer, L. (1968), *My Life in Court.* New York: Pyramid Publications.

Ramos, S. (1979), *The Complete Book of Child Custody.* New York: G.P. Putnam's Sons.

Rand, D.C. (1989), Munchausen syndrome by proxy as a possible factor when abuse is falsely alleged. *Issues in Child Abuse Allegations,* 1(4):32-43.

Riskin, L.L. (1982), Mediation and lawyers. *Ohio State Law Journal,* 43:29-60.

Sopkin, C. (1974), The roughest divorce lawyers in town. *New York,* Nov. 4, 1974.

United States Census Bureau (1991), *Current Population Reports,* Series P-25. Washington, D.C.: U.S. Census Bureau.

Varendock, J. (1911), Les teroignanes d'enfants dans un proces retinisant. *Archives of Psychology,* 11:129.

Watson, A.S. (1969), The children of Armageddon: problems of custody following divorce. *Syracuse Law Review,* 21:55-86.

Weiss, P.S. (1975), *Marital Separation.* New York: Basic Books, Inc.

Author Index

Alexander, G. J., 3
American Bar Association, 33
Bazelon, D. L., 47
Berger, S. J., 48
Brodie, H. K. H., 148
Campbell, R. J., 147, 148
Coogler, O.J., 6, 304
Derdeyn, A. P., 37, 53
Encyclopedia Britannica, 3, 36
Epstein, M. A., 148
Fisher, R., 304
Folberg, J., 6, 304
Forer, L. G., 46
Freud, S., 151
Gallo, D. M., 148
Gardner, R. A., 47, 57, 61, 77, 82,
    106, 120, 126, 129, 139, 146,
    151, 154, 157, 161, 164, 183,
    207, 223, 237, 258, 263, 269,
    280, 290, 292, 304, 315, 322
Gettelman, S., 44
Glieberman, H. A., 45
Goleman, D., 195
Gryboski, J. D., 148
Haynes, J. M., 304
Holmes, J. W., 148

Kolb, L. C., 148
Kopetski, L. M., 133
Landsman, S., 3
Libow, J. A., 148
Lieberman, J. K., 31, 324
Lindsley, B. C., 47, 48
Markowitz, J., 44
Markowitz, R. L., 148
McIsaac, H., 313
Money, J., 148
Murray, H., 201
Nagel, S., 3
Neef, M., 3
Nizer, L., 43
Ramos, S., 40
Rand, D. C., 148
Riskin, L. L., 301
Scherier, H. A., 148
Sopkin, C., 44
Taylor, A., 6, 304
United States Census Bureau, 33
Ury, W., 304
Varendock, J., 195
Watson, A. S., 295
Weiss, P. S., 44
Werlwas, J., 148

Subject Index

Adversary system
  and abolishment of Star
    Chamber, 28
  criticism of, 48–52, 56–57, 185
  and custody litigation, 43–44,
    46–57
  definition of, 1
  and failure to allow direct
    confrontation between
  accused and accuser, 288–293
  and Fourth Lateran Council,
    16–17
  and Greek society, 6–8
  historical development of, 1–36
  and inquisitional system, 17–21
  and issue of conviction for
    client's position, 293–296
  and issue of emotions and
    objectivity, 296–300
  judges' past and present roles in,
    24–26
  juries of, 21–23
  lawyers' past and present roles
    in, 26–28
  and lies of omission vs. commis-
    sion, 15, 286–288
  and primitive societies, 3–6
  reasons for development of,
    18–21
  and Roman society, 8–9
  rules developed for governing
    the, 29
  teaching lawyers about deficien-
    cies of, 285–300
  testimony of witnesses, 23–24
  and training in child psychology,
    56–57
  and trial by combat, 11–14
  and trial by ordeal, 9–11
  and trial by wager, 14–16
Albigenses, 18, 19
Appeals panel, 316–318
Arbitration panel, 314–316
Asian societies, dispute settlement
  of, 5–6
Attorneys (see Lawyers)

Best evidence rule, 24

Best-interests-of-the-child presumption, 53, 54, 61–62
Best-interests-of-the-family presumption, 266–267
Bonds (see Psychological bonds)
Borrowed scenarios, 77–80, 177
Brainwashing (see Programming)

Catholic church (see Religion)
Child advocates, 188
   provisions for serving as, 332–334
   and guardian ad litem, 231
Child custody disputes (see Custody disputes)
Child Labor laws, 40
Children
   absence of guilt in, 76–77
   and borrowed scenarios, 77–80
   and campaigns of denigration, 64–68
   cognitive immaturity of, 192
   and differentiating fact from fantasy, 192–197
   fear of disruption of primary psychological bond, 115–117
   and fears of contamination in mother's home, 65–67
   and hatred of a parent and parent's extended family, 64–82, 84–99, 107–121, 140–149
   identification
      with aggressor, 117–118
      with an idealized person, 118–119
   in-camera interviews with, 190–192
   independent thinker phenomenon in, 74–75
   individual interviews with, 171–178, 197–198
   infectiousness of emotions in, 120
   lack of ambivalence in, 73

and lying, 193–197, 231
   mothers' maneuvers used in programming of, 85–105
   overprotection of, 129–131, 137
   with parental alienation syndrome, 63–82, 59–156
   interviewing of, 212–213, 212–217
   reaction formation in, 117
   and reflexive love of the loved parent, 75–76
   release of hostility in, 119–120
   and separation anxiety, 78
   sex-blind custody decisions and best interests of, 305–309
   sexual rivalry in, 120–121
   therapy of moderate and severe cases, 226–228, 236–242
   and transition periods, 238–239
   types of interview questions to ask, 174–177, 199–208, 207–217
   underlying psychodynamics in, 115–121
   weak rationalizations for alienation, 68–73
Church (see Religion)
Circumstantial evidence, 17–18
Confidentiality, 198–199, 224
Constitution of the United States, 319–321
Cross-examination, 29
Custody disputes
   and adultery and atheism, 38–39
   and best-interests-of-the-child presumption, 53, 54
   and best-interests-of-the-family presumption, 266–267
   changing attitudes regarding parental preference, 37–57
   and development of psychopathology, 47, 50–51
   evaluation of family in, 157–183
   and exclusionary maneuvers,

127-129
and joint custody concept, 54-56
judges' guidelines for decision
  in, 263-267
and parental alienation
  syndrome, 59-156
and parent culpability, concept
  of, 39
provisions for serving as impartial examiner in, 327-332
roles of legal professionals in,
  185-218
sex-blind decisions in, 305-309
and stronger-healthy-
  psychological bond
 presumption, 323
and Talfourd's Act, 38
and tender-years presumption,
  38, 41, 52-53, 305-306
use of adversary system in,
  43-44, 46-57
Women's Liberation movement,
  effects of, 39-40
Custody disputes, alternative
  system for resolving, 312-324
appeals panel, 316-318
arbitration panel, 314-316
benefits of, 318-319
and due process and constitutional rights, 319-321
mediation, 313-314
problems with, 321-323
Custody disputes, preferred
  parent in
1960s to mid-1970s, 51-52
ancient times to World War II,
  37-41
mid-1970s to present, 52-57
World War II to 1960s, 41-51
Custody evaluations
  (see Evaluations)

Disorders
folie à deux, trois . . . , 146-149,

157, 221
Munchausen syndrome, 148-149
paranoia, 150-151, 152, 169-170
parental alienation syndrome,
  59-156
Disputes, settlement of (see Legal
  systems and Custody
  disputes)
Divorce
effects of increase in, 41
granting of, 41-42, 44-46
laws concerning, 41
no-fault divorce laws, 51-52
and psychological deterioration,
  50
and witnesses in court, 42
Doctrine of parens patraie, 38

Economic disparity, 122-123
effects on fathers, 134-135
Education
importance of in child psychology, 56-57
of lawyers, 280-302
of nonlegal professionals,
  302-305
Emotions
infectiousness of in children, 120
England
development of adversary system
  in, 28-29
European legal system, 1-2
Evaluations
and court-appointed impartial
  examiners, 160, 162, 177,
  188-189
initial, 223-225
of psychological bonds, 164-165,
  173, 176-177
structure of, 158-164
use of grandma's criteria, 165,
  170, 173, 183
various types of interviews for,
  165-183

Evidence, rules for presentation of, 24

Evidence-gathering procedures, 185–218
and guardian ad litem, 217–218
of judges, 190–217
of lawyers, 186–190

Exclusionary tactics
in fathers, 137
in mothers, 127–129

Family
evaluation of in custody disputes, 157–183
extended, spread of animosity to the, 80–82
parental alienation syndrome, psychotherapy of, 219–260

Family evaluations (see evaluations)

Fathers
as being overprotective of child, 137
economic disparity, effects of on, 134–135
exclusionary tactics of, 137
new woman involvement in, 138–139
and power, 137–138
as programmers of children, 106–115
projection in, 136–137
psychological bonds in, 133
reaction formation in, 135–136
as scorned men, 134
therapy for, 228–230, 242–244
underlying psychodynamics of in, 132–140

Folie à deux, trois . . . , 146–149, 151–152, 155–156, 157, 221, 233, 269–270

Fourth Lateran Council, 16–17

Gender differences, effects of, 131, 136

Genetics
and child rearing, 308–309

God, judgment of, 10–11, 12, 14–17

Grandma's criteria, 165, 170, 173, 183, 208–209

Grandparents (see Family, extended)

Greek society
dispute settlement of, 6–8

Guardian ad litem, 217–218
and child advocates, 231
qualifications for, 276–277

Guardianship of Infants Act, 40

Guilt, absence of in children, 76–77

Hearsay rule, 24

Hostility, release of in children, 119–120

Housekeepers, interviewing of, 182–183

Impartial examiner, provisions for serving as an, 327–332

In-camera interviews, 190–192
weaknesses of, 190–197

Independent thinker phenomenon, 74–75

Inquisitional system, 17–21
compared to adversary system, 20–21
reasons for development of, 18–21

Interviewing
children with parental alienation syndrome, 212–213, 212–217
in-camera, 190–197
individual, 171–178, 197–198
types of questions to ask, 174–177,199, 208, 207–217
and confidentiality, 198–199
housekeepers, 182–183
individual with parents, 168–171

initial, 165–168
joint, 162–163, 178–182
multiple interviews, absence of,
191–192

Joint custody, 54–56
Joint interviews, 162–163, 178–182
Judges
evidence-gathering procedures
of, 190–217
guidelines for making custody
decisions, 263–267
guidelines in appointing therapists and guardian
ad litems, 268, 270–273,
276–277
and in-camera interviews with
children, 190–197
and interviewing children individually, importance
of, 197–198
and issue of confidentiality,
198–199
power of, 17–18
and questions to ask children,
199–217
roles of, 20, 24–26, 263–276
Juries
past and present roles of, 21–23
use of in ancient civilizations,
7, 8

Law school admissions procedures,
280–285
problems with, 280–285
solution for problem, 284–285
Lawyers, 49
education of, 280–302
evidence-gathering procedures
of, 186–190
and issue of conviction for the
client's position, 293–296
and issue of emotions and objectivity, 296–300

and law school admissions
procedures, 280–285
paranoid type of, 283–284
psychopath type of, 281–283
roles of, 26–27, 262–263
and teaching about adversary
system deficiencies, 285–300
Legal professionals
advocate, provisions for serving
as, 332–334
evidence-gathering procedures
of, 185–218
guardian ad litem vs. child
advocate, 231
guardians ad litem, 217–218
impartial examiners
(court-appointed), 188–189
provisions for serving as,
327–332
judges, 190–217
lawyers, 186–190
Legal systems
adversary system, 1–36
and inquisitional system,
20–21
and teaching lawyers about
deficiencies of, 285–300
alternatives for resolving custody
disputes, 312–324
in ancient Greek society, 6–8
Asian, 5–6
and constitutional rights,
319–321
in early Roman society, 8–9
European, 1–2
and evidence-gathering procedures, 185–218
and the Fourth Lateran Council,
16–17
and God, judgment of, 10–11,
12, 14–17
and guardian ad litem, 217–218
inquisitional, development of,
17–21

past and present roles of
professionals in, 21–27
in primitive societies, 3–6
and religion, influence of, 9–21
rules for presentation of
evidence, 24
three common methods of trial
in Middle Ages, 9–16
Lying
and children, 193–197, 231
during interviews, 167
lies of omission vs. commission,
15, 286–288

Mediation, 313–314
Mental health professionals
diagnostic considerations for,
157–183
Middle ages, legal systems in, 9–21
Mothers
as being overprotective of
children, 129–131
at a disadvantage in custody
disputes, 62
economic disparity, effects of
on, 122–123
elaboration of preseparation
exclusionary tactics
in, 127–129
maintenance of primary psychological bonds in, 121–122
maneuvers in programming
children, 85–99
paranoia in, 150–151, 152,
169–170
as programmers of children,
82–106
projection in, 125–127
reaction formation in, 123–125
as scorned women, 122
therapy of, 225–236
underlying psychodynamics of
in, 121–132
Munchausen syndrome, 148–149

No-fault divorce laws, 51–52

Opinion rule, 24
Overprotection of children,
129–131, 137

Paranoia, 150–151, 152
in mothers, 169–170
Parent culpability, concept of, 39
Parental alienation syndrome,
59–156, 325–326
and absence of guilt, 76–77
and anger, 139–140
and animosity toward extended
family, 80–82
borrowed scenarios, presence of
in, 77–80
campaigns of denigration,
64–68
and child's hatred of parent,
64–82, 84–99, 107–121,
140–149
child's underlying psychodynamics, 115–121
clinical example of, 245–258
definition of, 59–61
diagnostic considerations for,
157–183
and evidence-gathering
procedures, 185–218
father's underlying psychodynamics, 132–140
folie à deux, as an example of,
146–149
future recommendations
regarding, 279–324
and identification-with-the-
aggressor mechanism,
141–143
independent thinker phenomenon, 74–75
initial evaluation for, 223–225
interviewing children with,
212–213, 212–217

judge's role in dealing with,
263-276
and lack of ambivalence in
children, 73
lawyers' role in dealing with,
262-263
manifestations of in the child,
63-82
mild cases of, 245
moderate cases of, 230-245
mother's underlying psychodynamics, 121-132
and Munchausen syndrome, 148
programming father, 106-115
programming mother, 82-106
psychotherapy of families,
219-260
and reflexive support of the
loved parent, 75-76
severe cases of, 225-230
situational factors in, 140-146
three categories of contributing
factors, 63, 64
three types of, 149-154
two reasons for increase in,
61-62
and weak rationalizations of
children, 68-73
Parental preference in custody
disputes, 37-57
Parental programming (see
Programming of children)
Parents
individual interviews with,
168-171
preference of in custody
disputes, 37-57
Perjury (see Lying)
Priests, role of in legal matters,
8, 10
Primitive societies
dispute settlement of, 3-6
Programming of children, 82-115
conscious vs. unconscious, 82-84

fathers, 106-115
maneuvers of mothers, 85-105
mothers, 82-106
Projection
in fathers, 136-137
in mothers, 125-127
tests involving, 201-202, 205
Psychological bonds, 106-115,
115-116, 155-156, 164-165,
173, 176-177, 259, 307-308
in fathers, 133
fear of disruption of in child,
116-117
healthy-stronger, 227
and mothers, 121-122
stronger-healthy, 263, 265, 274,
309-312, 323
using grandma's criteria in determining strength of, 165
Psychotherapist (see Therapists)
Psychotherapy (see also Therapy)
of families with parental
alienation syndrome, 219-260
initial evaluation for parental
alienation
syndrome, 223-225
for mild cases, 245
for moderate cases, 230-245
for severe cases, 225-230

Reaction formation
in children, 117
in fathers, 135-136
in mothers, 123-125
Religion
influence on legal systems in the
past, 9-21
Roman society
dispute settlement of, 8-9

Separation anxiety in children, 78
Sex-blind custody decisions
and best interests of children,
305-309

Sexual abuse
  accusations of, 136–137, 169,
    180
  false allegations of, 126–127,
    237, 322–323
  and parental alienation
    syndrome, 142–143, 144
Sexual rivalry in children, 120–121
Star Chamber proceedings, 28
Stronger-healthy-psychological-
    bond presumption, 309–312,
    323

Talfourd's Act, 38
Tender-years presumption, 38, 41,
    52–53, 62
Tests
  projective, 201–202, 205
  Thematic Apperception Test
    (TAT), 201
Therapists
  qualifications for treating
    parental alienation
    syndrome, 220–222, 231–232,
    244–245, 268, 270–273
Therapy (see also Psychotherapy)
  court-ordered family, 221, 222

Torture, as method to elicit
    confessions, 19
Training (see Education)
Treatment
  and combining efforts of mental
    health and legal
    professionals, 261–262
  for parental alienation
    syndrome, 219–260
Trial, methods of
  adversary system, development
    of, 21–36
  and the Fourth Lateran Council,
    16–17
  inquisitional system, develop-
    ment of, 17–21
  trial by combat, 11–14
  trial by ordeal, 7–8, 9–11
  trial by wager or compurgation,
    14–16

Unconscious maneuvers, 99–105
United States
  adversary system, development
    of in, 30–36

Witnesses
  past and present roles of, 23–24

- Dad beats Mom
- Dad is a threat to Mom's life
- F. would restrict my time = the kids + then tell them
    "that all the time Dad wants = you."
- Dad tampers = breaks of family car - jeopdizing
    the children.
- Dad breaks into the house
- Dad is responsible for E's stabbing.

- Dad can't oversee medical management
    of the children
        - doesn't give Ritalin.
        - " know allergies.

- Dad is an atheist - and shouldn't get kids
        for religious holidays.

- Dad sodimized mom young (+ reportedly
        over the years)

- Dad spends x5. time drinking at Dr. Bwans.

- Dad leaves kids = multiple babysitters
        for long periods of time.

- Dad breaks orders of protection multiple times. (607)

- Dad "burns" Ricky's ankle + Mom takes
        Dad to Soc. Services Investigation.

F. - witholds schedules of children's events -
    threatens to call police if I come to hockey games